MODERNITY AND ITS MALCONTENTS

Modernity and Its Malcontents

Ritual and Power in Postcolonial Africa

EDITED BY
JEAN COMAROFF AND JOHN COMAROFF

THE UNIVERSITY OF CHICAGO PRESS
Chicago & London

The University of Chicago Press, Chicago 60637
The University of Chicago Press, Ltd., London
© 1993 by The University of Chicago
All rights reserved. Published 1993
Printed in the United States of America
02 01 00 99 98 97   2   3   4   5

ISBN: 0-226-11439-2   (cloth)
       0-226-11440-6   (paper)

Library of Congress Cataloging-in-Publication Data

Modernity and its malcontents :   ritual and power in postcolonial
   Africa   /   edited by Jean Comaroff and John Comaroff.
          p.   cm.
       Papers presented at a conference held in the winter of 1990 at the
   University of Chicago.
       Includes bibliographical references and index.
          1. Rites and ceremonies—Africa—Congresses.   2. Witchcraft—
   Africa—Congresses.   3. Africa—Politics and government—
   Congresses.   4. Power (Social sciences)—Congresses.   5. Africa—
   Social life and customs—Congresses.   I. Comaroff, Jean.
   II. Comaroff, John L., 1945–
   GN645.M57   1993
   303.4—dc20
                                                                93-17
                                                                CIP

CONTENTS

PREFACE

A DEFINITIVE SOCIOLOGY OF ACADEMIC CONFERENCES is yet to be written—although David Lodge's *Small World* comes tolerably close, give or take a genre. Some of these gatherings, as we all know, are largely recreational: subsidized opportunities for scholars to exchange gossip and to "network," one of those suspect pursuits made possible when nouns become verbs. Aside perhaps from phantasmic volumes of *Collected Airplane Tickets and Cab Receipts,* such meetings yield little. Others are somewhat more productive, of course. And a select few are especially memorable for the way in which they rupture the normal flow of intellectual life, disconcerting its discourses and energizing its imaginings.

A small conference of this last kind gave rise to the present volume. Held in the winter of 1990, it was the first of a series of symposia in African Studies convened at the University of Chicago. For the past five years, the Africanist circle at Chicago, a group of about twenty-five students and faculty, has supported a lively workshop. To it have come scholars of various disciplines and degrees of reputation, of various nationalities and theoretical persuasions, of various political commitments and intellectual obsessions. Within it, too, the work of local members of the circle—some of it fresh and new, some well known and mature—has been vigorously discussed and reshaped. The group has also expanded to include regular participants from the recently revitalized Program of African Studies at Northwestern University.

The workshop has become a major focus of the Committee on African (and, more recently, African-American) Studies at the University of Chicago. Its members, both faculty and students, together take responsibility for a large, year-long introductory course on Africa; recently they have also introduced a new college concentration in African and African-American Studies. These various sites of intellectual production and pedagogy are all quite closely articulated. They provide a context in which our graduate students—of whom we are very proud—do their scholarly apprenticeship; a context in which we have all come, with unusual collegiality, to learn from each other.

The opportunity to expand our activities yet further came three years ago, when the University of Chicago was awarded a grant from the Ford Foundation to develop its undergraduate curriculum on non-Western cultures. The funds allocated to the Committee on African Studies included provision for three conferences, the object being to tie our current research and writing more effectively to the content and techniques of our teaching. One product is the present volume, which, we hope, will be taught in our own classrooms. This will bring the process full circle; hence the use of the metaphor to describe our continuing collective existence. Some of those who, as undergraduates, attended our courses in African Studies have essays published here, essays that will now reanimate those same courses and, no doubt, many others elsewhere.

We hardly need say that our horizons also stretch beyond the purely pedagogic; that these essays are also intended as a contribution to African studies, to history and to anthropology at large. The theme of the conference expressed concerns shared in Chicago and elsewhere at the time: it emerged from the intersection of our teaching and writing in 1989—and it still vexes us as we try, in the shadow of a classical Africanist tradition, to forge a historical anthropology for the late twentieth century. We originally framed the topic in terms of "Ritual, Power, and History," although the title of the volume was subsequently changed to *Modernity and Its Malcontents: Ritual and Power in Postcolonial Africa*, which better captures its substance. As will become clear in the Introduction, each of these concepts—modernity, ritual, power, and (the making of) history—is treated as highly problematic in its own right and in its relation to the others. Some of the chapters address familiar anthropological issues (among them, witchcraft and purification rites), but situate them amid the polyphonies of modern Africa in strikingly novel ways. Others take on distinctly nontraditional phenomena (the Nigerian popular press, for example, or processes of commodification) and seek to make imaginative sense of them as they run up against the conceptual limits of Western social science.

The symposium was concerned to respond to the challenges posed by contemporary Africa to our understanding of social worlds everywhere. How, precisely, do we, scholars of the American academy, come to know this not-quite-decolonized continent, with all its diverse voices and complex subjectivities, its kaleidoscopic incoherences and its fragmentary realities? How can we speak of it with humility, insight, and self-reflection—indeed, engage with it in a dialectic of discovery—rather than presume to speak for it in the arrogant tones of a monologic science? How do we preserve the relative, provisional advantages of an external gaze without falling back into the self-deception of detachment and misplaced authority? These questions hover, often very close to the surface, in all the essays—half of which are by women and half by men, half by Americans and half by scholars of African and European extraction. In short, while it is the work of people who share intellectual conventions, this volume is also the product of a circle of differences. It is written from varying perspectives about a variety of phenomena—but with a view to searching out a coherent universe of discourse for the historical anthropology of Africa, present and future.

We should like to thank the Ford Foundation for its financial backing; also the Center for the Study of Politics, History, and Culture at the University of Chicago for the use of Wilder House. John Boyer, then Master of the Social Sciences Collegiate Division, made the conference possible in the first place. An esteemed colleague, he has long been an indefatigable supporter of African Studies at Chicago. Our most important acknowledgment, however, goes to our students. Some have their work published here, others played an active role in the conference, and all are participants in the lively, imaginative, and challenging milieu from which this comes.

John and Jean Comaroff

Chicago
January 1993

INTRODUCTION

Jean and John Comaroff

PERHAPS THE GREATEST VIRTUE of the recent Western scholarly pre-occupation with "postmodernity" is what it has revealed about "modernity" itself. Above all else, we have been made aware that the latter—and all it has come to connote—is profoundly ideological and profoundly historical. Much of the time, in fact, it is difficult to be certain exactly what "it" is. To be sure, our grasp of global modernity is still rather limited, often rather unspecific. And this in spite of the legacies of classic social theory, which grew, in part, out of an obsession with the problem. Among other things, these theoretical traditions agreed—from right and left, for good or ill—that modernizing social forces and material forms would have the universal effect of eroding local cultural differences. In the late twentieth century, however, grand European teleologies that hold "Western hegemony as human destiny" (Sahlins 1992:2) seem strangely out of date. Markets, money, and mechanical media extend across the planet. Transnational cultural movements burgeon. But, *pace* the predictions of modernization theory and historical materialism, not to mention the efforts of CNN and Sony, the world has not been reduced to sameness. Nor does it promise to be, at least not imminently. It remains, in the words of Louis MacNeice (1973:394), "incorrigibly plural." Thus, while we are confronted on all sides with evidence of global systems—systems of capital, technology, ideology, and representation—these are systems in the plural: diverse and dynamic, multiple and multidirectional (cf. Appadurai 1990).

Mythic Modernities

There are, in short, many modernities. Nor should this surprise us. With hindsight, it is clear that the cultures of industrial capitalism have never existed in the singular, either in Europe or in their myriad transformations across the face of the earth. Various Western governments might have extended their dominion over much of the planet in the high age of imperialism, giving graphic evidence of the expansive power of capitalism in the service of the nation-state—and vice versa. But such exertions had unforeseen outcomes. Conquered and colonized societies, to take the obvious example, were never simply made over in the European image, despite the persistent tendency of Eurocentric scholars to speak as if they were. Rather, their citizens struggled, in diverse ways and with differing degrees of success, to deploy, deform, and defuse imperial institutions. What is more, the colonizers were themselves transformed in the process, often in unexpected ways. Thus new political cultures were born from countless couplings of "local" and "global" worlds, from intersecting histories that refocused European values and intentions—thus rerouting, if not reversing, the march of modernity. Indeed, as we have shown elsewhere (J. L. and J. Comaroff 1992: chap. 10), this great historical process was also instrumental in remaking economy and society "at home." But that is a topic for another time.

Looked at up close, then, modernity itself all too rapidly melts into air. As an analytic term, it becomes especially vague when dislodged from the ideal-typical, neo-evolutionary theoretical frame that classically encased it, defining it less in reference to the "real" world than by contrast to that other chimera, "tradition."[1] Such binary contrasts, we would argue, are a widespread trope of ideology-in-the-making; they reduce complex continuities and contradictions to the aesthetics of nice oppositions. It should no longer need saying that the self-sustaining antinomy between tradition and modernity underpins a long-standing European myth: a narrative that replaces the uneven, protean relations among "ourselves" and "others" in world history with a simple, epic story about the passage from savagery to civilization, from the mystical to the mundane (see J. L. and J. Comaroff 1992). This story is, in fact, a Progress. It tells of the inexorable, if always incomplete, advancement of the primitive: of his conversion to a world religion, of his gradual incorporation into civil society, of improvement in his material circumstances, of the rationalization of his beliefs and practices.[2]

Nor is its telos limited to the optimistic models, the master narrative, of modernization theory, whose euphemisms have long been subject to trenchant critique. Those who turn that narrative on its head, pointing to the underdevelopment by the West of the rest, have not always escaped its Eurocentrism; in particular, its linear view of history-as-progress, a unidirectional movement orchestrated by and from the "complex" societies of the northern hemisphere. This history may be celebrated or excoriated, its ideological apparatus camouflaged or unmasked; such things depend, ultimately, on the politics of theory. But, for most Western social thought, modernity remains the terminus toward which non-Western peoples constantly edge—without ever actually arriving. Even the label "*non*-Western," to restate an old point in contemporary chic-speak, fixes the universal "other" into a conceptual space defined by negation, inversion, deficiency, absence. A poor farmer in rural Botswana once put it in more straightforward, pungent terms. "Things modern," he said, "seem always to be in the next village."

Precisely because it *is* so closely connected to Western ideologies of universal development, modernity serves ill as an analytic tool for grasping European expansion, most of all from the vantage of the colonized. Still, evaluative and imprecise though it often is—and it tends to be both, even where it masquerades as a technical concept—the term itself has come to circulate, almost worldwide, as a metaphor of new means and ends, of new materialities and meanings. As a (more-or-less) pliable sign, it attracts different referents, and different values, wherever it happens to land. But everywhere it speaks of great transformations that have reshaped social and economic relations on a global scale; transformations, indeed, that have made the very idea of the "global" thinkable in the first place. These processes are real enough, of course. It is their specific properties and effects—rather than their vague, value-laden representation—that are the focus of the essays in this volume: the impact, on various African communities, of expansive markets and mass media, of commoditization and crusading creeds, of books and bureaucracies. These, in their many guises, have interacted in diverse ways with local conditions and contingencies, giving rise to a wide range of cultural practices, spatial arrangements, material circumstances. They have also drawn a multitude of distinct voices into a worldwide conversation, a multilogue.

But, most of all, they have raised a number of critical questions. How, for instance, do we do justice to the fact that similar global forces have driven the colonial and postcolonial history of large parts of Africa, and yet recognize that specific social and cultural conditions, conjunctures, and indeterminacies have imparted to distinct African communities their own particular histories? How do we describe a set of dialectical processes between center and periphery, ruler and ruled, metropole and margins, whose form is broadly the same but whose content is often very different? How, in other words, do we write a historical anthropology of world systems that is not merely *the* History of *the* World System? Can we take sufficient account of the worldwide facts of colonial and postcolonial coercion, violence, and exploitation, yet not slight the role of parochial signs and values, local meanings and historical sensibilities? How do we read European imperialism and its aftermath without reducing it to crude equations of power, domination, and alienation?

Note that such questions do not merely shift the level of inquiry from general processes to particular instances, from the ideal-typical to embodied, historical "cases." They imply, rather, an argument *against* reified typologies *sui generis;* those typologies whose neat oppositions, nice determinations, and nefarious teleologies are preserved by short-circuiting the more complicated pathways of human practice. (It is also an argument against the reduction of "non-Western" realities to simple discourses—however sympathetic, reflexive, even confessional—about ourselves and "othering." But that, again, is something else.) The contributors to this volume seek, instead, to address the paradoxes they encountered in late twentieth-century African communities, communities that confound classical models of development. In them, "modernity" seems to have bred a heightened concern with "tradition"; "culture," now often objectified and commoditized, has become the subject of historical consciousness and contestation; "rationalization" has begotten an efflorescence of witchcraft and magic; "commodities" and "class formation" have spawned a complex commentary, neither simply "African" nor "European," on the costs and contradictions of postindependence "progress." These studies, in sum, present a rich ensemble of local discourses on the possibilities and perversities of the African present. Together, they show the extent to which modernity—itself always an imaginary construction of the present in terms of a mythic past—has its own magicalities, its own enchantments.

As this implies, their authors share a common orientation. It is to a historical anthropology that tries to dissolve the division between synchrony and diachrony, ethnography and historiography; that refuses to separate culture from political economy, insisting instead on the simultaneity of the meaningful and the material in all things; that acknowledges—no, stresses—the brute realities of colonialism and its aftermath, without assuming that they have robbed African peoples of their capacity to act on the world. This historical anthropology focuses centrally on the interplay of the global and the local, treating as problematic the shifting line between them. It pays particular attention to the processes by which transnational signs and practices are welded into the divers cultural configurations, into the contested realities and multiple subjectivities, of most late twentieth-century social scapes. In so doing, moreover, it seeks to disentangle the dialectics of continuity and change that characterize all social milieus—and the intricate threads that join meaningful structures to creative action, authoritative institutions to the politics of difference and contestation.

As we said in the Preface, we recognize that these perspectives are partial and provisional; we are all too aware of the very complicated social realities, the polyphonies, that make up contemporary Africa. Here, moreover, we narrow our analytic gaze, turning it upon a quite specific phenomenon: the role of ritual in African modernity—and, especially, in the efforts of people to empower themselves, thus to assert a measure of control over worlds often perceived to be rapidly changing. But why *this* choice of topic for a volume dedicated to breaching the division between tradition and modernity, to resisting the Western tendency to separate simple, sacral societies from those with Reason and History (cf. Dirks 1990:25)? Does not such a focus on "ritual"—with its own evocation of the opposition between the enchanted and the secular—inevitably return us to the typologies, teleologies, and theoretical discourses from which we seek to escape? The answer, of course, depends on the manner in which we conceive of ritual—and on the way in which we inscribe it, methodologically, in the historical scheme of things.

Rites of Rapprochement

Ritual has long been a mark, in Western social thought, of all that separates rational modernity from the culture(s) of tradition.[3] Whether as magic or mystery, as pseudoscience or social sacrament, it conjures up the very inverse of practical reason. Yet despite (or, perhaps, because of) this, its study has, for some time now, been the site of an unusually creative rapprochement between the perspectives of anthropology and history (see, e.g., Evans-Pritchard 1949; Ginzburg 1983, Darnton 1985; Sahlins 1985; Davis 1981; Bloch 1986, 1989; Bogucka 1992). There seems, in fact, to have opened up an analytic space—often charted by such fashionable phrases as "the politics and poetics of . . ." (after Stallybrass and White 1986)—in which everything from medieval carnivals to first fruit rites, royal progresses to technologies of colonial rule, may be considered as comparable kinds of symbolic action.

How has this come about?

Ritual, Edmund Leach once noted (1968:521), lies largely in the eye of the beholder. It tends to be a quality that we attribute to the activity of "others," be they at home or abroad. Among modern social scientists, not coincidentally, it is anthropologists who have made ritual most uniquely their own, seeing it as meaningful practice that exceeds brute necessity or instrumental reason (Sahlins 1976). Classically defined as "formal action directed at the sacred" (see, e.g., V. W. Turner 1967:19), it was fetishized in both structural functionalist and symbolic anthropology. For the former, it served as an "all-purpose social glue," a Durkheimian mechanism that made desirable the socially obligatory (V. W. Turner 1957; 1967:30)—thereby collapsing individual agency to social determination, personal experience to collective consciousness. The flawed genius of this perspective lay in its intriguing vision of a world of enduring difference, a world composed of self-sustaining "societies." It was also a world in which ritual, in its various forms and formulations, was "quintessential custom," the *deus ex machina* that could assure solidary sentiments and redress corrosive conflict. What is more, its numinous potential guaranteed that, in these "simple" societies, structure would triumph over inherent social tensions; indeed, over the disruptive forces of history *tout court*.[4]

It is hardly surprising, then, that the rise of historical anthropology, with its stress on the dialectics of social life, would raise difficult questions about the nature of ritual in particular. Or that the latter would pose a formidable challenge to historical anthropology (Kelly and Kaplan 1990:120).

A growing number of revisionist scholars have responded by repudiating the idea that ritual is (or ever was) the hostage of "custom"; that it is properly confined to sacred practice, to formal symbolic processes, or to the solemn enactment of social structure; that its function is to secure the continuity of social systems, especially when their integrity is threatened. Nor should we abandon our concern with the phenomenon, goes the argument; we ought rather to historicize it, taking it down from its hallowed pedestal and putting it to work in the everyday world. The papers collected in this volume are examples of this continuing effort. Their authors are no longer content to regard ritual as the mere reflection of a transcendent "tradition." They try, instead, to make the concept embrace more mundane meaningful practice, practice often meant to transform, not reproduce, the environment in which it occurs (Lan 1985; J. Comaroff 1985). Indeed, "rites" are increasingly being treated, alongside everyday "routines," as just one form of symbolic practice, part and parcel of the more embracing "discourses" and "technologies" that establish or contest regimes of rule (Cohn and Dirks 1988).

As a result, ritual has, for many, become almost synonymous with "signifying" practice; "the practice," Kelly and Kaplan (1990:141) say, "that that defines and authorizes." The stress here on signification evokes Leach's (1968:524) classic yet still controversial statement that ritual is "the communicative aspect of all social behaviour" (see also 1954: chap. 1). Such catholic formulations themselves raise problems, as shown below. But they have distinct virtues, too. For by demystifying and detaching it from the sacred, they allow the possibility that ritual may be creative, constitutive practice—and, hence, an instrument of history in all human societies at all times. Rather than being reduced to a species of ceremonial action that insulates enchanted, self-reproducing systems from the "real" world, then, ritual may be seen for what it often is: a vital element in the processes that make and remake social facts and collective identities. Everywhere.

Anthropologists have not been alone in rethinking ritual. Some historians, also concerned with signifying practice and the meaningful construction of social worlds, have done so too. In tune with a rising humanism in the social sciences, these "newer social historians," as Davis (1990) dubs them, have increasingly written accounts not confined to the Promethean, the Political, the Ecclesiastical, or the Economic. Far from being chronicles of courts, constitutions, or kings, such accounts seek to penetrate the lives of those "[without] proper names" (de Certeau 1984:vii). As this suggests, the historiography of the ordinary, of the meaningful-in-the-mundane, has become ever more preoccupied with "popular" culture; with the everyday experience of common people; with the routine forms of symbolic action that configure their social existence and their identities.[5] And it has posed its analytic problems in terms thoroughly familiar to anthropologists. If peasant and proletarian communities were rooted in the practices of everyday life—practices that were *not* a mere sediment of ruling institutions or elite ideas—wherein lay their coherence? Whence came their power to reproduce themselves? How might, for example, fairs, market festivities, or carnivals have given voice to local cosmologies, or have contested dominant discourses? How might the logic of, say, witchcraft have figured in a moral economy capable of addressing the raw realities of misfortune and inequity? Not unexpectedly, in broaching these questions, historians often found themselves turning to standard anthropological works on the role of ritual in "simple" societies, many of them in Africa.[6]

Relevant also, albeit a little later, were developments in British cultural studies, itself a less diffuse and more left-leaning field than its North American counterpart. Critical of received orthodoxies in literature and sociology, the likes of the so-called Birmingham School turned their attention to the expressive practices of women, underclass youth, and minorities. Here, too, a focus on "ritual," loosely defined as "intentional communication" or "signifying practice," seemed productive, especially in discerning the politics and history of unconventional subcultures (Hall and Jefferson 1976; Hebdige 1979, 1988). At first glance, this may appear to return us to the perception that ritual is primarily the means of the marginal, albeit now our own "others" in the West. At the same time, however—in a somewhat different meeting of cultural studies, the "newer" social history, historical sociology, and anthropology—a companion literature insisted that rites were not just weapons of the weak (Hobsbawm and Ranger 1983). In *The Great Arch*, for instance, Corrigan and Sayer (1985) show that the making of modern British nationhood was, above all, a cultural project; one in which the authoritative rule of the state was gradually effected by the ritualization—and, thereby, routinization—of conventional practices of citizenship and subjectivity. Similarly, accounts of European regimes abroad increasingly stressed their reliance on "the ritual idiom" in making imperial authority "manifest and compelling" (Cohn [1983] 1987: 677; T. Mitchell 1988; Trexler 1984; Kelly and Kaplan 1990:133). The "thin white line" that enclosed the colonial state was hardly power from "the barrel of a gun" (Fields 1985:12, 31). Its force inhered in a welter of bureaucratic ceremonials, exemplary aesthetics, and portentious pilgrimages (Ranger 1987; J. and J. L. Comaroff 1991). This, once more, speaks to a notion of ritual which, while not tied to tradition or the sacred, remains faithful to a basic Durkheimian tenet: rites are persuasive practices that enjoin a reality and an authority stretching far beyond the immediacies of the present.

Rather than divide students of the West and the rest, then, ritual has come ever more to unite them. Or at least some of them: those skeptical of grand theories that make modernity a passage from rite to reason; those concerned to plumb the polyvalent, subtle ensembles of elements that situate (often humdrum) human practice in time and space. The convergence is evident in a rising rate of intertextual and comparative references, and in the appeal to shared scholarly ancestors like Victor Turner and, more recently, Mikhail Bakhtin (Kelly and Kaplan 1990:137). The essays in this volume attest to the value of all this. They argue, explicitly or implicitly, that an open, dynamic approach to the study of ritual may yield surprising results, expanding the horizons of popular history, throwing new light on old ethnographic concerns, and promoting conversation across disciplinary lines.

In treating ritual as an integral dimension of everyday existence—of the routine, secular practices of both "public" culture and "private" life—we do not deny the importance of major, elaborately orchestrated rites; of Ritual, so to speak, in the upper case (cf. J. Comaroff, in press). These are the totalizing moments when kings or chiefs, presidents or priests, may (re)make history by their actions; their capacity to do so arising from the cultural fact that, in some places and times, such heroic figures embody, metonymically, the worlds they (re)present (Sahlins 1985:35). In the lives of most ordinary late twentieth-century Africans, however, such moments are rare. And yet, for them, the work of ritual—of the building and contesting of social realities by way of formally stylized, communicative action—is unceasing. Which is all the more reason to regard it as a pervasive aspect of ongoing activity, to perceive the "ritual in all politics, and the politics in [all] ritual" (Kelly and Kaplan 1990:141), to dispense with the old Eurocentric dichotomy between the sacred and the profane.

This has the added advantage of allowing us to comprehend, in their own right, phenomena like "magic and witchcraft" without having to force them into ill-fitting Western categories. Indeed, from the vantage of those categories, such "mystical" activities seem to lurk anomalously between religious ritual and pragmatic technique; and they appear meaningful only in redressing traditional tensions or in dealing with cultural "disintegration." As it turns out, this is a crippling limitation. For witchcraft—a central concern of several of our essays—may be seen to have played a complex, even contradictory part in the making of modern African history. Its changing moral discourses and purifying practices have intervened, diversely, in conquest and colonialism, in state building and stratification, in the advent of markets and the marginalization of local economies. Thus understood, implies Austen (chap. 4 this vol.), witchcraft is less a reified analytic category than a situated moral discourse about which anthropologists and historians might profitably converse. For, thus conceived, its study reveals telling similarities and differences in the experience of Africans and early modern Europeans as their communities became enmeshed in market economies centered elsewhere (see also Auslander, chap. 7 this vol.; Bastian, chap. 6; Apter chap. 5; Schmoll, chap. 8).

We are, of course, aware of the problems involved in the expansive view of ritual for which we argue here. Apart from all else, the concept itself would seem to become so unspecific as to be virtually coterminous with any and all social action. This danger is not trivial. Take, for instance, *Resistance through Rituals*, an imaginative, pathbreaking study of the "ritualised and stylised form" of everyday cultural expression among working-class youth in Britain (Hall and Jefferson 1976:47). Here "ritual" is allowed to become a self-evident synonym for collectively meaningful action; it is not even listed in the index. The effort to escape definitions that tie the phenomenon to sacred, awesome action has made the term increasingly into a polyvalent qualifier, a commonsense equivalent of the "cultural," "symbolic," or "discursive." Whatever its intent, this move sacrifices all explanatory rigor, all analytic discrimination. And it leaves us with a real conceptual problem.

Similarly and simultaneously, while many anthropologists insist on treating ritual as "inherently historical" (Kelly and Kaplan 1990:119), few have ventured to specify what this might actually mean. Even fewer have succeeded in explaining how we might redefine its properties in such a way as to show, quite literally, that it can "authorize action" outside of itself and thereby "make history." Yet this seems essential if the analytical power of the concept is not to be lost, if ritual is to mean more than the poetic quality of any social act. All we can hope to do here is to stimulate a conversation on these issues, thus to introduce the ethnographic accounts to come. We turn, then, to consider some of the implications of historicizing ritual practice in light of those accounts.

Doing the Rite Thing

For all the bitter arguments in the social sciences over the nature and meaning of ritual, one thing is widely shared: a stubborn preoccupation with substance over form, with the content of rites rather than with their constitutive modes of practice (J. Comaroff, in press).[7] In the past, ritual was usually identified as action addressed to spiritual values and mystical forces. Even now, it is rarely treated as action of a distinctive sort: the sort that might, in fact, produce the very power it purports to draw from elsewhere. This stress on substance is arguably part of the general, post-enlightenment Western tendency to divide reality from its representations, messages from the media that bear them (W. J. T. Mitchell 1986; J. L. and J. Comaroff 1987).

Anthropologists have paid more attention than most to the efficacy of ritual, of course. Yet, as Silverstein (1981) notes, even they have shown far greater sensitivity to its symbolic content than to its formal properties, to *what* it says rather than to *how* it says it. Some have seen the primary significance of rites to lie in the fact that they epitomize—indeed, give active voice to—cultural values (e.g., Wilson 1957; Geertz 1973). Others have underscored their ability to transform experience and/or to resolve contradiction by re-presenting the paradoxes of social life as so many narratives or dramas (e.g., Lévi-Strauss 1966; V. W. Turner 1969; La Fontaine 1977). Still others have emphasized their capacity to empower the normative by stating it in incontrovertible terms (Bloch 1986) or by inverting it in carefully bounded moments of parodic license (Gluckman 1963). Their differences notwithstanding, all of these perspectives refract a broader concern with the stuff of the ritual process as it unfolds—condensing, intensifying, and motivating meaning along the way.[8] This is not to imply that matters of form are always ignored. To the contrary, it is now coming to be recognized that rites deploy such things as poetic tropes, juxtaposition, and redundancy to implode and (re)order experience. But precisely *how* they are mobilized to work their magic typically goes unexplored.

Put another way, to those who take ritual at face value—at least, the face it puts on in our own religions and among the few others to whom we attribute "great traditions"—its capacity to make meaning is a consequence of its awesome referents; it is expressive, and empowered, *because* it invokes the sacred and the transcendent. To those of a "neo-Tylorian," intellectualist bent, rites do their work *because* they explain and control the perplexities, even the meaninglessness, of human existence (Horton 1971). And to those of Durkheimian disposition, they are significant *because,* in making society into God, they animate and represent enduring social value. Yet none of these classic approaches, in and of itself, gives account of how ritual actually generates the very power it presupposes, how it actually conjures up the presence of absent potential.

True, there have been a few who have sought to analyze ritual processes, and to account for their dynamics, in terms of either their constituent elements or their formal construction. Most notable perhaps—certainly the most noted—was Victor Turner (e.g., 1967).[9] For him and for those who share his methodological orientation, the symbol is[10] ritual in microcosm: the "smallest unit of ritual which still retains . . . its . . . properties" (19). And the premier property of ritual symbolism is the capacity to "condense meaning," to unite "disparate significata" (29) by infusing social norms with visceral emotion. The organic images here are appropriate: the symbol has twin poles, the sensory and the ideological. It is Turner's molecular unit, his particle of meaningful matter, whose two atoms are everywhere joined by a covalent bond; the bond, that is, through which the poles are joined, thus ensuring that the obligatory becomes desirable, the desirable obligatory. The symbol, in short, contains the basic chemical processes that impart social life to complex orders of signification—and significance to the complex life of social orders. Yet these processes are taken always to be repetitive, their outputs fixed. Symbols reproduce and re-present normative meanings: meanings that (i) derive from a received "social structure" and (ii) are expressed in the values, utilities, and conflicts to which it gives rise.

Ironically, despite Turner's concern with the social and experiential dynamics of process and paradox, his symbols are allowed to conjure only with a finite and fixed range of referents. The latter—the relations, forces, and things for which these signs are held to stand—are predetermined by the social order of a putatively unchanging, tightly bounded society, a human island with no history to speak of. Africans like "the" Ndembu might have been part of an expanding late colonial world at the time of Turner's fieldwork in the 1950s. But, so far as we are told, little awareness of transformed signs, objects, or values insinuates itself into their richly textured rites. Ritual is not here conceived as something that may actively refigure meanings in line with changing perceptions of the universe. Nor does it press fresh associations, fashion visions for worlds yet unborn, deploy the pragmatics of language to invest contemporary practice with new force, or call upon the power of poetics to subvert unfamiliar forms of authority.

Yet it is just here—in the unification of diverse, shifting significata— that ritual ought to be at its most creative. If, as anthropologists claim, it is a species of activity that deploys the poetic properties of signs to the fullest, it should also be a fecund medium for making new meanings, new ways of knowing the world and its workings. Note that those who wish to return ritual to history stress precisely this: its pragmatic, innovative qualities. Rites, says Tambiah (1985:123–24; cf. Kelly and Kaplan 1990:126), are not formulaic restatements of mystical, sacred truths. Nor are they mechanistic invocations of conventional values that serve merely to regulate recalcitrant realities. Intricately situated performances with complex historical potential, they intensify and enrich meaningful communication among human beings by calling upon what Silverstein (1981) has termed the "metaforces" of poetic form: the positioning, contrast, redundancy, and tropic play of images.

The creative power of ritual, in other words, arises from the fact that (i) it exists in continuing *tension* with more mundane modes of action, of producing and communicating meanings and values; (ii) its constituent signs are ever open to the accumulation of new associations and referents; and (iii) it has the capacity to act in diverse ways on a contradictory world. These, to be sure, are the things that make it always so responsive to history. As Matory offers by way of example (see chap. 3 this vol.) an enduring knot of Oyo Yoruba images may long have been tied together by the figure of a vessel filled with potent contents. But these images—a possession priest, the fertile female body, and a brimming pot—have been made to carry a changing semantic load as they have been borne along by the shifting tides of Nigerian history. Having been variously (re)situated in different texts and contexts, their meanings have altered visibly over both time and space.

This is not an isolated case. From the precolonial epoch, through the colonial era, and into the advanced capitalist age,[11] the ongoing revaluation of signs has always been palpable feature of African creativity. Everyday experience is ever recasting prior meanings as it confronts new signifiers, themselves variously empowered; among them, books and money, lenses and looking glasses, paper and photographs, the tools of trade and common domestic commodities. Ritual innovators have long redeployed these—as they have redeployed the terms of Christianity, the mission classroom, and the market in goods and skills—to craft novel forms of practice and to offer critical commentaries on African history as it unfolds. Creative figures—be they poets, prophets, even witchfinders; whether they work with mirrors, medicines or the written word—are *experimental* practitioners. They try to make universal signs speak to particular realities. As we argue elsewhere (1989:290), their activities are in fact a means of *producing* historical consciousness: they seek to shape the inchoateness, the murky ambiguity of colonial encounters into techniques of empowerment and signs of collective representation.

These signs and techniques often come to be potent precisely because of the historical circumstances in which they acquire their meanings; that is, the processes that hitch local cultures and communities to the increasingly global forces that encompass them. Born in the encounter between inner and outer worlds, along frontiers opened up in their interstices, they tend to become the currency of ritual that seeks both to preserve endangered values and to give birth to new possibilities (Munn 1973). This juxtaposition of the unfamiliar with more enduring tropes establishes new fields of signification, newly nuanced notions of evil and affliction, new incipient identities, new modes of practice. And so, over time, the exogenous becomes indigenous, the strange is synthesized into the "established" order—itself evanescent, of course, even though it may not seem that way from within. It is to be stressed, in all this, that those symbolic processes that give concrete form to emerging consciousness often do so in nonnarrative terms, *sans* written word or text; which is why they commonly escape conventional historiographies. A colonial coin, a Christian gesture, a bureaucratic rite, or an imported commodity may serve to situate people in wider regional, national, and international landscapes: once woven into local performances, practices, or costumes, they have the power to impart a sense of presence through which distant horizons become tangible realities.

The essays in this volume focus on rural communities, on the role of ritual in articulating their horizons with more expansive forces and collectivites, including those of translocal elites and the nation-state. They prove that such processes are politically complex, sometimes revelatory and resistant, sometimes accommodating, sometimes positively reactionary. Typically, however, they express ambivalent and ambiguous motives, seeking at once to contest and affirm aspects of the dominant order(s). Indeed, the historical significance of local ritual practice always requires careful and situated reading. On occasion, it seems in harmony with national maps and hegemonies, on occasion it forges moral economies that dispute the authority of the modern state, even while trying to capture its techniques of producing and reproducing value (see Austen). Auslander shows, for instance, that the appeal of the remarkable witchfinder, Dr. Moses, lay in his promise to restore productivity and self-determination to a divided community in rural Zambia, using the bureaucratic tools of government surveillance—rubber stamps, identity cards, and the like—to detect witches. But his magic mirror reflected fragmented images (see also Apter); for this was a community torn by its troubled, uneven incorporation into a fitful market economy. Some hoped to find a form of redemption in the looking glass, expecting others to be exposed by it as selfish and antisocial, as primitive accumulators who had blocked the mysterious march of modernity. This case dramatizes a very general feature of ritual as historical practice. It is less about giving voice to shared values than about opening fields of argument; about providing the terms and tropes, that is, through which people caught up in changing worlds may vex each other, question definitions of value, form alliances, and mobilize oppositions.

This is especially clear in Masquelier's account of the "ritual economy" of a Hausa market, where material transactions are inseparable from a moral traffic in human and superhuman powers. Here the adepts of the local *bori* possession cult contest the growing control of Muslims over the terms of trade in their community; to their great dismay, the Islamic ascendancy has effaced a symbolic map that anchored indigenous history and identity in the immediate landscape. Yet the followers of *bori* have also reconfigured themselves in the course of protesting these alien Islamic signs, purposefully purloining some of them for their own ends. Again, as Austen says, the production of new wealth often depends on appropriating the reproductive resources of others while collaborating—at least to some degree—in their authority. Thus, in an effort to redirect the power of the followers of the Prophet, *bori* adepts have built houses for their own spirits in Muslim architectural style, and have buried within them a melange of symbols of market prosperity, hoping thereby to divert some of the wealth that flows into Islamic coffers. They do this, Masquelier insists, without actually buying into the ideology that authorizes such wealth—a

Muslim ideology that resonates with neocolonial values of private property and the work ethic, from which *bori* remains largely estranged.

Ritual, in short, has played an obviously significant role in the articulation of local and global orders of production and exchange; the latter being understood, here, as simultaneously material and moral, social and symbolic. Equally obvious is the fact that such processes of articulation have long histories (see Wolf 1982). They predate European colonialism and extend beyond it into the postcolonial age of advanced capitalism, in which much of Africa has suffered renewed political and economic marginalization, ecological devastation, and the impact of AIDS (see Austen). Under such conditions, ritual tends to address not only the dubious embrace of alien powers but also the equivocal status of national elites, who appear as the visible face of cosmopolitan culture. Rural Africans widely acknowledge the fatal attraction of that culture, and of the urban centers that direct the capricious flow of its commodities. They also are often quick to appreciate two things: that the (relative) well-being of the cities is usually gained at the expense of the countryside (see Hart 1982); and that people such as themselves lack control over the worldly workings of the modern state.

Such insights have often led to incisive critiques of the rapacity of international capital ("business") and its African beneficiaries—though rarely to practical means for reversing its effects. Chewa children, says Kaspin (see chap. 2 this vol.), fear the cannibalistic inclinations of white people, but adults are fascinated by their gluttonous consumption of meat, a quality associated with callous predators and monsters. This, together with activities like the transfusion of blood,[12] is enough to suggest that Europeans wield dangerous, even superhuman powers over life itself. In addition, they appear to enjoy mastery over motorized and airborne movement—and, with it, the capacity to fuse the realms of above and below, to collapse time and space, and to control the velocity of value. Nevertheless, while such skills are incontrovertible proof of great potency, they remain, to many rural Chewa, alien and alienating. Western technologies might be manageable by Malawian Christian elites, who are suspected of having struck a Faustian deal with the whites. For the rest, however, these technologies remain auguries of otherness, increasingly intrusive signs against which to assert a defiant, ritually marked identity. In fact, Kaspin notes, Nyau ritual has come to be opposed to the church as are Chewa country folk to Christian literati. It has come to embody "not only the enduring legacy of [Chewa] precolonial culture, but also their immediate experience on the political margins of the neo-colonial state." Is it surprising, then, that, in the effort to tie these margins to a culture of national consensus, government should try to appropriate Nyau, using it as a means to define and regulate "Chewa ethnicity"?

It is in the context of just such processes—where, as Apter puts it, local communities, regional economies, state structures, and global markets collide and are realigned—that we come upon our most elaborate ritual discourse about modernity and its malcontents: that concerned with witchcraft. This discourse, significantly, often takes on national, even international proportions. For, as Austen notes, it involves a totalizing moral economy, an economy in which the acquisition of money and power links parochial means for producing and destroying human value to potent foreign sources of wealth. Far from merely being a homeostatic feature of precolonial societies, as some earlier anthropologists were wont to suggest, the signs and practices of witchcraft are integral to the experience of the contemporary world. They are called on to counter the magic of modernity. And to act upon the elusive effects of transnational forces—especially as they come to be embodied in the all-too-physical forms of their local beneficiaries.

As the essays in this volume confirm, African witches have a long legacy. Their signifying potential, moreover, has proven to be unusually dynamic and versatile. They travel across broad horizons, take up residence in towns, become mistresses of money, markets, and motorized transport, wear makeup and modish attire (Bastian, n.d.; Masquelier 1991). They also become the personification of capricious commodities, the sirens of selfish desire. Thus Schmoll shows that Hausa "soul-eaters" in rural Niger consume the life essence of their fellows out of insatiable, uncontrolled craving. Theirs is an antisocial lust that finds its "meat" in the bodies of children, and hence subverts the process of social reproduction itself—this, Austen reminds us, being a very general motif in African witchcraft. Soul-eating is thought to be driven by an appetite for money, a hunger unleashed, as local commentators stressed, by European colonialism. And while its "seeds" are held to have been inherited in earlier times, they are now a widely circulating, purchasable commodity on their own account. In fact, soul-eaters themselves become like commodities, being capable of changing their physiques into innumerable material forms; they take on a life of their own and, ultimately, threaten to devour Hausa heritage *in toto*. As this implies, the notion of soul-eating, along with the practices that seek to counteract it, amounts to a powerful disquisition against those who "pursue their fortunes blinded by the glitter of 'modernity' to the moral reality of what 'modernity' means." Nor is its plausibility limited to country folk. It also provides a viable vocabulary for describing the world of those beyond the village—civil servants, for example—who must chase scarce employment in state bureaucracies crippled by financial uncertainty. Likewise in Nigeria, observes Apter, where witchcraft thrives among elites as well as in the population at large. Its "immoral economy" is inflated, in that context, by the experience of government-engineered boom-and-bust, and by the failed dream of "development."

The poetics of predation, it seems, have become particularly salient in coping, imaginatively and practically, with the encounter between local and translocal worlds. That much is clear from Bastian's account of an altogether new category of witchfinders: writers for the Nigerian popular press. *Pace* the predictions of some rationalist theorists (e.g., Horton 1967), literacy has proven to be highly hospitable to magic. (It has, itself, often been seen as such by those subjected to the power of inscription; J. Comaroff 1985:250). Condensing diffuse forms of historical consciousness in plainspoken (usually English) prose, some Nigerian newspapers make it apparent that witchcraft has come to permeate everyday conversation about politics, the pursuit of power, and the complex interdependence of urban and rural life. Neither, it seems, is the appeal of such spectral stories limited to West Africa; the very same "reports" are readily recycled, alongside parallel Western ones, in the yellow presses of Britain, North America, and Europe.

Witches, shows Bastian, serve as ready referents in a many-sided debate about the shifting moral margins of "community." It is a debate framed within the wider process of rethinking the relation of the country to the city, African style (Williams 1973; J. L. and J. Comaroff 1987; cf. Ferguson 1988). In reciprocal ripostes between growing urban masses and their rural relatives, witches have become Janus-faced signifiers. From the town, they seem to epitomize the grasping resentment of reactionary villagers, who greedily "eat" the patrimony of those absentees compelled to mine sources of wealth in the world outside. To the village, they appear as the city incarnate, feeding off the countryside for their own selfish ends, absorbing people, goods, and money with no return, and robbing peripheral populations of their means of reproduction. The fact that these conceptions often find voice in Nigerian English is predictable, Bastian points out. For, in putting witches into words, journalists fuse qualities and constructs of the *lingua franca* with the vernacular, their narratives representing each in terms of the other. And so they attempt to unite both in a new synthesis—just as their readers must do in their daily lives.

As a signifying economy, then, witchcraft is broad and supple in its conceptual scope. But its signs work by rooting expansive moral meanings in the naturalizing ground of human bodies. The latter are made to speak disturbingly, viscerally, about ultimate values: about life, death, wealth, power, misappropriation, domination, and so on. Thus procreation and abortion serve as metonyms for social reproduction and its abuse; gluttony and cannibalism signify unnatural consumption and accumulation; the commoditization of vital physical properties and functions is the archetypical image of capitalist exploitation. As bodies—human energy? labor power?—come to fuel elusive processes of production and enrichment, flesh becomes meat, blood becomes petroleum (Schmoll; Kaspin; Bastian, in press). All this, in turn, underscores a crucial point, one that is confirmed over and over in these essays: witchcraft is not simply an imaginative "idiom." It is chillingly concrete, its micropolitics all-too-real. As Evans-Pritchard (1937) long ago maintained, its occurrence is explicable only with reference to its particular pragmatics: to the ways in which, in specific contexts, it permits the allocation of responsibility for, and demands action upon, palpable human inequities and misfortunes.

In exploring these pragmatics, the essays below affirm that the female form is a particularly fertile site for the "night battles" of contemporary African witchcraft. Take, for instance, the Atinga witchfinding movement among Yoruba (see Apter). Here women were sought out as agents of destruction because they seemed to embody contradictions in an unsettled world of intensified market production, sharpening class divisions, and growing competition between male commercial elites and established female traders. Held to be guilty of cannibalism—of consuming their children and agnates—the accused were made to confess in large numbers; the rites that purged their malign influence appear to have been a collective attempt to efface the diffuse dangers they so vividly objectified. Apter shows how the Atinga movement drew upon a long-standing Yoruba ambivalence toward women's economic activities, an ambivalence gradually retuned in the face of world capitalism and the expanding power of the Nigerian state. That females would be good to think with in such a context was, as Matory also insists, culturally overdetermined.

But it is not merely the threat posed by newly empowered women that evokes the image of the witch. In rural Ngoniland it seems, relict older females are most frequently accused of perverting "progress." Here is further evidence that, in attempts to concretize a collective consciousness of malaise, women have become ever more ubiquitous signs of mystical malevolence.[13] African men are sometimes suspected of nefarious practices too (see Austen). However, their activities are widely regarded as an extension of their public pursuits, as politics by other means (cf. Bastian on the Igbo case). Often this takes the form of sorcery; that is, the intentional manipulation of medicines, now sold on the "black market," that may contain female body parts as active ingredients (see Matory). Women, by contrast, are said to bewitch out of an innate capacity, as a function of the ambiguous values, the ambivalences, naturalized in their very substance. In this, they share qualities with their sisters in early modern Europe (Austen; cf. Thomas 1971). Such "natural" qualities are culturally constructed, of course. Nonetheless, it is the tendency to embody ambivalence that has made females particularly liable to personify contradictions in troubled times and places in the history of expanding capitalism.[14] Thomas (1971: 568), for one, demonstrates how, in sixteenth-century England, the equivocal predicament of peasant women rendered them prime objects of the signifying gaze. As feudal communities felt the impact of merchant capital, these women, marginalized as "unproductive," became sites of the conflict in a new social order.

There has, in this respect, been a wealth of recent work on the objectification of women's persons and bodies with the development of capitalism; especially of industrial capitalism, whose culture rests on asymmetric, often gendered contrasts between such things as the public and the domestic, production and reproduction, the city and the country, reason and intuition, work and leisure. Alongside this, there is growing evidence to show that the ideologies associated with the concomitant rise of "modernity" grouped their counterimages under feminized signs: the rural, the preindustrial, the ritualistic, the irrational, the primitive. The old witch in the attic with her deadly spinning wheel was an apt icon of social inequities engendered by intensified market production in early modern Europe (cf. Schneider 1989). Her kinship with the old Ngoni woman of the 1980s, who hid a medicine horn in her roof thatch, is striking. For Africa has been drawn inexorably into the world of capitalist production. And while it has hardly been made over entirely in European image, it *has* been subjected to forceful social change—of which the marginalization of the domestic, the rural, the "primitive," and the female has been a crucial, if complex component.[15] This process of marginalization has many sides to it. Perhaps most poignant is the fact that those displaced along the way tend quickly to become signs and ciphers with which others make meaning. A final point here: lest we think that such phenomena belong merely to the early beginnings, or to the exotic fringes, of the "modern" European world, let us remind ourselves of contemporary forms of Western witchcraft, witchcraft that addresses the contradictions of advanced capitalist societies. A clutch of images in the recent popular culture of North America are especially revealing in this respect: the "Fatal Attraction" of the corporate harridan who would use sexual and professional wiles to destroy home, husband, and family—and will not die; the dangerous market woman of Wall Street, a trader in the vortex of voodoo economics, who will consume all before her, including the honest "Working Girl"; the standardized nightmare of child abuse, embodied in the callous babyminder, whose "Hand . . . Rocks the Cradle" and aborts social reproduction.

Although African witchcraft clearly predates colonialism, it is not the intention here to reconstruct or recuperate its earlier forms. As it happens, there is clear evidence that, in precolonial polities, it also gave human expression to structural contradictions (e.g., Wilson 1951); but probably less is known about its "traditional" workings than anthropologists often suppose. In its late twentieth-century guise, however, witchcraft is a finely calibrated gauge of the impact of global cultural and economic forces on local relations, on perceptions of money and markets, on the abstraction and alienation of "indigenous" values and meanings. Witches are modernity's prototypical malcontents. They provide—like the grotesques of a previous age—disconcertingly full-bodied images of a world in which humans seem in constant danger of turning into commodities, of losing their life blood to the market and to the destructive desires it evokes. But make no mistake: these desires are eminently real and mortal. And some people are indeed more vulnerable than others to their magic allure. Nor, it should be stressed again, are witches advocates of "tradition," of a life beyond the universe of commodities. They embody all the contradictions of the experience of modernity itself, of its inescapable enticements, its self-consuming passions, its discriminatory tactics, its devastating social costs.

IN SUM, THEN, THE OBJECT OF THIS BOOK is to bring together, in methodological counterpoint, the topics of modernity and ritual. Each of these terms is regarded critically in its own right. Each is treated at once as a space of (often contested) ideological discourse, as a trope of signifying practice, and as an analytic problem. Each is taken to be both a medium and a product of the (relatively) empowered—and empowering—actions of human beings. The relationship of modernity and ritual itself, we have also said, is historically wrought. It is animated by men and women as they seek to make their worlds manageable and meaningful—giving vent in the process to their imaginings of the past, present, future.

In this respect, the central theses that underlie the various chapters may be condensed into two general propositions. First, *pace* the long, persistent tradition that sees ritual as conservative and conservationist, as a (indeed, *the*) prime mechanism of social reproduction, cultural continuity, and political authority, we presume differently: that it may as well be, and frequently is, a site and a means of experimental practice, of subversive poetics, of creative tension and transformative action; that, under its authorship and its authority, individual and collective aspirations weave a thread of imaginative possibilities from which may emerge, wittingly or not, new signs and meanings, conventions and intentions. It is in this sense that ritual is always a vehicle of history-in-the-making: at times it conduces to sustain and legitimize the world in place; at times it has the effect of changing more-or-less pervasive features of that world; at times it does both simultaneously. (We need hardly add, any longer, that social reproduction and cultural continuity are as much a *historical* business, an effect of human intervention, as is the most turbulent and transformative of processes.) Of course, consequences do not invariably follow envisaged scripts and scenarios: some ritual practices aimed explicitly at changing received circumstances do not do so at all—in fact, some may become downright reactionary. Some turn out to be highly significant, others insignificant; some become saturated with meaning, others languish in meaninglessness; the impact of some is enduring, others fleeting. Such things are never fully predictable. If they were, history would lack all surprise, all contingency.

We do not pretend to be the first to speak of the capacity of ritual to change the world, or to insist on its quintessentially historical character. Such assertions, however, are easy. It is altogether more difficult to demonstrate *how* ritual actually works its transformations; how, in practice, it actually (re-)makes social predicaments and (re-)casts cultural orders. For that, we require detailed historical ethnographies of exemplary cases, sensitive social histories of specific signs. This is exactly what the contributors to this volume set out to offer. In so doing, they seek not simply to give support to our first proposition but also to make good the methodological promise implicit in it—thereby to add something creative and interesting to the analytic agenda of both contemporary African Studies and the historical anthropology of modernity.

This brings us back to where we began—with mythic modernities—and to the second of our general theses. It may be phrased as follows: ritual, as an experimental technology intended to affect the flow of power in the universe, is an especially likely response to contradictions created and (literally) engendered by processes of social, material, and cultural transformation, processes re-presented, rationalized, and authorized in the name of modernity and its various alibis ("civilization," "social progress," "economic development," "conversion," and the like). For modernity, a Eurocentric vision of universal teleology, carries its own historical irony, its own cosmic oxymoron: the more rationalistic and disenchanted the terms in which it is presented to "others," the more magical, impenetrable, inscrutable, uncontrollable, darkly dangerous seem its signs, commodities, and practices. It is in this fissure between assertive rationalities and perceived magicalities that malcontent gathers, giving rise to ritual efforts to penetrate the impenetrable, to unscrew the inscrutable, to recapture the forces suspected of redirecting the flow of power in the world. These forces also create huge chasms between material enticements and the often diabolical costs of new forms of transnational cultural capital; between, as some would have it, desire and (im)possibility. In these circumstances, ritual practice typically appears to its practitioners as an entirely pragmatic, secular means to bridge those chasms, to plumb the magicalities of modernity.

Here, by choice and expertise, we take a variety of African contexts as sites in which to explore the phenomena of modernity and its malcontents, of ritual and the technologies of power in the making of history. The processes we interrogate occur everywhere, of course, and have done so periodically since time immemorial. They are, in short, part of the condition of being-in-the-world, of humanity-in-time. We privilege Africa, then, not only to understand better its contemporary predicament. We do so also to make the point that its modern history illuminates the very general, dialectical workings of global processes and transnational forces as they encounter human beings where they live: in local communities, that is, be they in Chicago, Shoshong, or shanty-town South Africa, in Onitsha, Oyo, or oases in the Sahel, in London, Lagos, and countless little villages all over our planet.

Notes

1. In an older vintage of anthropological writings—mainly of structural functionalist provenance—the major trope of contrast with "the modern" was "the primitive." Note the titles of such basic texts as *Structure and Function in Primitive Society* (Radcliffe-Brown 1952), *Primitive Government* (Mair 1962), *The Law of Primitive Man* (Hoebel 1954), *Theories of Primitive Religion* (Evans-Pritchard 1965), even *Primitive and Peasant Economic Systems* (Nash 1966). These titles were not ironically intended, unlike others, many of them published later, that used the term "savage."

2. Although we speak here of "the primitive" as man, the gender politics of modernity—and, by extension, of images of premodernity—is a very complicated issue. While sometimes, in some Western discourses, "the primitive" is male, the feminization (and subjection) of colonized bodies and landscapes, of colonized polities and "traditions," was a consequential feature of European imperialism; see below (also J. and J. L. Comaroff 1991: chap. 3).

3. This section draws heavily upon J. Comaroff (in press).

4. For many structuralist, functionalist, and interpretive anthropologists, in fact, the essence of any "other culture"—including the principles underlying its social order—was best captured by describing its rituals. See Bloch (1989: 15–16) for further discussion of the anthropological equation of ritual with social structure.

5. Among major historical works of this genre read widely by anthropologists, perhaps the earliest is Thompson (1963). For more recent examples and/or methodological discussion, see Le Roy Ladurie (1979a, 1979b); Davis (1981); Ginzburg (1980, 1983); Hobsbawm and Ranger (1983); de Certeau (1984); Levi (1988); and Samuel (1989). For a critical evaluation of work from this perspective done in Germany, see Lüdtke (1982).

6. See, for instance, the influence of Evans-Pritchard and Douglas on Keith Thomas's now classic *Religion and the Decline of Magic* (1971), or of Turner on Natalie Zemon Davis's *Society and Culture in Early Modern France* (1975).

7. In a provocative essay on ritual for the *International Encyclopedia of the Social Sciences*, Leach, e.g., concludes (1968:526) that "[n]o attempt has been made to discuss the *forms* of ritual" (emphasis added).

8. For notable exceptions, see Hanks (1990); and Silverstein (1981).

9. Like many students of ritual before and since, Turner himself relied at times on Van Gennep's (1960) formal model of rites of passage. That model, of course, is a descriptive one; it does not amount to an explanatory theory, *sensu stricto*, of anything. As is well known, Van Gennep described three stages through which those undergoing life-crisis ceremonies pass. But he did not account for *how* the triparte scheme—or, for that matter, any formal feature of the ritual process—actually achieves its effects. (For a critical reformulation of his approach in just this respect, see T. S. Turner [1977].) On another note: while we highlight the work of Turner here, it is not, we repeat, our intention to imply that he is the only anthropologist to have considered the formal construction of rites. For example, Bloch (e.g., 1989) explains the power of ritual—which, for him, stands at the opposite pole, on a continuum, from politics—by appeal to the formalism of its linguistic and paralinguistic features; this, he argues, is what makes it impossible to contest the messages conveyed in ritual communications—and hence gives them unquestionable authority. For Bloch, as for Turner, therefore, rites can only be instruments of social reproduction. His position has received a good deal of critical attention of late (see, e.g., Kelly and Kaplan 1990); but, because it is not in our direct line of inquiry, it is only addressed here in passing (see below).

10. Our switch from the past to the present tense here is meant to reflect the fact that, while Turner died some years ago, his approach to ritual and symbolism is still very much alive—as much outside as within anthropology.

11. We use "advanced" rather than "late" capitalist, as we are uncomfortable with the teleology implied by the latter term.

12. The potency of blood transfusion as an image of the extraction of value by Europeans seems widespread in Africa; see, e.g., White (1992); Weiss (1992).

13. See, for instance, Fields's (1985:80ff) account of Zambian *Mucapi* witchfinding during the colonial era. Her material shows that jealousy among the relict co-wives of migrants served as fuel for a growing number of accusations. But she also gives plenty evidence of male witches, often the older rural kinsmen of returned workers, who demanded their share of urban wages. Auslander's later ethnography, in contrast, indicates that aged women made up the bulk of the accused in postcolonial witchcleansing movements.

14. Obviously, it need not only be women who come to signify ambivalent values or social ambiguity in capitalist societies. See Newborn (in prep.) for a cogent account of how Jews—and, in particular, Jewish bodies—came to embody critical contradictions in Nazi Germany.

15. This is not to deny that, in precolonial Africa, women were marginalized in political, economic, and ritual terms (J. Comaroff 1985; J. L. Comaroff 1987). They certainly were—*pace* Ali Mazrui's startling assertions to the contrary in his tele-

vision documentary series, *The Africans*. Rather, it is to (re-)assert the fact that colonialism, and global market forces, played into existing African social arrangements to produce far more thoroughgoing processes of marginalization.

References

Appadurai, Arjun. 1990. Disjuncture and Difference in the Global Cultural Economy. *Public Culture* 2:1–24.

Bastian, Misty L. Forthcoming. Blood and Petrol: The Dangerous Eroticism of Transport in Southeastern Nigeria. *Africa*.

Bloch, Maurice. 1986. *From Blessing to Violence: History and Ideology in the Circumcision Ritual of the Merina of Madagascar*. Cambridge: Cambridge University Press.

————. 1989. *Ritual, History and Power: Selected Papers in Anthropology*. London: Athlone Press.

Bogucka, Maria. 1992. Gesture, Ritual, and Social Order in Sixteenth- to Eighteenth-Century Poland. In *A Cultural History of Gesture*, ed. J. Bremmer and H. Roodenburg. Ithaca: Cornell University Press.

Cohn, Bernard S. 1987. Representing Authority in Victorian India: Cultural Contradictions in the Construction of a Ritual Idiom. In *The Invention of Tradition*, ed. E. J. Hobsbawm and T. O. Ranger. Cambridge: Cambridge University Press. Reprinted in *An Anthropologist among the Historians and Other Essays*, B. Cohn. New Delhi: Oxford University Press, 1987.

Cohn, Bernard S., and Nicholas B. Dirks. 1988. Beyond the Fringe: The Nation State, Colonialism, and the Technologies of Power. *Journal of Historical Sociology* 1:224–29.

Comaroff, Jean. 1985. *Body of Power, Spirit of Resistance: The Culture and History of a South African People*. Chicago: University of Chicago Press.

————. In press. Defying Disenchantment: Notes on Religion, Resistance, and the "Modern" State. In *Communities in Question: Visions of Authority in Asia*, ed. C. F. Keyes, L. Kendall, and H. Hardacre. Honolulu: University of Hawaii Press.

Comaroff, Jean, and John L. Comaroff. 1989. The Colonization of Consciousness in South Africa. *Economy and Society* 18:267–96.

————. 1991. *Of Revelation and Revolution: Christianity, Colonialism, and Consciousness in South Africa*. Chicago: University of Chicago Press.

Comaroff, John L. 1987. *Sui Genderis:* Feminism, Kinship Theory, and Structural "Domains." In *Gender and Kinship: Essays toward a Unified Analysis*, ed. J. Collier and S. Yanagisako. Stanford: Stanford University Press.

Comaroff, John L., and Jean Comaroff. 1987. The Madman and the Migrant: Work and Labor in the Historical Consciousness of a South African People. *American Ethnologist* 14:191–209.

————. 1992. *Ethnography and the Historical Imagination*. Boulder: Westview Press.

Corrigan, Philip, and Derek Sayer. 1985. *The Great Arch: English State Formation as Cultural Revolution*. Oxford: Basil Blackwell.

Darnton, Robert. 1985. *The Great Cat Massacre and Other Episodes in French Cultural History*. New York: Vintage Books.

Davis, Natalie Zemon. 1975. *Society and Culture in Early Modern France: Eight Essays*. Stanford: Stanford University Press.

————. 1981. Sacred and the Body Social in Sixteenth-Century Lyon. *Past and Present* 90:40–70.

————. 1990. The Shapes of Social History. *Storia della Storiografia* 17:28–34.

de Certeau, Michel. 1984. *The Practice of Everyday Life*. Translated by S. Rendall. Berkeley: University of California Press.

Dirks, Nicholas B. 1990. History as a Sign of the Modern. *Public Culture* 2:25–32.

Evans-Pritchard, Edward E. 1937. *Witchcraft, Oracles and Magic among the Azande*. Oxford: Clarendon Press.

————. 1949. *The Sanusi of Cyrenaica*. Oxford: Clarendon Press.

————. 1965. *Theories of Primitive Religion*. Oxford: Clarendon Press.

Ferguson, James. 1988. The Country and the City on the Copperbelt. Paper read at the annual meeting of the American Anthropological Association, Chicago, November.

Fields, Karen E. 1985. *Revival and Rebellion in Colonial Central Africa*. Princeton: Princeton University Press.

Geertz, Clifford. 1973. *The Interpretation of Cultures: Selected Essays*. New York: Basic Books.

Ginzburg, Carlo. 1980. *The Cheese and the Worms: The Cosmos of a Sixteenth-Century Miller*. Translated by J. and A. Tedeschi. Baltimore: Johns Hopkins University Press.

————. 1983. *The Night Battles: Witchcraft and Agrarian Cults in the Sixteenth and Seventeenth Centuries*. Translated by J. and A. Tedeschi. London: Routledge & Kegan Paul.

Gluckman, Max. 1963. Rituals of Rebellion in South-East Africa. In *Order and Rebellion in Tribal Africa: Collected Essays*, by Gluckman. London: Cohen & West.

Hall, Stuart, and Tony Jefferson, eds. 1976. *Resistance through Rituals: Youth Subcultures in Post-War Britain*. London: Hutchinson.

Hanks, William F. 1990. *Referential Practice: Language and Lived Space among the Maya*. Chicago: University of Chicago Press.

Hart, Keith. 1982. *The Political Economy West African Agriculture*. Cambridge: Cambridge University Press.

Hebdige, Dick. 1979. *Subculture: The Meaning of Style*. London: Methuen.

————. 1988. *Hiding in the Light: On Images and Things*. London: Routledge.

Hobsbawm, Eric J. and Terence O. Ranger, eds. 1983. *The Invention of Tradition.* Cambridge: Cambridge University Press.

Hoebel, E. Adamson. 1954. *The Law of Primitive Man: A Study in Comparative Legal Dynamics.* Cambridge: Harvard University Press.

Horton, Robin. 1967. African Traditional Thought and Western Science. *Africa* 31:50–71, 155–87.

———. 1971. African Conversion. *Africa* 41:85–108.

Kelly, John D., and Martha Kaplan. 1990. History, Structure, and Ritual. *Annual Review of Anthropology* 19:119–50. Palo Alto: Annual Reviews Inc.

La Fontaine, Jean S. 1977. The Powers of Rights. *Man,* n.s. 12:421–37.

Lan, David. 1985. *Guns and Rain: Guerrillas and Spirit Mediums in Zimbabwe.* London: James Currey.

Leach, Edmund R. 1954. *Political Systems of Highland Burma: A Study of Kachin Social Structure.* London: Bell.

———. 1968. Ritual. In *International Encyclopedia of the Social Sciences,* vol. 13, ed. D. L. Sills. New York: Macmillan Co., Free Press.

Le Roy Laudurie, Emmanuel. 1979*a. Carnival in Romans.* Translated by M. Feeney. New York: G. Braziller.

———. 1979*b. Montaillou: The Promised Land of Error.* Translated by B. Bray. New York: Vintage Books.

Levi, Giovanni. 1988. *Inheriting Power: The Story of an Exorcist.* Chicago: University of Chicago Press.

Lévi-Strauss, Claude. 1966. *The Savage Mind.* London: Weidenfeld & Nicolson.

Lüdtke, Alf. 1982. The Historiography of Everyday Life: The Personal and the Political. In *Culture, Ideology and Politics: Essays for Eric Hobsbawm,* ed. R. Samuel and G. Stedman Jones. London: Routledge & Kegan Paul.

MacNeice, Louis. 1973. Snow. In *The Oxford Book of Twentieth-Century English Verse,* ed. P. Larkin. Oxford: Clarendon Press.

Mair, Lucy. 1962. *Primitive Government.* Baltimore: Penguin Books.

Masquelier, Adeline M. 1991. Consumption, Prostitution, and Reproduction: The Poetics of Sweetness in *Bori.* Paper read at a conference on Meaningful Currencies and Monetary Imaginations, University of Chicago, March.

Mitchell, Timothy. 1988. *Colonising Egypt.* Berkeley: University of California Press.

Mitchell, W. J. Thomas. 1986. *Iconology: Image, Text, Ideology.* Chicago: University of Chicago Press.

Munn, Nancy D. 1973. Symbolism in a Ritual Context: Aspects of Symbolic Action. In *Handbook of Social and Cultural Anthropology,* ed. J. J. Honigmann. Chicago: Rand McNally.

Nash, Manning. 1966. *Primitive and Peasant Economic Systems.* San Francisco: Chandler.

Newborn, Jud. In prep. "Work Makes Free": Nazi Anti-semitism and the Transformative Labor of Genocide. Ph.D. diss., University of Chicago.

Radcliffe-Brown, Alfred R. 1952. *Structure and Function in Primitive Society*. London: Cohen & West.

Ranger, Terence O. 1987. Taking Hold of the Land: Holy Places and Pilgrimages in Twentieth-Century Zimbabwe. *Past and Present* 117:158–94.

Sahlins, Marshall D. 1976. *Cultural and Practical Reason*. Chicago: University of Chicago Press.

———. 1985. *Islands of History*. Chicago: University of Chicago Press.

———. 1992. Goodbye to Tristes Tropes: Ethnography in the Context of Modern World History. Ryerson Lecture, University of Chicago, 29 April.

Samuel, Raphael. 1989. Heroes below the Hooves of History. *The Independent*, no. 902 (31 August):23.

Schneider, Jane. 1989. Rumpelstiltskin's Bargain: Folklore and the Merchant Capitalist Intensification of Linen Manufacture in Early Modern Europe. In *Cloth and Human Experience*, ed. A. B. Weiner and J. Schneider. Washington, D.C.: Smithsonian Institution Press.

Silverstein, Michael. 1981. Metaforces of Power in Traditional Oratory. Paper read to the Department of Anthropology, Yale University, February.

Stallybrass, Peter, and Allon White. 1986. *The Politics and Poetics of Transgression*. Ithaca: Cornell University Press.

Tambiah, Stanley J. 1985. *Culture, Thought, and Social Action: An Anthropological Perspective*. Cambridge, Mass.: Harvard University Press.

Thomas, Keith. 1971. *Religion and the Decline of Magic*. New York: Charles Scribner's Sons.

Thompson, Edward P. 1963. *The Making of the English Working Class*. London: Gollancz.

Trexler, Richard C. 1984. We Think, They Act: Clerical Readings of Missionary Theatre in 16th Century New Spain. In *Understanding Popular Culture*, ed. S. Kaplan. Berlin: Mouton.

Turner, Terence S. 1977. Transformation, Hierarchy and Transcendence: A Reformulation of Van Gennep's Model of the Structure of Rites de Passage. In *Secular Ritual*, ed. S. F. Moore and B. Myerhoff. Assen: Van Gorcum.

Turner, Victor W. 1957. *Schism and Continuity in an African Society: A Study of Ndembu Village Life*. Manchester: Manchester University Press.

———. 1967. *The Forest of Symbols: Aspects of Ndembu Ritual*. Ithaca: Cornell University Press.

———. 1969. *The Ritual Process: Structure and Anti-structure*. London: Routledge & Kegan Paul.

Van Gennep, Arnold. 1960. *The Rites of Passage*. Translated by M. Vizedom and G. Caffee. Chicago: University of Chicago Press.

Weiss, Brad L. 1992. Electric Vampires: Haya Rumors of Wealth. Paper read at the annual meeting of the American Ethnological Society, Memphis, March.

White, Luise. 1992. Bodily Fluids and Usufruct: Controlling Property in Nairobi,

1917–1939. Paper read at the African Studies Workshop, Northwestern University, February.

Williams, Raymond. 1973. *The Country and the City.* New York: Oxford University Press.

Wilson, Monica. 1951. Witch Beliefs and Social Structure. *American Journal of Sociology* 56:307–13.

———. 1957. *Rituals of Kinship among the Nyakyusa.* London: Oxford University Press, for the International African Institute.

Wolf, Eric R. 1982. *Europe and the People without History.* Berkeley: University of California Press.

PART I

(Re)visions of Power, Ritual (Trans)formations

1

Narratives of Power, Images of Wealth: The Ritual Economy of *Bori* in the Market

Adeline Masquelier

BECAUSE THE *BORI* CULT OF POSSESSION HAS BEEN REIFIED as an "epiphenomenon" whose practices are merely symbolic and whose impact is restricted to the sphere of ritual, its historical and political significance has been largely overlooked. Many have viewed the cult as a thinly disguised protest movement for marginalized and deprived individuals eager to redress grievances and exact concessions from their superiors (Lewis 1971; Besmer 1983; Onwuejeogwu 1969). Other scholars, who have dismissed the "deprivation" theory, have interpreted *bori* as a positive assertion of value by the powerless (Monfouga-Nicolas 1972) or as "sub-culture" (Callaway 1984). Though they point to the salient issue of protest, all these approaches have failed to treat the *bori* as a source of potency of wide social relevance. By viewing possession as a problem-solving process rather than a discourse about power, they have often narrowly interpreted the practices of *bori* as a way to redress social dysfunction and treated the cult's symbolic statements as historically insignificant. As the incident I am about to recall will show, *bori* is not a symbolic alternative to an estranging reality, or an idealized refuge whose claims can be dismissed on the basis that the cult accomplishes nothing, or that it has no lasting impact on the society at large.

Despite their failure to account for the social impact or the political significance of healing cults, most approaches to mediumship nevertheless attempt to deal with power as a dimension of human experience crucial to the understanding of possession and ritual. In the context of spirit possession, power has been defined as domestic strife (Lewis 1971), competition between co-wives (Wilson 1967), "cultural resistance" (Stoller 1984), or rebellion against political domination (Fry 1976). Possession also has been analyzed as a struggle between spirits and humans for control of mediums' bodies and minds. In this essay, power is the creative energy focused through ritual and the imagined community of spirits. As agents of mediation between human and supernatural realms, and through their partner-

3

ship with one or several spirits, cult adepts have the knowledge and
authority to tame or exorcise the spirits afflicting their victims. Their roles
as healers enable them to channel and manipulate forces that threaten to
invade individual and social bodies. This form of power is opaque, diffuse,
and multidirectional. It cannot be translated as a concrete quantum of
agency or domination. Elusive, yet effective, it is not easily located and
circumscribed in time or space. To account for the social and historical
relevance of spirit possession, we can no longer view power as inherently
negative, unidimensional, repressive, and subjugating. We must recognize, along with Foucault, that power can be creative and productive, as
is shown in the way that cultural signs, categories, and relations are manipulated and transformed in rituals, implicitly reordering the social system in the process (1977). This transformative capacity of power (Arens
and Karp 1989), and the subtle ways people devise to act upon the world,
will be the focus of this essay.

Understanding the poetics and politics of *bori* thus presupposes relinquishing the view that "bullets are more effective weapons than spirits in
the struggle against . . . colonizers" and construing power as an elusive
force which takes many forms (Lewis 1971:117). As Comaroff and Comaroff have said:

> . . . power also presents, or rather hides, itself in the forms of every-
> day life. Sometimes ascribed to transcendental, suprahistorical forces
> (gods or ancestor, nature or physics, biological instinct or proba-
> bility), these forms are not easily questioned. Being "natural" and
> "ineffable," they seem to be beyond human agency, notwithstanding
> the fact that the interests they serve may be all too human. This kind
> of *nonagentive* power proliferates outside the realm of institutional
> politics, saturating such things as aesthetics and ethics, built form and
> bodily representation, medical knowledge and mundane usage . . .
> Yet the silent power of the sign, the unspoken authority of habit,
> may be as effective as the most violent coercion in shaping, direct-
> ing, even dominating social thought and action. (1991:22)

Drawing on the notion that the instrumental value of *bori* signs, images,
and practices cannot be abstracted from their meaningful dimension, and
that "reality" and "representation" are inseparable components of people's
experience of history, I will discuss a particular event that occurred in a
rural town of Niger and is revealing of the ways *bori* provides a voice for
a minority of Mawri who have been silenced by Islam, the religious establishment. I will show that though they have been estranged from the tangible structures of wealth and authority, *bori* devotees have successfully
managed to channel their own forms of potency through the ritual manipulation of empowering signs and techniques. In attempting to reassert

their independence from the hegemony of Islam, *'dan bori* (members of *bori*) are in effect reworking the bases of a moral economy which rejects the rules and principles laid down by Muslim clerics and merchants. The *'dan bori's* reaction to Muslim structures of economic, religious, and political control remains a largely inarticulate and implicit protest which rarely takes the form of a cogent political discourse, but the cult's images and narratives are nevertheless a powerful vehicle of collective consciousness. Because they are rooted in indigenous cosmologies the veneer of Muslim practices has not managed to erode, these images and narratives become an instrument of persuasion and coercion in the hands of a marginalized faction seeking to transform alienating structures of control.

Encounter with the Spirit of the Market

During my fieldwork in the Arewa region of Niger, people often made striking comments about the market (*kasuwa*). One statement in particular had puzzled me for a long time. I had been told that "those who go to the market are not afraid" (*Du wanda ya zaka kasuwa bai jin tsoro ba*). I would spend hours walking among the stalls of the Dogondoutchi market but could never see what made the market such a dangerous place.[1] When I asked my friends what the phrase meant, some would shrug their shoulders and answer that they were not afraid of anything but Allah. Others would say that since so many strangers came to the market, you could never know about the people with whom you spoke, implying that the old woman who had sold you a liter of peanut oil might actually be a witch or a spirit in disguise and not an old woman at all. I supposed that might be why one should always remain on guard when entering the marketplace.

But I also knew that men, especially those who professed to be devout Muslims, would often strictly prohibit their young wives from going to the market, preferring to entrust their unmarried daughters or their mothers with the task of purchasing the weekly household necessities. Some men would even do the marketing themselves rather than allow any women of the household to venture into the marketplace. It seemed that a husband's fear of having another man cast an eye on, or even seduce, his wife could hardly justify the deep-seated, yet unspoken, fear I felt pervading Mawri attitudes regarding the market. If seduction was the primary reason for women to avoid the market, any public place where young, married women were not supposed to be seen should have been perceived as equally dangerous. Yet that was not the case. Moreover, in my experience, men would express reservations about going to the market as often as women would. As months went by, I got more involved in the *bori* cult of possession and put aside my investigation of the mysteries the market held.

In June 1989, however, an incident occurred in the area that was to shed some light on the dangers of marketing. On the first Friday of the month, the weekly market of Dogondoutchi, traditionally held on the west side of town, was transferred south to the outskirts of the city. The newly appointed mayor, eager to make some innovative changes, had decided that the closer proximity of the market to the highway would improve the economic prospects of the area. Holding the market at a place along the highway linking all the major cities of southern Niger would undoubtedly increase the flow of prospective merchants and customers and facilitate access to, and transportation of, locally unavailable or perishable goods.

Such a major transformation in the spatial organization of the town did not meet with everybody's approval, however. Added to the inconvenience of having to walk an extra half-mile to reach the market, proximity to the highway implied a whole array of new dangers. People were especially concerned with the rise in theft and robbery they perceived as the inevitable outcome of having to venture by the *kwalta* (tarmac road). The weeks preceding the event nevertheless witnessed the feverish activity of carpenters busy setting up stalls in the newly apportioned market space.

I was eagerly awaiting what I thought would be an important celebration that a great many people would attend. But as I was sharing my excitement with my neighbor, Halima, on the eve of the opening of the new market, she warned me not to go to the market the next day because evil things happened the first time a *kasuwa* was held at a new site. When I attempted to press the issue further, Halima just said she really did not know much about it and that I should ask my *bori* friends.

The next day, still resolved to go to the market in spite of (or maybe because of) Halima's intriguing warning, I made my way to my friend Mamu's house to see if her eldest daughter Rabi would come with me. Even though Mamu is one of my most valuable *bori* informants, I did not consciously go to her on my way to the market in order to ask about why I should not go, as Halima had suggested. Upon learning of my intentions, however, Mamu became very alarmed and told me not to go to the new marketplace. When I asked her why she and Halima both tried to prevent me from accomplishing such a mundane task, she seemed to be at a loss for an answer. After I insisted that attending such an important event was crucial to my overall research project, again she could say only that it would be very dangerous for me to go there that day. She then added that she could not tell me anything more at this point, but that if I promised not to go she could perhaps explain later what was so threatening about the *kasuwa* that day. In spite of my intense curiosity, I agreed to forgo the day's main attraction and limit my activities to visits and interviews.

It was not until the next day that I learnt what had motivated Mamu and Halima's mysterious warnings. That morning, right after sunrise, I was informed that the day before three people from the nearby village of

Kieche had died in an auto crash soon after leaving the Doutchi market-place. Their deaths were not accidental, I was told. They had been the victims of a bloodthirsty spirit (*iska;* plural: *iskoki*) which I came to know as the *doguwa*² of the market. In Arewa, each market has its *doguwa*. And each time a market is transferred to a new site, the spirit of that market has to be propitiated by an offering of blood so that commerce thrives. People say that a new market requires the shedding of blood (*ya kamata a wace jini*). Theoretically, the chief of Arewa should provide the sacrificial ox for the establishment of the market (*kashin kasuwa*). I have been told often that in the past *doguwa* would not associate with mere commoners but only with chiefs, since only chiefs were rich enough to be able to satisfy the voracious appetites of these fearful *iskoki* (spirits). Legend has it that human blood was the *doguwa*'s favorite sustenance. It is believed that the chiefs kept some slaves whom they would regularly sacrifice to appease the *doguwa*. Fulfilling the *doguwa*'s request through the ritual killing of an ox would nowadays ensure the prosperity of the market, the fulfillment of which would constitute a sign that the spirit was satisfied and agreed to protect the *kasuwa* and its people.

Concomitant with such belief was the idea that on the first market day the *doguwa* would kill a young man and a young woman, or a *budurwa* (un-married girl) and a *samari* (unmarried boy), regardless, in fact, of whether or not an ox was sacrificed. If the spirit did not kill two such persons, the market would not "take"—become a place of prosperity. Hence, individ-uals who belonged to these categories ran the risk of becoming the spirit's next victims should they venture to enter the new marketplace on the first day of its siting. This meant that I could have been the *doguwa*'s prey had I not been warned about the potential danger.

My friends' fears were heightened by the fact that no offerings had been made to the deity. Unlike the *'yan bori* whose role was often scorned by the administration, the *malamai* (Muslim teachers/healers) had pow-erful connections with city officials. Eager to demonstrate their loyalty to the representatives of Islam and to promote their own agenda, the mayor and the *mai gari* (customary chief of town) thus agreed to pay the *malamai* for their services and forgo the traditional sacrifice of an ox. Thus, on the eve of the market day, the Imam of Doutchi led his assembly of followers to prayer and called on Allah to make the new market prosperous. After this ritual was accomplished, the *'yan bori* swarmed the marketplace to hold a possession ceremony and call on the spirits whose support they saw as essential for the success of the town's enterprise. Every one of them was bitter and angry that the town's officials had ignored their claims to a part of the money that had been turned over to the *malamai*. Besides seeing their prospects of getting free meat ruined, *bori* leaders felt insulted by the fact that their roles and responsibilities in promoting the market's prosperity had been so grossly overlooked. In their eyes, it was a dramatic sign that times had changed irretrievably.

Were the spirits angry as well for not having been offered a sacrificial ox? Nobody could say. But the fact that all the spirits declined to possess their devotees during the possession ceremony that day was taken by some as an inauspicious sign of the evils that were yet to come. It did not take long for these premonitions to be realized. The sun was still high up in the sky when the three unfortunate passengers of a Peugeot 404 had a fatal accident on their way back from the market. Among them were a young man and a young woman.

The following Friday, the tragedy was, if not forgotten, at least no longer the main topic of gossip in Doutchi households. If the week before the newly established market had had a limited attendance due to people's fears of the *doguwa*'s requirements, in its second week it presented, in the opinion of onlookers, all the signs of becoming a prosperous institution. Muslim leaders had been vehemently denying that the death of the three travelers had been caused by anything else than the will of Allah. The *'yan bori*, on the other hand, were eager to erase from their memory the painful humiliation they had just suffered. At the same time, they were reluctant to acknowledge that their defeat implied the abandonment of yet another non-Muslim communal ritual. Yet, to them and to all those who, in spite of their adherence to Islam, believed in the power of the *iskoki* (spirits), the fatal car crash was an unmistakable confirmation of the *doguwa*'s potency and of her fierce temper. It, therefore, provided *bori* devotees and sympathizers with an effective weapon to challenge the supremacy of Muslim authority. It was clear to them that the Imam's prayers, no matter how convincing, had been of no avail against the *doguwa*'s anger.

A number of studies have discussed the importance of trade and markets in Hausa society (Cohen 1969; Hill 1969; Works 1976). Yet, those who have explained the institution of *kasuwa* in relation to pre-Islamic religious practices have done so only in passing, usually reducing the market to a field of socioeconomic forces (Nicolas 1966, 1975; M. G. Smith 1962). Overplaying the economic dimension of this cultural enterprise at the expense of the immaterial and the symbolic has only obscured what the market has come to stand for and signify for those Mawri like the *'yan bori* who feel cast out from the poles of economic and political activity. In particular, such an approach ignores how the *'yan bori* tap into their stock of traditional concepts and historical imagery to accommodate the new demands of their market economy, and to mediate their understanding of wider social forces they cannot clearly pinpoint, much less control. Besides alerting me to the crucial role played by the spirits in the seemingly mundane sphere of commerce and trade, the market incident convinced me that a very real battle was being waged in the *kasuwa* between *'yan bori* and Muslims. The fight involved no overt confrontation of palpable power but found expression in an "argument of images" whose impact on the collective imagination remained long after the *doguwa*'s victims were buried (Fernandez 1982).

Spirits, Arziki, and Precolonial Cosmologies

Despite the repeated efforts of the *malamai* to discredit the *bori* cult at every opportunity, the belief that spirits intervene in people's lives to increase or decrease their *arziki* (a complex word-bundle which simultaneously means well-being, good fortune, prosperity, and favorableness) is tacitly accepted by a great many members of the community. According to the ideology surrounding *arziki*, life is nothing but a game of chance; some individuals, being more fortunate, have more chance of winning than others (Nicolas 1964). By securing the protection and assistance of one spirit, or several, it is believed that a person will ensure his chances of staying, or becoming, healthy and prosperous. Although agricultural production is the main source of income for villagers, its unreliability has turned trade into the only avenue to *arzkiki* for those who do not practice a craft or work as civil servants. According to my Mawri friends, engaging in trade is one, if not the best, way to enhance one's economic position and prestige. The fact that most, if not all, of the rich and prosperous *alhazai* (Muslims who have accomplished the pilgrimage to Mecca) are merchants is testimony to that in people's minds. Because life is a lottery and because success in any human enterprise, whether it be a commercial transaction, marriage plans, or the taking of an exam, is mostly credited to the favorable intervention of a spirit, it follows that only after having promised allegiance to a spirit will a person achieve wealth and prosperity through trade.

Up until the French colonization of Niger at the turn of the century, war was the backbone of Mawri socioeconomic and political order (Piault 1975; de Latour 1982, 1984). For the Mawri, war implied pillage. It meant extorting millet and cattle and capturing slaves.[3] As such, it constituted the basic source of wealth and power for the ruling aristocracy as well as a unique avenue to fame and fortune for commoners. Whether it was to gain political power or to ensure one's subsistence, however, waging a battle was never simply a matter of military power or tactics: a crucial step in achieving victory and bringing back booty involved securing the trust of a protective *iska* (spirit) before engaging in combat. Just as it is believed by *'yan bori* that a trading venture cannot be a successful and fruitful enterprise without the approval of the spirits, so legend has it that in the past victories on the battlefield could never be achieved without the intervention of spirits. More than simple struggles in which human strength and courage were measured, battles engaged supernatural forces whose protective powers were put to test. Certain deities were intimately associated with the landscape (certain landmarks such as caves, rocks, ponds, or trees were, and still are, tangible objectifications of the spirit world) and revered by an entire community in exchange for the protection they afforded the village; others actually would take part in actual battles, and their memories are cherished for the many victories they helped achieve.

Preparing for battle meant acquiring protective medicines which would either make the recipient invisible, rendering enemy arrows inoffensive, or turn bullets into water. Because such medicines could only by acquired by promising allegiance to a spirit, the wealth and fame that were inevitably associated with success in war would not only prove the strength of a warrior and make him into a hero but also demonstrate the power of the *iskoki*. Though no battle could be safely planned and won without having recourse to the spirits' assistance, credit was always given to these supernatural interventions. Upon successful return from a battle, the chief and his warriors would each thank their protective deities by performing a sacrifice. Through these periodic offerings of blood, villagers reinforced the timeless bond established between the people and the supernatural agencies. Failure to propitiate one's protective spirit would inevitably result in ill luck and heavy losses during battles. But warriors who regularly fulfilled the *doguwa*'s request for offerings had nothing to fear. Each spirit had particular qualities and particular ways of intervening in a warrior's life as long as he could prove his devotion and commitment to the deity.

The Emergence of a Market Economy

The imposition of peace, the abolition of slavery,[4] and the introduction of a market economy by French colonial forces all contributed to the erosion and reshaping of the political, economic, and religious institutions of Mawri society. The colonial administration not only imposed a heavy burden through taxes, forced production, forced labor, and military enrollment; by ruining the political and economic bases of the ruling aristocracy, it profoundly upset the elaborate alliances and rivalries, exchanges and redistributions that constituted Mawri social order (de Latour 1982:259). In the realm of religious faith and practice, the ignorance, incompetence, and limited means of the French administration often led to a complete realignment of the *rapport de forces*. Although official policies toward Islam vacillated considerably according to politicohistorical circumstances as well as the motivations and assumptions of individual administrators, they seemed to have made little difference to the situation on the ground. Hostile measures taken against Islam often proved beneficial to the Muslim cause because they fostered a resurgence of the tradition of revitalist holy wars and stimulated religious conversion. Tolerance of Islam and cooperation with Muslim leaders similarly, but for different reasons, encouraged adherence to Islam. The French administration, which had no clearly defined Islamic policy, hence succeeded where commerce and religious imperialism had both failed: by upsetting the generative dynamics of the politicoreligious order and breaking down local economic structures, it helped propagate the Coranic message among a people who had until then staunchly resisted conversion to Islam.

Faced with the necessity to minimize administrative costs and to generate revenues from a territory that offered scarce resources, the French introduced policies that were purely exploitative. The objective was to break the circuits of subsistence in the rural economy in order to restructure the production toward fulfilling the needs of an expanding capitalist economy in France (Collion 1982:2). Instructed to extract as much of the local material and human resources as possible, French officers often left the population impoverished and vulnerable to epidemics and hunger (Fuglestad 1983). In addition to having to pay the head tax in cash, taxable individuals were required to plant a minimum area (0.6 hectares in 1943) in groundnuts (Collion 1982). Such measures would have unforeseen consequences for the viability of the household as an economic unit. When the drought of 1913–15 and the locust invasion of 1931 produced famines of massive proportion, the breakdown of indigenous economic structures was highlighted by massive population migration to Nigeria (Egg et al. 1975).

Whether defensive or offensive, war had traditionally unified aristocrats and commoners against the outside and insured that lineages maintained their coherence (de Latour Dejean 1980:108). War required solidarity among people, lineages, and ethnic groups no longer necessary in times of peace. With the imposition of colonial rule, the incidence of divorce became higher and the organization of the lineages progressively disintegrated (de Latour 1982:261–62). As a result of its inability to financially provide for all its members, the extended family fragmented into smaller economic units. In tandem with the nuclearization of the farming unit, the organization of the sacred evolved to address and express the complexity of emerging identities and relations of power. *Bori* deities became more personalized as religious practice evolved toward a greater individualization (Piault 1970:59). The *bori* pantheon expanded to include a diverse array of Mawri and non-Mawri spirits whose appearance expressed the Mawri's experience of political domination and drastic social change (Masquelier 1989).

Although Arewa remained impermeable to the influence of Islam and the Mawri were spared from invasion and proselytization at the hands of the Fulani in precolonial times, the colonial period saw the timid beginnings of Islamic practices. A colonial report (Belle 1913) stated that the handful of Muslims that could be seen in Arewa in the 1910s were foreign merchants from Nigeria. Around 1940, the number of Muslims had risen to 3000 in a total population of 72,400, according to colonial sources.[5] All the Muslims in the region were either Zarma or Fulani, and no one, not even the *malam* (Muslim teacher/healer) who enjoyed a certain degree of prestige in Doutchi, had managed to make converts among the local population. Whether or not these specific figures are reliable, it is clear that at independence Islam had won hundreds of adherents among the local population. In fact, in the last fifty years, conversion to Islam has intensified to the extent that the followers of the Prophet now outnumber the *'yan bori* in the Doutchi region.

The progress of Islam is perceived by many as a direct outcome of the suppression of war and a symptom of the society's malaise. One of de Latour Dejean's informants touched on a crucial point when he declared that "Islam has spread because of peace (1982:264). War necessitated recourse to the spirits." The advent of peace is thus experienced as one of the many evils brought about by colonialism because the pax colonial brought about the breakdown of the socioreligious mechanisms that ensured the survival of local communities in times of hardship. Conversely, the improvement of communications and the expansion of commerce within, and outside of, pacified Arewa paved the way for Islam: those Mawri who perceived the potentials of trade probably converted to the Muslim faith to legitimize their activity and earn the trust and consideration of the French who generally favored the Islamic status.

With the penetration of money and the introduction of such new notions as private property, individuality, and free enterprise, members of society became increasingly self-oriented instead of relying on the pooled resources of the extended family unit. According to Sutter,

> . . . collective ties, based on reciprocal responsibilities centered on the extended family production and consumption unit, have become progressively replaced by social relationships mediated through money. The family as an economic unit has become less important in supplying the needs of the individual, who has become more isolated and responsible for his own subsistence. (1979:1)

Youths were given the means to produce their own income by selling not only the crops of their personal fields but their labor as well. No longer depending upon their elders for putting together a bride-price and paying their taxes, they gradually escaped the tutelage of the extended family which was, in any case, less and less able to support all of its members (de Latour Dejean 1980:123).

Sutter notes that "It [was] the need for money that pushe[d] young men, and even family heads, into working as salaried laborers and into selling land" (1979:1). Groundnut production and commercialization, which the French had encouraged by imposing a head tax payable in cash (Pehaut 1970:64), particularly hastened the breakdown of the extended-family farming unit and led to the privatization of landholdings. When increasingly fragmented landholdings could no longer sustain them as farmers, men would turn to migration as a means to earn the necessary cash and relieve the demand made on the food supply of their household.

Moving away from the extended household also implied neglecting one's heritage and one's ties and ritual obligations to the lineage's spirits. In the eyes of many Mawri, this is where the crux of the matter lies. I was told over and over again that people had forgotten the spirits and turned to Islam because, once peace was established, they felt no need to call on their protecting *iskoki* and just wanted to get on with their lives. Ironically, Islam contributed to the increasing individualization and monetarization of the economy by favoring the notions of private property and social differentiation and by encouraging the accumulation of wealth (de Latour Dejean 1975:200).

The spirits were thus neglected, and consequently they ceased to intervene in human existence except to cause diseases, poverty, and degradation as punishment. In fact, incurable afflictions and repeated misfortunes are often taken to be the spirits' way of reminding people of their heritage, whether they be Muslims or *'yan bori*. While people see their struggles as originating in the French domination and in the profound changes that have come in its wake, they nevertheless impute a great part of the responsibility for such a state of affairs to their own lack of fidelity and honesty. "It is our own fault," they say, "if things have become so bad." This widespread sense that it is ultimately people themselves who "ruined everything" is shared mostly by *'yan bori* who, thus, can put the blame on those who have strayed from the path of the ancestors, the Muslims. Yet, one finds some followers of the prophet who are also convinced that the troubles they are experiencing stem from their disregard for traditions and the "way" of their forefathers.

In a sense, it is as if the *bori* priests see their role as having shifted from a focus on prospective propitiation to one of retrospective amelioration. Punishment is dispensed by the *iskoki* who, by denying wealth and good fortune (*arziki*) to an individual, are thought to strip him of all he possesses in the form of money, land, offspring, and social prestige. A formerly prosperous villager lacking *arziki* will not only lose all the traces of his fortune; he will also have to abandon all hope of enhancing his economic standing, his social status, and the enjoyment derived from being rich and wealthy (Nicolas 1964:105). On the other hand, a person who is endowed with *arziki*, thanks to having nurtured his relationship with spirits, must risk everything in the game of chance.[6] Besides card games and lottery, the best way for a villager to try his luck and test the power of his *arziki* is to go to the market.

The market is now a fundamental institution of Mawri society, but it was not so in the precolonial past. On the eve of colonization, Mawri society had a limited orientation toward trade. The administrator Belle reports the following in 1913:

> Non-existent before our occupation, commerce in this sector only started to develop at the end of 1908 with the transport of telegraphic materials. Though the transport of such materials required a considerable effort from them at the beginning, indigenes have now realized what profits can be gained from such activities. The transport service has been an economic and political benefit for the region. It has stirred a people which was previously unwilling to move away from the corner of earth to where it confined itself. It has given villagers the desire for acquiring possessions, and the idea of engaging in trade. By convincing, Mawri and Azna[7] that they could work, it has rendered them bold enough to speculate. (My translation)

With the imposition of peace and the introduction of money through the levying of taxes, the indigenous war economy was progressively replaced by a market economy. When taxes were first introduced in 1914, they were paid in cowries and centimes. Cowries were suppressed in 1920 and replaced in 1921 by silver coins.[8] This region, in which twenty years before no foreign merchant would have ventured for fear of being attacked, robbed, or captured as a slave began to welcome Nigerian merchants and foreign traders (Belle 1913). Many tradesmen who left for Madaoua, Niamey, or Gaya exchanged in these towns parts, or all, of their salaries to acquire goods that could be sold on Arewa markets. Others, who traveled to Nigeria, would stock up on cloth, wrappers, and turbans which they would then resell at an inflated price in Dogondoutchi (ibid.). Belle noted that as early as the 1910s the

> traffic of Dioulas is heavy; they bring back from Nigeria, sometimes from Dahomey: wrappers, *boubous* [Muslim robes], turbans, British or German knick-knacks, showy cloth manufactured in Europe, needles, thread, pearls, copper or glass bracelets, etc. Kola nuts, which used to be in scarce supplies and solely for chiefs, are now plentiful, markets have been created and are flourishing . . . A commercial movement has been created, it can only grow. (1913; my translation)

By that time, six weekly markets had been created in the villages of Matankari, Dogondoutchi, Doumega, Tibiri, Lokoko, and Lougou; they gave signs of continued growth, affluence, and prosperity (ibid.).

By 1941, the number of markets in the subdivision of Dogondoutchi had risen to nine, providing further evidence of the growing role of money in the local economy.[9] The main commodities traded in the markets of Fadama and Nassarawa were millet, wrappers, cattle, sheep and poultry, and goods imported from Nigeria. In the markets of Dogondoutchi, Matankari, Bagaji, and Sukukutane, villagers could sell or purchase millet, cattle, skins and salt. At the lesser markets of Ligido, Kilia, and Bougou, the main goods were millet and wrappers (ibid.). Aside from animals and millet, one could acquire locally grown cotton, tobacco, cloth, peanut oil, butter, eggs, milk, and locally dyed wrappers. The money obtained from the sale of cash crops also enabled villagers to purchase the Western goods which eventually replaced locally produced items. Kola nuts, white cloth, matches, colored cloth, sugar and *chechia* (Sudanese hats) figured most prominently among the imported goods available at local markets.[10] As people were forced to sell their labor, or a portion of their harvest or herds to take care of tax requirements, more coins began to be used in transactions and barter gradually died out (de Latour Dejean 1980:110).

In a geographic area already subject to periodic natural disasters, the new colonial economy deepened the peasant's vulnerability to climactic changes and price fluctuations, and increased his dependence on cash-crop revenues. Forced to buy manufactured goods of generally poor quality at high prices in return for the sale of unprocessed products grown or collected locally, villagers were continually indebted. In their attempts to surmount the contradictions of the capitalist economy and meet the never-ending monetary needs of their families, they would inevitably fall back on the market to find the necessary cash (ibid., 124–25). This was the beginning of a vicious circle from which the peasants could never disentangle themselves.

Take, for instance, the case of a villager who derived his subsistence from field cultivation. Sowing more peanuts (at the expense of his millet field acreage)[11] to get cash meant that the man would be faced with a shortage of millet before the next harvest. If he hired himself out as a laborer to buy extra millet with his wages, he would wind up having little or no time to tend his own field. To make ends meet, he would often be forced to sell parts of his livestock, an option that resolved short-term demands for cash but, since animals were the currency for bride-price, also prompted greater long-term needs for money. The last recourse available to a peasant faced with the fearful prospects of ruin and famine was the sale of his land or labor and, possibly, emigration. These were commonly chosen alternatives as more and more households found it increasingly difficult to sustain themselves solely from their agricultural revenues.

Faced with increasing monetary obligations and decreasing, or unstable, revenues, peasants were obliged to resort to the market, even if

the market absorbed not simply surpluses but also what was indispensable
to the cyclical reproduction of labor and resources. The market thus became, to paraphrase de Latour Dejean (1980:124), a trap. Added to the
fact that money had become the indispensable instrument of exchange
without which one could not survive, let alone prosper, in this new
economy was the problem of the limited amount of currency available in
the colony. This only made the need for money more acute. On one occasion, it also deeply upset the entire economic structure laid out by the
French: according to a colonial report of 1913, the rarity of bronze coins
in the Territory induced some villagers to desert the market and revert to
barter (ibid., 110). Besides raising the question of African resistance to
new economic policies, the incident is significant for it shows how the
market was perceived by villagers. For them, indeed, the market was a
trap, and money was the embodiment of what they could not have and was
the source of their many problems. Solving their immediate difficulties
implied abandoning the market as the main locus of trade and exchanging
goods and services without using cash as an intermediary.

Money was such a symbol of the alienation from traditional values and
of the uncertainties of the future that it was feared as much as it was coveted. I was told that up to a few years ago those who would hire themselves out as day laborers often insisted upon being paid in grain rather
than in cash. In these people's minds, millet would go a long way, whereas
money literally burnt holes in their pockets. The comments of one of
de Latour Dejean's (1980:140) informants expresses these fears very vividly: "We prefer millet to money. Money gets spent right away; millet is
kept into our gullet." As villagers became increasingly controlled by the
market economy and helpless in the face of adversity, there was the sense
that money only made the poor poorer and the rich richer. Such a feeling
still prevails today in Arewa as money has invaded virtually every area of
Mawri life. It was not just only nostalgia for the "good old days" that im-
pelled an eighty-year-old man to observe that "before the Whites, we had
no money and everybody was rich. Now, we have money but everybody
is poor."

From the Battlefield to the Marketplace

Earning money, by any means and at any cost, has nevertheless become a
major concern of the Mawri, whether they be rich or poor, peasants or
civil servants, nobles or commoners. If in 1913 a handful of villagers decided to eliminate the market and its chief instrument, money, in an attempt to regain control over the means of production, there is no sign
today that their rebellious action had any historical impact. The kasuwa is
now a thriving and popular institution in Arewa.

Villagers and merchants from nearby or faraway communities attend the market not simply to sell or buy goods but to meet friends and relatives and to renew acquaintances. In fact, the need to make a purchase is irrelevant to whether or not someone will go to the market. One goes to the market to see and to be seen. Men parade in their most elegant gowns, and women show off their newest outfits. The market is the place to hear news and gossip and to discuss marriage plans. It is the place where new fashions and trends are started. In the past, chiefs would inform their subjects of their general orders or important decisions in the market (M. G. Smith 1962:309). In the past, the *kasuwa* was also the scene of official executions. According to informants, the individual who had been found guilty of witchcraft would be beheaded there and his body left to hang from a tree so that all would have a chance to witness the punishment inflicted upon witches. Village and neighborhood chiefs in charge of tax collection often visit the market for the sole purpose of collecting the money from family heads or remind them of their monetary obligations.

The establishment and growth of a market is not simply a matter of allocating a space, laying out stalls, and inviting everyone to come. Attendance at the market may fluctuate dramatically; when everyone might expect a market to be flocked by traders, customers, and onlookers, it could nonetheless fail to attract anyone. Market performance is so unpredictable that people say: *Da kogi da sarki da kasuwa ba a ba da labarinsu* (A river, a chief, and a market are too capricious to prognosticate about them) (also noted by Abraham 1962:532). So capricious are markets, in fact, that no matter how experienced, cunning, and calculating traders might be, there is no telling what the future of a market will be. For a market's success essentially depends upon the good fortune (*arziki*) of the community founding it. According to the *'yan bori*, this *arziki* is contingent upon the power and goodwill of the spirits (Nicolas 1975:390). For this very reason, choosing the site of a new market should never be conducted haphazardly. A divinatory rite should be held in order to determine the most auspicious location for a market. For should the site chosen for a new market be on the customary path of a spirit or too close to the stone or tree in which an *iska* dwells, the *kasuwa* will never become a successful enterprise (Nicolas 1975:391). If the spirits like the place for the new market, they will make it thrive, but in the manner of a river; sometimes full and flowing, sometimes dry and empty.[12]

Spirits are thought to enjoy attending people's markets. Although they have their own markets, where they can sell and buy goods, they never miss an opportunity to mingle among a crowd of humans for the sole pleasure of contemplating piles of colorful enamel bowls or of smelling the fragrant aroma of ripe mangoes and guavas. Spirits are attracted by fragrant smells and beauty,[13] and they are said to be curious, envious, and sometimes greedy, just like humans. As Mary Smith's informant Baba recounts,

> The market is the people's, but it belongs to the spirits also. If you give them alms, you please their hearts, then they settle down and cause men to come with their loads, they draw people and draw people—lots of people. (M. F. Smith 1981:220)

Propitiating spirits before the first market day is, in the eyes of the *'yan bori,* essential to the prosperity of the establishment. In the past, *bori* ceremonies, whose purpose was to invite one or several *iskoki* to settle at the marketplace, were held with the tacit, if not complete, approval of city officials. If Muslim authorities interfered and prevented the propitiation of benevolent spirits, disastrous consequences would generally follow. We know from Baba that

> there was also no market at Old Giwa [Nigeria]. The market refused to take. The *bori* adepts danced for fourteen days, and it looked as if the market might settle, but since there was no water, it did not take . . . They [the spirits] said that they were to be given a black bull and black goats and black cloth, but Fagaci [the chief of Kano's scribe, a Muslim] would not give them their things. After that they were here, they went on living here, but the market wouldn't go. They didn't go anywhere else, they were here, they just put a stop to the market. (M. F. Smith 1981:188–89)

Since the market is so full of spirits (this is where they are said to often reside when they are not in the bush or participating in a *bori* ritual), it is a potentially dangerous place. There are evil as well as benevolent spirits who stroll in the *kasuwa* in search of human company. These *iskoki* may take on the appearance of a harmless animal, such as a donkey, a horse, or a goat, to trick humans. They can also make themselves look like somebody a person is familiar with, such as one's sister or one's neighbor, in order to communicate with this person. More often than not, they look like pretty Fulani women, pacing the market alone or walking in pairs. One should be especially suspicious of these creatures, I was told, because their beauty is equaled only by their cruelty and fierceness. The only way to find out whether or not they are real women is to take a look at their feet: these female spirits have camel, donkey, or horses hooves in place of feet.

While an encounter with a spirit can be beneficial and fruitful, meeting a spirit also can have tragic consequences if the *iska* turns out to have evil intentions. Many dreadful incidents, which resulted in the ailing, or death, of a villager and involved an evil spirit, were said to have originated in the marketplace where the victim had gone to buy a calabash or some tomatoes. This is why one should not go to the market without protection. It is thought that those who have one or several spirits never enter a marketplace without them. Thanks to her spirits, a woman will know what dangers await her, and she will see through others to find out what their intentions are. Moreover, just as one does not walk into the arena of a *bori* ceremony without having washed with, or ingested, powerful medicines, one never enters a market without being protected by *magunguna* (medicines). Some *magunguna* act as a protection against evil spirits, blows, metallic weapons, etc., while the aim of others is to ensure that the people having used them will be liked by everybody and, therefore, be offered a profitable exchange for every transaction they undertake.

Besides the evil spirits who visit the marketplace, one must also fear the presence of mean old women who practice medicine only to hurt and gain power over individuals. Men in particular should be especially careful not to leave any hair and nail clipping on the ground of the *kasuwa* if they have resorted to the services of a barber. After everyone has gone home, these old hags are thought to roam the marketplace in search of forgotten hair and nail clippings with which they will prepare potent and harmful medicines. When the medicine takes effect, the man to whom the shaved hair belonged may, for instance, become impotent.

The dangers of markets do not reside solely in the fact that one may cross the path of a dangerous spirit or become the victim of an evil healer; markets are inherently dangerous by virtue of their unboundedness. Usually located on the periphery of a town or a village, there are not enclosed within walls like houses.[14] Because there are no boundaries to limit access, and no restrictions as to the identity of visitors, anybody is free to walk in and out of the *kasuwa*. Although the pre-Islamic installation of a market aims at ritually circumscribing a space that will be protected from external evil forces and where benevolent agencies will converge (Nicolas 1966), there is no telling who enters the *kasuwa* and under what disguise.

Part of the attractions that a market holds for Mawri seems to reside in these very dangers. Just as in past battles, wealth and fame could only be achieved by taking risks and courting death, so in the market, one must be willing to expose oneself to certain threats in order to conduct trade and hope to attain prosperity. Visiting the market is seen as a risky, yet potentially rewarding venture if one knows when and how to seize opportunities. One way to enhance one's chance of becoming prosperous is, of course, to obtain supernatural powers. This is achieved, Nicolas tells us, by spending one or several nights within the deserted marketplace in order to meet the spirits and become infused with their potency (1975:345–46). Since, as the proverb goes, "a market isn't anybody's home" (*kasuwa bai gidan kowa ba*), people who are found to wander in the market at odd hours are generally suspected of "messing with the spirits." Marketplaces, like cemeteries and garbage dumps, are avoided outside of neatly circumscribed times and activities, for they are situated on the community's spatial and ritual boundaries (Douglas 1966).

In spite of, or perhaps because of, its inherent dangers, it is tacitly acknowledged that the market is where "things happen." [15] It is where wealth, in the form of goods, animals, people, spirits, and information, converges in a seemingly inexhaustible flux. The concept of market is synonymous, in Mawri eyes, with abundance and opportunity. [16] If in precolonial times war was the sole avenue to riches and social advancement, it is now the market that has taken on that role for many unschooled Mawri. The saying that states that "anything one sees in the chief's house can be found in the market" (komi an gani gidan sarki akwai shi kasuwa) (in Whitting 1967:112) speaks to such a view. Some villagers seem to set up a trade business with almost no capital and end up rich a few years later. Ironically enough, most of them have turned their backs to the spirits to embrace Islam and its social values.

The Market as a Muslim Institution

Trade in Doutchi is mainly in the hands of Muslims. In fact, as several studies have pointed out for the rest of Hausaland, the development of trade went hand in hand with the spread of Islam (Lovejoy 1971; Works 1976). Trade provided the avenue for the spread of Islam because adherence to the Muslim faith maintained ties between dispersed trade settlements as well as enabled merchants to feel part of an "imagined community" and to experience the "consciousness of connectedness," to apply Anderson's concepts to this situation (1985:57). Conversely, Islam paved the way for commerce by providing a religious rationalization to economic motivations and success just as the Protestant ethic provided an ethical justification to the hardworking and successful European capitalists. Like the Protestant ethic, Islamization represented a marked shift away from the past: it facilitated the region's opening to the vaster world by locking local history into the framework of a universal time scale and linking it to world geography (see Anderson 1985). It enabled the new converts to communicate at a distance, to record the passage of the years, and to learn about the history of past centuries or faraway lands (Goody 1971:460). It also subjected them to moral judgment by an external, monotheistic standard of values (Hiskett 1973:81). This had important implications for the way Muslims have dealt with the increasing monetarization of their economy in colonial and postcolonial Arewa. Besides the fact that French colonial policies reflected an overriding preference for Islam, Muslims seemed to be more advantageously adapting to the newly emerged cultural order and better equipped to deal with a nascent capitalism than *'yan bori*.

Today, the social veneer provided by Islam is a crucial element in successful trading. Only those who openly profess allegiance to the Prophet will see doors open up before them; only those who enjoy visibility and conspicuously parade at the mosque for the Friday prayer will be able to establish the network of relationships needed to practice commerce on a large scale. It is through ostentatious displays of piety and sobriety that one may claim membership in the universal and egalitarian brotherhood that, in theory at least, recognizes no tribal, racial, or geographical cleavages. As Hausa merchants striving to maintain social and commercial ties far away from their home base realized long before the nineteenth-century Islamic *jihads*, becoming a Muslim can be purely a matter of wearing Islamic garb, taking a Muslim name, and professing some knowledge of Arabic. By conforming to Islamic custom, adopting Islamic values, and following an Islamic schedule, one can soon earn the prestige and recognition needed to enter the world of trade.

It is not surprising, then, that all the successful traders in Doutchi are Muslims. More often than not, these *attajirai* (wealthy merchants) have accomplished the pilgrimage to Mecca and are highly respected, and powerful members of their community. For their fellow Muslims, their achievements—highlighted by the trip to Mecca—are a measure of their commercial abilities and a sign of God's will. In the eyes of the *'yan bori*, however, their material success stems from their faithful allegiance to their lineage's spirit. Just as rich and powerful Muslim leaders allegedly owe their *arziki* to a spirit whom they secretly propitiate, so wealthy merchants are thought to regularly sacrifice to their spirit in the privacy of their home to ensure their continued prosperity. The annual commemoration of Abraham's sacrifice is also interpreted by some of the *'yan bori* as another disguised attempt on the part of the Muslim community to propitiate the spirits. Pious Muslims would, of course, never admit to such practices, but that does not make these customs any less real to the *'yan bori*. In fact, for the *'yan bori*, these practices only exemplify the proverbial bad faith of the Muslims. It is common knowledge within the *bori* community that the followers of the Prophet lie about their dealings with the spirits and hide behind the deceptive facade of Islamic conventions.

Despite popular perceptions that commerce is the sole avenue to riches for those who have no political connections and little education, not everyone who trades ends up rich and respectable. In fact, wealthy merchants remain a minority among the multitude of petty traders who resell the goods they have bought from a wholesaler for a nearly insignificant profit. The increasing commoditization of their economy has forced many farmers to fall back on trade as a secondary occupation during the dry season in an attempt to supplement their meager agricultural revenues. Studies conducted in the eastern part of Hausaland have shown, for instance, that three-fourths of the traders interviewed in markets were cultivators or herders seeking to earn cash through market transactions (Arnould in Horrowitz et al. 1983). Like their counterparts in Dogondoutchi, they hold limited inventories and usually buy and resell goods in the same market in a single day (ibid.). Whether they sell cigarettes, kerosene, kola nuts, candies, or laundry soap, their profit margins are usually narrow. Because farming is no longer an adequate means of livelihood, many Mawri go to the market to sell as much as to purchase in the hope that their (often speculative) transactions will bring the much needed cash. It is as if "more and more part-time traders are competing for a decreasing share of the limited 'surplus' in the country" (ibid.).

Bori *in the Market and Market in the* Bori

The apparent bad faith of the Muslims, who openly condemn the rituals which the *'yan bori* suspect them of secretly resorting to, only exacerbates the mounting tension between the Islamic and the *'yan bori* communities. For if Muslims are thought to have a monopoly over the market, the *'yan bori* would like to retain unlimited control over the realm of spirits. With the growing disappearance of once popular pre-Islamic rituals in the Doutchi area, the *'yan bori* see the extent of their authority and the sphere of their power diminish progressively. In their attempt to retain what remains and perhaps to regain control over what was once theirs, they blame the Muslims for all the evils of this world. Hence, the source of profit to which they had little access, the market, became identified by the *'yan bori* as the source of misfortunes after the Muslims denied them the ritual powers they once held over the institution. Because the new market was a triumphant symbol of Islamic hegemony rather than an emblem of unity and cooperation between opposing factions, the tragedy associated with its opening provided *bori* devotees with the perfect occasion to brandish the fearful images of a not-so-distant past and shake up the villagers' admiration for Muslim ways. By conjuring up the powerful vision of the *doguwa* which spoke to all Mawri and resonated with the forgotten images and symbols of the precolonial past in all its glorious and legendary dimensions, the *'yan bori* were also attempting to rework the historical roots of their predicament and locate the source of their misfortunes (of which the death of three innocent villagers was only a facet) in the practices of those who sought to overpower them.

Reclaiming the marketplace as a "place of, and for, the spirits" was also a way to redefine the market location as part of the moral landscape in which were encoded so many beliefs and practices relating to *bori*. In the Doutchi region, for instance, certain rocks, trees, and caves are inhabited by the spirits who guided the foundation of many local settlements and became the protective deities of these communities. Annual offerings were (and still are to a certain extent) made to the spirits at the particular site where they reside to ensure the village's protection and prosperity for another year. As tangible objectifications of the interconnections between the world of humans and the world of the *iskoki*, these various landmarks constituted a moral topography within which a sense of history and identity was anchored (see Munn 1970). Each redefinition of this topography through an offering at the various sites not only promoted good relations between humans and spirits; it also symbolically reenacted the historical pact made between the deity and the first settlers. Like the caves, anthills, and mounts that had been imaginatively appropriated by early settlers to domesticate and historicize the local landscape (see Ranger 1987 for a similar case among the Shona), the market had become part of this mystical geography. In the eyes of the *'yan bori*, denying the *doguwa* of the market her ritual offering essentially amounted to relinquishing one's identity and consciousness of the past because it meant letting Muslims erase yet another sacred site in the landscape and redraw a new moral topography that would only bear the imprint of Islam.

Cast out from what they see as the main avenue to economic prosperity, the *'yan bori* have attempted to change the real world and recreate their own inherent source of wealth through the ritual manipulation of signs, objects, and relations capable of channeling riches and potency. A recent practice of *bori* adepts involves building houses for spirits who are allegedly Zarma. Spirits are more likely to remain with their devotees and to help them become (or remain) healthy and prosperous if they can be physically anchored to the land. In the past, this anchoring was done by erecting one or two stones in a place chosen by the spirit. Some deities had their homes in the village, inside or just outside the compound where their devotees lived, while others, who were considered wild and dangerous, had their stone in the bush, away from the human community. Ritually apportioning a site the spirits could call home for as long as they wished, and usually long after the stone's first keeper had died, insured the spirits fixity both in space and time. Anybody could go to the houses of these spirits to request their intervention in times of need or desperation. The spirits' devotees periodically held a possession ceremony at the stone site and made offerings of blood to the deity by slaughtering animals on the altar. The stone was both a timeless reminder of the spirit's presence, and a marker of the finitude of human lives: seven days after a *'yan bori* had died, the stone would be dug up and replanted in the ground upside down to warn the spirit that one cycle had been brought to an end and that another was about to begin if the spirit chose a new adept among the descendants of the deceased.

The last decade or so has seen the emergence of a new kind of house for spirits whose appearance in Arewa coincides with the end of the colonial period. These houses look just like the thatch roofed huts in which many villagers are living themselves, except that they are the object of an elaborate and costly ritual during which the spirits are invited to take possession of their new homes. From then on, anybody in need of a spirit's assistance is free to come to the hut and ask for the spirit's support, usually promising payment in the form of a piece of cloth or an animal after the request is granted. One of the most significant aspects of the ritual marking of the hut as the *iska's* home involves filling a minuscule earthenware cooking pot with a long series of ingredients before burying it on the right-hand side of the hut entrance. Over the pot is erected the sacrificial stone on which animals are ritually slaughtered to propitiate or thank the spirit.

What *bori* specialists use to fill the little cooking pot varies from one village to the next, but they usually include tufts of cotton, which stand for clothing and which are supposed to elicit gifts of cloth from those who come to the house of the spirit in search of help. There is also grain, which represents the food the spirit's medium will receive from those who are thankful to the *iska*. A handful of sand from an anthill, referred to as *uwa yawa* (the mother of many), is often included. The anthill, where a crucial part of initiation into the *bori* cult takes place, is a major symbol of fertility and abundance for the Mawri. The visions of growth and fertility associated with water are also contained in the pot by including a handful of sand from a riverbed, usually that of the Niger, which flows in the extreme southeastern part of the country.

Each time an ingredient is placed in the cooking pot, the *bori* specialist supervising the ritual whispers the words that will define the purpose of this performance while imbuing the object with the necessary potency. By assembling together these potent elements and by describing how each symbolizes a type of *arziki* or stands for a spatial landmark of ritual importance, the *bori* priest is weaving together familiar images to create a powerful instrument of wealth. Juxtaposed with these symbols of prosperity is the image of the market which evokes notions of plentiness and draws forth visions of unlimited commodities: among the ingredients which are always included are seven handfuls of sand collected from seven different marketplaces.[17] While this sand is poured into the cooking pot, the priest supervising the ritual whispers the following:

the soil of the market will be poured (a market will be set up)
anyone who comes with his things

when the market is over
he goes home
the thing that we want
anyone who comes to the house of spirits
whether man or woman
the one who comes with good intentions
whether it be night or day
may he receive that which he wants
this is what one wants for a market
the soil of the market,
the soil that they will put in the cooking pot
the soil of the market
the one who comes to look for prosperity
may he receive it in a flash
that which he came to look for at the house of spirits
may he receive in a flash[18]

I would suggest that by concentrating these images of abundance, wealth, and growth into a cooking pot which is then buried to the right of the doorway, the priest is actually bringing the market into the *bori* devotee's house or perhaps making that house into a market. Through this condensation of symbolic wealth, he is recreating and redefining a source of prosperity for the *'dan bori*. For the burial of the pot is thought to ensure that the *'dan bori* who owns the house will never be wanting. Following the ritual, there should be a never-ending stream of "customers" who, in return for the spirit's protection or forgiveness, will amply reward the devotee with money, clothes, animals, or the *iska*'s favorite perfume.

By manipulating the signs of wealth and diverting the flow of market goods to their houses, the *'yan bori* are drawing on the signs and symbols of Islamic superiority to justify new claims to authority. They are also laying the bases of their own moral economy, an economy that remains anchored in a mystical landscape of hills, rocks, and caves, and objectified through the myths and ceremonies mapping out moral and material relations of power. But more than simply an attempt to recreate their own networks of exchange and power, these new houses of spirits must be seen as an objectification of the interconnection of human and spirit worlds. As more practices and institutions (such as the marketplace) progressively fall in the hands of the fast-growing Muslim community, *'yan bori* feel an urgent need to reassert their connection with the realm of spirits by physically inscribing this connection on the landscape for all to see. While planting stones as spirits' altars is a practical and efficient way to redesign a moral topography, erecting a costly house to store the material possessions of a spirit is a far more vivid and powerful testimony to the strength and lastingness of the alliance established between people and deities. The fact that in the last thirty years mosques have sprouted like mushrooms to accommodate the ever-expanding crowds of Muslim believers may have influenced 'yan bori in building these costly dwellings. Perhaps the houses of spirits emerged as a direct response to the Muslim erection of monuments that celebrated the almightiness of Allah. Inspired by the success of the Muslims in "taking hold of the land" to create holy sites (Ranger 1987), the 'yan bori borrowed freely from a Muslim tradition whose monuments and symbols spelled prestige and authority. This is suggested by the fact that a villager I knew actually built a mosque for his spirit, a spirit who was a Muslim preacher and who taught his devotee how to write verses of the Koran. After witnessing the Muslims remapping towns and villages by destroying spirits altars,[19] erecting mosques, and forbidding the indigenous rituals that closed off village entrances to sorcerers and evil spirits,[20] 'yan bori needed to objectify their control over local networks of moral, spiritual, and material relations by physically imprinting on the landscape the visible signs and symbols of the wealth and potency they wanted for themselves.

Thus we see how a marginalized minority's response to Muslim hegemony is not overt resistance but rather a complex and enduring process of rejecting and accommodating the dominant order whose signs, practices, and values sometimes provide the terms for indigenous expressions of contestation. Hence, while Muslim attitudes toward spirits are openly condemned by bori members, Muslim architecture provides models for spirit devotees eager to rechannel the might of pious followers of the Prophet. Though Muslim policies are criticized by the bori minority for causing much evil and suffering, one of the most triumphant symbols of Muslim domination, the market, is symbolically brought to the house of the spirits to divert the flow of its goods and riches to 'yan bori.

Although satisfying the spirit's desire for a home is taken to be the major reason prompting the construction of a hut for the bori, visions of the wealth the iska's house will bring to its human owner is a powerful incentive that usually outweighs the actual cost incurred through the entire ceremony. No matter how few and small the gains really are for some, they remain convinced that their hard-earned income is boosted thanks to the gratefulness of occasional villagers who have come to the spirit's house and seen their requests fulfilled. All of the 'yan bori who owned a house for one of their iskoki told me that, if it were not for this extra revenue, they would never be able to afford to buy new clothing for their families every year. In their eyes, the ritual aimed at capturing the essence of health by burying a "little bit" of the marketplace under their spirit's altar was an efficient and meaningful way to regain control over local contexts of power and redefine the source of their prosperity without sacrificing to the Muslim worldview and its concomitant work ethic.

Conclusion

When French colonizers imposed peace and a cash economy in what is today the republic of Niger, villagers of Arewa who had at first shunned the market and ignored its laws progressively came to the hard realization that the *kasuwa* had now become one of the only avenues to power and wealth for those who were unable to get a job in the administration, or unwilling to emigrate. Together with the increasing monetarization of Mawri society, the last fifty years witnessed the rise of Islam which paved the way for capitalism by promoting a moral economy based on individual success, private property, and the accumulation of wealth. Converting to Islam meant adopting a worldview that provided better ideological tools for coping with the complexities introduced by the emergence of a market economy. It also meant straying from the paths of one's forefathers and relinquishing the traditional view that individuals' well-being depended essentially upon the nature of their relations with spirits.

Confronted with the fast disappearance of pre-Islamic beliefs and practices, and constantly provoked by the members of the ever-growing and powerful Muslim community, the *'yan bori* can only blame the followers of the Prophet for the far-reaching disruptions that have come in the wake of colonialism and capitalism. Feeling increasingly pushed aside and dominated by Muslims in the sphere of politics, economy, and ritual, they are desperately trying to reassert their control over the market—the area they see as a crucial locus of power and a source of infinite wealth. When Muslim officials denied them the religious responsibilities they traditionally held over the marketplace, the *'yan bori*'s response, though seemingly inarticulate, proved a potent weapon with which to question the legitimacy and supremacy of Islamic values. Drawing on a notion of authority rooted in ritual practice and legitimated by the weigh of history and tradition, the *'yan bori* conjured up a fearful figure of the past, a figure that spoke to all Mawri regardless of their religious affiliation. That the shadow of the *doguwa* hung over the town of Doutchi several weeks after the tragedy connected with the opening of the market testifies to the viability of such mystical figures in the collective conscience and speaks to the effectiveness of *bori* images and conventions in dominating the moral imagination of a community. The *bori* cult's mixed response of identification with, and rejection of, Muslim values and ethics, its largely inchoate protest of the structures of domination, and its creative efforts to understand a world threatened by forces beyond local control all point to the elusive and subtle forms that power, history, and agency can take in the context of ritual practice.

Notes

1. Dogondoutchi is a rural town of approximately 21,000 inhabitants and the administrative seat for the *arrondissement* bearing its name. People often refer to it as Doutchi. This is the appellation that will be used in this essay.

2. Although most spirits belonging to the *doguwa* "family" bear proper names, I was not able to find out what this *doguwa* was called. Nobody, out of fear or ignorance, could tell me whether or not she had a name. Let me add that it would only be fitting for her to retain some measure of anonymity because it is said that the *doguwa* who kill people at random and are involved in witchcraft remain forever nameless. They are considered too mean and vicious to be named, that is, to be properly tamed and socialized so as to interact with humans in a benevolent and fruitful manner.

3. Slaves were captured only during battles waged against non-Mawri opponents. When fighting against other Mawri, warriors seized millet, cattle, blankets, and other goods. Mawri women were neither captured nor raped because it would "spoil" the medicines with which combatants protected themselves against iron weapons (Piault 1975:326).

4. If, in the nineteenth century, slavery had become a major dimension of the socioeconomic structures in the rest of Hausaland—during his stay in Kano, Barth estimated that there were as many slaves in the city as there were free men (1857: 510)—it never played but a secondary role in the Mawri economy. According to Piault (1975), there was never any systematic exploitation of slave labor in Arewa. The embryonic character of the Mawri state and the persistence of a lineage mode of production promoted the progressive integration of most war prisoners into their masters' lineages. Noble prisoners could be exchanged against a ransom from their families. Commoners made up the bulk of the slaves who were exported to Songhay country to serve as a means of exchange, but most became members of one's lineage. The slave trade in this region appears to have been very limited, which is probably why colonial administrators often reported the quasi-absence of market relations in Arewa.

5. In Republique du Niger, Monographie de la Subdivision de Doutchi (between 1936 and 1940), document 6.1.6, n.d. (*a*).

6. The widespread practice of gambling (in the form of card games) which attracts a crowd of players and onlookers during *bori* ceremonies is testimony to such a belief.

7. Azna ("masters of the land") is the Hausa name given to those who worshiped the deities associated with the land. Descendants of the first group which settled in Arewa, they are locally known as Gubawa (as opposed to the Arewa who con-

quered the area in the seventeenth century and subsequently imposed their political dominion).

8. Republique du Niger, Calendrier Historique de l'Arrondissement de Doutchi, document 6.1.11, n.d. (*b*).

9. Republique du Niger, Monographie du cercle de Dosso, document 5.1.8, 1941.

10. In ibid.

11. In the southeastern part of the country (Hausaland), farmers responded so enthusiastically to colonial propaganda destined to promote the cultivation of groundnut that production soared from above 9000 tons in 1945 to nearly 200,000 tons in 1957 (Charlick 1991:39). Because raising cash crop for the market inevitably meant decreasing the amount of acreage used for millet or sorghum cultivation, the French became alarmed about the possibility of chronic famine and potential political unrest ensuing from a shortage of food crop (ibid.). Storage of surplus grain production and the implementation of modern farming techniques were seen as remedies to the threat of food shortage. Mention is made in colonial reports of the legendary "lack of foresight" of villagers who sell all their millet in Nigeria to obtain cash and who find themselves obliged to later buy it back at a higher price or struggle to survive on wild roots and berries (see, for instance, Republique du Niger, Revue des evenéments du 2eme trimestre, cercle de Dosso, document 5.5.7, 19477).

12. This is aptly conveyed in the following proverb: *Kasuwa kogi ce* (The market is a river).

13. This is why one should never take one's spirit to a museum (*gidan kallo*, i.e., housing of seeing) for fear that the *iska* will want to remain there, forever gazing at beautiful objects and rich artifacts.

14. A notable exception is the new *Grand Marche* (big market) of Niamey which was constructed on the site where the previous one burnt down approximately ten years ago.

15. None of my male neighbors in Doutchi ever missed the Friday market unless they were sick or out of town. Failing to attend the market would have been akin to a dyed-in-the-wool gambler missing a day at the races. Added to the fact that it was *ran salla* (prayer day) for the Muslims, Friday was clearly the most important day of the week for Mawri living in, or within travelling distance of, Doutchi.

16. It is interesting to note, in this respect, that one of the markets of Niamey, Niger's capital, has been named *wadata*. As a noun, *wadata* can be translated as "wealth." As a verb, it also means "to become rich" or "to have sufficiency" (Abraham 1962:914).

17. As the union of three (associated with maleness and male elements, cycles and activities) and four (its female counterpart), the number seven is extremely important in Mawri culture. It is the product of the joining of male and female principles—principles that provide the foundation for Mawri conceptions of the

universe and its reproduction. As such, it is intimately associated with concepts of growth and generation. That seven markets, no more or less, are needed for the successful completion of the hut heightens the significance of the ritual as an attempt not only to create wealth but also to ensure its subsequent reproduction.

18. *Za'a sa kasa kasuwa / wanda ya zaka da abinshi / da kasuwa ya kare / shina zuwa gida / abin da aka so / du wanda ya zaka gidan bori / ko namiji ko mace / wanda ya zaka da abin kwarai / ko da dare ko da rana / shi samu abin da shika bida / shi ne abin da aka so ga kasuwa / kasa kasuwa / kasa da za su sa cikin tukunya / kasa kasuwa / wanda ya zaka in bida alheri na / maza da zahi shi samu alheri / abin da ya zaka bida wurin bori / maza da zahi shi samu shi.*

19. In 1988 and 1989, there were rumors that in northern Nigeria, *malamai* went around systematically destroying spirit houses in an attempt to discourage villagers from practicing *bori.*

20. See Masquelier (1991).

References

Abraham, Roy C. 1962. *Dictionary of the Hausa Language.* London: University of London Press.

Anderson, Benedict. 1985. *Imagined Communities: Reflections on the Origin and Spread of Nationalism.* London: Verso Editions.

Arens, W., and Ivan Karp. 1989. Introduction. In *Creativity of Power: Cosmology and Action in African Societies.* Washington, D.C.: Smithsonian Institution Press.

Barth, Henry. 1857. *Travels and Discoveries in North and Central Africa.* Vol. 1. New York: Harper and Bros.

Belle. 1913. Monographie du secteur de Dogondoutchi. Document 6.1.2, Archives Nationales de la Republique du Niger.

Besmer, Fremont. 1983. *Horses, Musicians and Gods: The Hausa Cult of Possession-Trance.* South Hadley, Mass.: Bergin and Garvey.

Callaway, Barbara. 1984. Ambiguous Consequences of the Socialization and Seclusion of Hausa Women. *Journal of Modern African Studies* 22, no. 3: 429–50.

Charlick, Robert. 1991. *Niger: Personal Rule and Survival in the Sahel.* Boulder, Colo.: Westview Press.

Cohen, Abner. 1969. *Custom and Politics in Urban Africa: A Study of Hausa Migrants in Yoruba Towns.* London: Routledge & Kegan Paul.

Collion, Marie-Helene J. 1982. Colonial Rule and Changing Peasant Economy in Damagherim, Niger Republic. Ph.D. diss., Cornell University.

Comaroff, Jean, and John L. Comaroff. 1991. *Revelation and Revolution: Christi-*

anity, Colonialism and Consciousness in South Africa. Chicago: University of Chicago Press.

de Latour, Eliane. 1982. La paix destructrice. In *Guerres de Lignages et Guerres d'États en Afrique*, ed. Jean Bazin and Emmanuel Terray. Paris: Editions des Archives Contemporaines.

———. 1984. Maitres de la terre, maitres de la guerre. *Cahiers d'Etudes Africaines* 95, no. 24:273–97.

de Latour Dejean, Eliane. 1975. La transformation du regime foncier: Appropriation des terres et formation de la classe dirigeante en pays Mawri (Niger). In *L'Agriculture Africaine et le Capitalisme*, ed. Samir Amin. Paris: Editions Anthropos.

———. 1980. Shadows Nourished by the Sun: Rural Social Differentiation among the Mawri of Niger. In *Peasants in Africa: Historical and Contemporary Perspectives*, ed. Martin Klein. Beverly Hills, Calif.: Sage Publications.

Douglas, Mary. 1966. *Purity and Danger: An Analysis of the Concepts of Pollution and Taboo.* London: Routledge & Kegan Paul.

Egg, J., et al. 1975. *Analyse descriptive de la famine des annees 1931 au Niger et ses implications methodologiques.* Paris: Institut de Recherches des Nations Unies pour le Developpement Social.

Fernandez, James W. 1982. *Bwiti: An Ethnography of the Religious Imagination in Africa.* Princeton: Princeton University Press.

Foucault, Michel. 1977. *Discipline and Punish.* New York: Pantheon Books.

Fry, Peter. 1976. *Spirits of Protest: Spirit-Mediums and the Articulation of Consensus among the Zezuru of Southern Rhodesia (Zimbabwe).* New York: Cambridge University Press.

Fuglestad, Finn. 1983. *A History of Niger: 1850–1960.* New York: Cambridge University Press.

Goody, Jack. 1971. The Impact of Islamic Writing on the Oral Cultures of West Africa. *Cahiers d'Etudes Africaines* 11, no. 43:455–66.

Hill, Polly. 1969. Hidden Trade in Hausaland. *Man* 4, no. 3:392–409.

Hiskett, Mervyn. 1973. *The Sword of Truth: The Life and Time of the Shehu Usuman dan Fodio.* New York: Oxford University Press.

Horrowitz, Michael M., et al. 1983. *Niger: A Social and Institutional Profile.* Binghamton, N.Y.: Institute for Development Anthropology.

Lewis, Ioan M. 1971. *Ecstatic Religion: An Anthropological Study of Spirit-Possession and Shamanism.* New York: Penguin.

Lovejoy, Paul E. 1971. Long Distance Trade and Islam: The Case of Nineteenth-Century Hausa Kola Trade. *Journal of the Historical Society of Nigeria* 5, no. 4:537–47.

Masquelier, Adeline. 1989. Ritual as Historical Practice: The Cult of *Bori* in Arewa. Paper presented to the African Studies Association meeting, Atlanta.

———. 1991. Lighning, Death and the Avenging Spirits: Images of Power and

Morality in *Bori*. Paper presented to the Workshop on Spirit Possession and Universal Religions, Harvard University.

Monfouga-Nicolas, Jacqueline. 1972. *Ambivalence et culte de possession: Contribution a l'étude du Bori Hausa*. Paris: Anthropos.

Munn, Nancy. 1970. The Transformation of Subjects into Objects in Walbiri and Pitjantjajtara Myth. In *Australian Aboriginal Anthropology*, ed. R. M. Berndt. [Nedlands]: University of Western Australia Press.

Nicolas, Guy. 1964. Etude de marches en pays Hausa (Republique du Niger). Documents Ethnographiques, Universite de Bordeaux.

———. 1966. Structures fondamentales de l'espace dans la cosmologie d'une société Hausa. *Journal de la Societe des Africanistes* 36, no. 2:65–107.

———. 1975. *Dynamique sociale et apprehension du monde au sein d'une société Hausa*. Paris: Institut d'Ethnologie.

Onwuejeogwu, Michael. 1969. The Cult of the *Bori* Spirits among the Hausa. In *Man in Africa*, ed. Mary Douglas and Phyllis Kaberry. New York: Tavistock Publications.

Pehaut, Yves. 1970. L'arachide au Niger. *Etudes d'Economie Africaine*, Serie Afrique Noire 1:11–103.

Piault, Marc-Henri. 1970. *Histoire Mawri: Introduction a l'étude des processus constitutifs d'un état*. Paris: Editions du Centre National de la Recherche Scientifique.

———. 1975. Captifs du pouvoir et pouvoir des captifs. In *L'esclavage en Afrique precoloniale*, ed. Claude Meillassoux. Paris: Maspero.

Ranger, Terence O. 1987. Taking Hold of the Land: Holy Places and Pilgrimages in Twentieth-Century Zimbabwe. *Past and Present* 117:158–94.

Republique du Niger. n.d. (*a*). Monographie de la subdivision de Doutchi (entre 1936 et 1940). Document 6.1.6, Archives Nationales.

———. n.d. (*b*). Calendrier historique de l'arrondissement de Doutchi. Document 6.1.11, Archives Nationales.

———. 1941. Monographie du cercle de Dosso. Document 5.1.8, Archives Nationales.

———. 1947. Revue des evénements du 2eme trimestre, cercle de Dosso. Document 5.5.7, Archives Nationales.

Smith, M. G. 1962. Exchange and Marketing among the Hausa. In *Markets in Africa*, ed. Paul Bohannan and George Dalton. Evanston: Northwestern University Press.

Smith, Mary F. 1981. *Baba of Karo: A Woman of the Muslim Hausa*. New Haven: Yale University Press.

Stoller, Paul. 1984. Horrific Comedy: Cultural Resistance and the Hauka Movement in Niger. *Ethos* 12, no. 2:165–88.

Sutter, John. 1979. Social Analysis of the Nigerien Rural Producer, vol. 2, Part D of the Niger Agricultural Sector Assessment. Niamey: USAID.

Whitting, C. E. J. 1967 [1940]. *Hausa and Fulani Proverbs.* Farnborough,
  Hamts.: Gregg Press.
Wilson, Peter J. 1967. Status Ambiguity and Spirit Possession. *Man* 2:366–78.
Works, John A. 1976. *Pilgrims in a Strange Land: Hausa Communities in Chad.*
  New York: Columbia University Press.

2

Chewa Visions and Revisions of Power: Transformations of the Nyau Dance in Central Malawi

Deborah Kaspin

IN CHEWA VILLAGES OF CENTRAL MALAWI, a focal institution of community life is the Nyau dance, also known as "the great dance" (*gule wamkulu*).[1] It is performed at the request of Village Headmen on the occasion of funerals, puberty initiations, and the installations of chiefs, and is part of the legacy of royal ritual inherited from the precolonial period. As such, Nyau legitimates chiefship by linking it to precolonial Chewa polities and by reproducing the symbolic elements of an older cultural order. Yet the chiefships that Nyau ritual supports were radically transformed by colonial and now independent rule and eroded by the development of a market-oriented, Eurocentric state system. The performance of an old ritual of chiefship in Malawi's modern rural periphery is inherently contradictory. And yet Nyau ritual thrives.

Ranger (1986) observes that traditional rituals of this sort often provide their practitioners with fixed reference points in the shifting sands of social history. As such they are sustained by nostalgia for an idealized past that is symbolically dissociated from a troubled present, while the present is represented in new ritual forms such as Africanized Christianities. At a certain level, this generalization does fit the Chewa case: Chewa do claim Nyau as their own "tradition" (*miyambo ya Chewa*) in contrast to the Christian practices they associate with a relatively new and imported political presence. A simple opposition of "the traditional" and "the modern," however, cannot adequately explain either the durability of Nyau or its relationship to alternative ritual idioms. Thus Nyau not only conjures up images of a bygone era but also reflects and redesigns the political and economic realities of contemporary circumstances. And Christianity not only signifies modernity in the Chewa mindset but also derives its utility as a sign from its relationship to the conceptual categories of Nyau.

The purpose of this paper is to place this archaic ritual in the contemporary context of rural Malawi. This means examining Nyau from several perspectives, as symbolic type and social event, as fixed form and fluid formula, as received culture and revised practice. To do so, this chapter will be divided into five principle sections. First, the historical transformations of the Chewa chiefdom will be outlined to show how Nyau has emerged from its precolonial background to claim operational value in the modern setting. Second, the contours of Nyau ritual as it is currently performed will be summarized and the cosmology that shapes its interior logic drawn from it. This will elucidate the symbolism of rural chiefship and of the chief-centered community. Third, the social implications of the ritual system will be explored in terms of the cohorts it consolidates and the means of expression it provides them. Fourth, the relation between Nyau and Christianity will be investigated as twin doorways that lead into, out of, and back into the parallel milieus with which they are associated. Fifth and finally, the threads of analysis will be drawn together to show that Nyau is not an artifact of cultural nostalgia, nor a discrete feature of Chewa society, but part of a repertoire of conceptual categories with which the modern world(s) is continually imagined and revised.

A Brief History of Nyau

Nyau is today, as precolonially, an essential feature of the Chewa countryside; more than a dance form, it is a men's organization and ritual system that is woven into the fabric of the community. As a men's organization, the Nyau society can be defined in two senses. In its most restricted sense, it is a group of dancers who disguise themselves as spirits and animals, collectively called wild beasts (*zilombo*), to perform at the chief's invitation in his village. In a less restricted sense, the Nyau society is the widest community of male initiates. Every Chewa boy undergoes initiation between the ages of ten and fourteen, and thereafter considers himself a member of Nyau, since he is privy to its secrets and has free access to the dancers' private meeting place in the graveyard. Thus in its more expanded sense, the Nyau society includes virtually half—the male half—of the adolescent and adult community.

Yet to define Nyau solely as a male association, even in its expanded sense, too narrowly limits its range of social significance. Nyau provides the basic ritual needs of men and women both, officiating at funerals, at puberty initiations, and at the installations of chiefs. Although each rite requires its own personnel—Nyau officials in one instance, the chief's sisters in another—each rite is coordinated by the Nyau dance troupe. Similarly informed by Nyau symbolism, all rites cohere as elements of a single cosmological order, differentiating and conjoining male and female, spirits and people, chiefs and commoners. Thus Nyau is a totalizing ritual system which defines the contours and categories of the Chewa community.

Nyau is also an essential feature of chiefship at the village level. It is the Village Headman who invites Nyau to his village, who sends boys to the graveyard for initiation, and who provides for each girl initiated in his village. Nyau and Village Headmanship are virtually synonymous, hence the first official act of any new headman is the clearing of his own courtyard (*bwalo*) for its performance. Nyau more than anything else makes the chief, for Nyau more than anything else makes his constituency.

The Nyau society, its rituals, and their linkages to chiefship predate the colonial era (Langworthy 1972a; Schoffeleers 1976; Schoffeleers and Lindgren 1985). Yet Nyau and the chiefship have undergone radical transformations since their precolonial origins, transformations that make their present linkage in the rural setting appear, at first glance, disjunctive: How can old rituals of Chewa royalty be relevant in the present context of the rural underclass? Although the answer to this question must be found in the Chewa countryside today, the analysis of the present must be prefaced by a glance at the transitions of the past century, a history from which the modern production of Nyau is inseparable.

In the precolonial context, the chief's ritual authority was part and parcel of his authority over all life-sustaining processes: land, rain, agricultural products, and trade goods all came from networks of chiefs who controlled paths of exchange with various outsiders, be they human traders or superhuman spirits. Networks of high- and low-ranking chiefs consolidated large territories, motivating political contests, and, in the seventeenth and eighteenth centuries, sustaining centralized kingdoms that extended from the Shire Valley to the Zambezi basin to the Luangwa River (Langworthy 1969, 1972b; Phiri 1975).

The political economy of these central African states was permanently undermined by colonial rule. The British regime cut Africans off from their larger political cohorts and co-opted control over their most essential valuables. Under indirect rule, kingdoms were subdivided into numerous administrative districts, these in turn subdivided into many small territories, and these allocated to indigenous chiefships that were identified—or invented—to assist in the administration of the colonial order. No longer forging polities through other chiefs, African chiefs under the new order served only the needs of the colonial state, assisting in the collection of taxes, the imposition of labor regulations, and the enforcement of various efforts at various times to "modernize" agricultural practices. Less a conduit for valuables than a mouthpiece for the British regime, the rural chiefship was hamstrung, tied to but distinct from the emerging center of power (Kaspin 1990:59–82).

The diminishment of chiefly authority continued under independent rule, as the new government subdivided the chief's territories into ever smaller units and superimposed several new layers of authority over the colonial system of indirect rule. This included several new government ministries created to oversee social services as well as the branching cells of the Malawi Congress Party. The elaboration of civil bureaucracy was undertaken both to aid rural development and to secure the new government's authority in all corners of the republic. The result was the intensification of rural Malawi's focus on the metropole both politically and economically, leaving rural chiefs with less autonomy, not more.

Although the transformation of kingdoms into peripheries eroded the political and economic foundations of Chewa chiefship, the ritual dimensions of chiefship were left intact. Moreover, the colonial regime and the missionary enterprise that accompanied it established the grounds for recreating old rituals of kingship into new rituals of resistance. This began when Christian missionaries sought to bring the colonized Africans to Christ by freeing them from their more barbaric proclivities. In Chewa areas, as Linden (1974, 1975) and Schoffeleers (with Linden 1972) have shown, both Catholic and Presbyterian missionaries targeted Nyau as unChristian and set out to eradicate it so that Christian society could flourish. Preaching against the evils of these obscene dances, at times even seizing drums and masks as dances were underway, the missionaries made conversion contingent upon the repudiation of Nyau as they tried to entice Chewa into their own sphere of influence.

Ironically, the missionaries succeeded not in eradicating Nyau but in identifying for Chewa the means to retaliate against European incursion. Although some Chewa were drawn into the orbit of the missionaries' influence, far more followed the directives of their own chiefs who reacted to Christian proselytizing by recruiting more members to Nyau. To do so, they authorized more chiefs to own Nyau courtyards, lowered the age of entrance from eighteen to eight, and mandated the performance of Nyau on any and every occasion. As a result Nyau proliferated under missionary pressure, limiting the flow of potential recruits to the missions, while expanding the ranks of Nyau chiefs and Nyau members.

While the political and economic authority of chiefs diminished, the rituals of chiefship reemerged as a forum of rural resistance: Nyau became emblematic of African defiance against white rule. In this way, Nyau detached itself from its moorings in the precolonial kingdom and reattached itself to the colonial periphery: a sign of centralized power became a sign of decentralized opposition. As such, Nyau claimed its place in the swelling anticolonial movement led in the 1950s and 1960s by the Nyasaland African Congress. These political meanings were epitomized in the celebratory dances performed on the steps of the Catholic mission at Mua on the occasion of Malawian independence (Linden 1974:131).

In the early heady days of independence, the renamed Malawi Congress Party (MCP) claimed Nyau as its own icon. After all, Nyau and MCP were both African organizations that had thwarted European rule; and Nyau was particularly useful as a sign of the MCP's base of popular support in the countryside. To this day, Nyau dancers are required to perform in the president's honor on national holidays. But as the independent government established itself as the new ruling elite, it came to look upon Nyau as a threat to civil security and by extension its own capacity to govern. Once again Nyau found itself in conflict with the elite.

The government's principal concern with Nyau was the threat that it posed to the security of the rural citizenry, as Nyau members exercised their license as "wild animals" to attack the uninitiated. According to Nyau symbolism, this behavior was essential to the dancers' mystique as beasts and spirits, creatures ungovernable by the laws of mere people. According to Malawi officialdom, however, Nyau "animalism" was not a ritual entitlement but an act of defiance against civil law. And so in the late 1960s, the police and the MCP included the "Nyau problem" within their general programmatic for maintaining security in the countryside and initiated a campaign to domesticate Nyau once and for all. Combining their resources, they identified Nyau's more disruptive members and brought them to court, publically stripping "wild animals" of their masks and issuing criminal convictions and prison sentences to the more defiant. Nyau did not cease to exist as a result of police pressure, but its membership did become sedate and subdued. By 1980 only the memory of their animalistic license survived.

The domestication of Nyau by the Malawian government had important consequences both for Nyau and for rural understanding of state power. Unmasked by the police, the dancers lost their mystique as spirits and were soon understood within their own milieu to be "only" men in disguise. As such, they became more comical than dangerous. At the same time, the authority of the chief was further diminished, as the state laid down its rules and regulations over and against rural protocols. Contrary to the symbolic logic of Nyau ritual, "power" came less from the bush than from the metropole, less through local chiefs than from the new elite. But who exactly were the new elite?

The MCP continues to proclaim populism as the basis of rule, invoking images of Malawi traditionalism—like Nyau dances—to assert that a commonality of culture binds the national whole to its political center. But the cohesion of the whole is underwritten by class stratification—strata that, like the polity itself, were created under colonial rule, and have under independent rule reopened the rift between the ruling elite and the countryside. In the hierarchy of offices that link the first to the second—from District Officer to Traditional Authority (territorial chief) to Village Headman—the Traditional Authority literally straddles the line between them. But the Village Headman is wholly identified with the rural periphery where, at the bottommost rung of the bureaucratic ladder, he has little political capital wield.

In this social and political location the Village Headman provides his community with Nyau, a ritual of the old Maravi royalty, now a ritual of the underclass. It is in this context that we consider the ambiguous status of Nyau and its practitioners today. Nyau cannot be explained as an arcane artifact of cultural nostalgia, for it persists as a more subtle transformation of the hegemonic precolonial order into the counterhegemonic order of the modern Chewa periphery. Yet neither is Nyau adequately explained by reducing it to an expression or vehicle of resistance, devoid of cosmological meaning and sociological depth. As noted earlier, Nyau is not a dance but a ritual system, inextricable from the community and synonymous with chiefship at the most local level. Here it provides an integrating framework within which the rural world creates itself, both in terms of its internal coherence as community and in its relationship to external loci of power.

As counterhegemony, Nyau redesigns the Chewa countryside as a world with its own center, symbolically inverting the relationship between itself as periphery and the metropole as core. This is given in the logic of Nyau cosmology, which transfigures the familiar world into zones of inclusion that face an unknown and external presence. While the ritual dramas represent the outside world as the bush and spirit realm, the logic of opposition is sufficiently elastic to permit the representations of numerous outsiders in the guise of beasts: colonial officials, missionaries, and state agents have all appeared at one time or other in the chief's courtyard, seamlessly woven into Nyau ceremony.

To unravel the many threads of Nyau, I propose to return to the chief's village for a view of the periphery as center as it is formulated within the framework of Nyau ceremony. This means beginning with Nyau as a ritual system that consolidates a community around local chiefs and imposes on that community the conceptual categories that make its internal composition coherent. From there I will consider how the ritual provides an arena and format for creating new images of the outside world, while its interior logic extends beyond the ritual into everyday consciousness to motivate the questions Chewa ask of the powers that today impinge on them.

A Ritual Center of the Rural Periphery

The life cycle rites conducted under the aegis of the Nyau society constitute a major part of social experience, drawing an extended community together on numerous occasions to create the largest arena of sociality that rural Chewa know. This community is forged through the linkages of perpetual kinship among Village Headmen, linkages that mandate the exchange of ritual duties and entertainments, embracing their villages within a ceremonial circuit. As I often heard: "The people of our village go to funerals at Ch—— Village just as the people of Ch—— Village come to funerals at ours." Like Chewa youth, I came to know the contours of the community beyond my own village, as that community came to know me, by following the pathways of Nyau ceremony from one chief's courtyard to the next. Nyau ritual places everyone within this extended social field, giving each a same sex, same age cohort that transcends homestead and village and that dictates one's social responsibilities beyond one's own home. Yet Nyau also reasserts one's personal bond to one's own chief—the chief in whose village one was born, in whose courtyard one was initiated, in whose name one attends Nyau at other villages, and in whose graveyard one will eventually be buried.

Nyau is thus the pivot of a totalizing ritual that defines the boundaries of and cleavages within the Chewa social universe. As such it demarcates chiefly territories and differentiates within them the categories of gender, age-grade, and rank. As we shall see later, Nyau also demarcates the class cleavages that orient the Chewa community within a larger political context, that of the nation-state. But to grasp how Nyau is implicated in the second we must first ascertain how it is entailed in the first, namely, how Nyau creates a community of ritually informed experts who are versed in the secret language of its own performances.

At each rite of passage, the provision of ritual services is the responsibility of the entire assembly, who separate into men's groups and women's groups to perform the ceremonial duties assigned them. The men congregate in the graveyard to dig graves, build coffins, prepare Nyau masks and initiate boys, while the women congregate in the village to cook food, bathe the dead, comfort the bereaved, and initiate girls and chiefs. In the meantime, all perform for their own entertainment the songs and dances of their "side," art forms that are laced with the imagery of Nyau animalism to proclaim their distinctive attributes as men and as women.

These duties, songs, and dances are all identified by a single term, *mwambo*. Loosely translatable as "secret knowledge," *mwambo* is the ancestral wisdom that everyone learns at puberty initiation and that is the unique possession of each person's rank and gender: adult men have their *mwambo*, adult women have theirs, chiefs have their *mwambo*, and chief's wives and sisters have theirs. The boundaries of secrecy around these bodies of ritually transmitted knowledge assert and reify the principle social categories of the community. Thus children are excluded from adult ritual because they do not yet know about Nyau, while men and women are excluded from each other's domains because they do not know each other's ancestral esoterica. As one woman said when a man came too close to

the women's funeral dances, "You can't be here! You don't know our secrets! (*musangakhale kuno osadziwa mwambo*)." Knowing (*adziwa*) and
not knowing (*osadziwa*) create lines of differentiation, orienting everyone
within the social whole.

Although each body of secret knowledge contains its own symbolism,
collectively they cohere as elements of a single subliminal order, a hidden
cosmology that defines the complementarities of gender, rank, and life
status. This subliminal order is the key to the ritual complex and to the
differentiated social universe that the ritual creates; it is the invisible text
which becomes partially visible each time someone moves through a rite
of passage, whether as an adolescent, a new chief, or in death. To comprehend its universe of meaning we must place the dancers, as initiated
Chewa do, within this semantic frame, making explicit what the Nyau
ceremony leaves largely implicit.[2]

Nyau presupposes a symbiotic relationship between human society
and a mysterious other world, the latter depicted both as the bush and the
invisible realm of spirits. The graveyard (*manda*), a thicket of trees and
brush, marks its point of articulation where the dead are buried and Nyau
convenes to make masks and to initiate new recruits. The quintessential
male meeting place, the graveyard is not an endpoint but a halfway point,
lying between parallel worlds, linking the village to the bush and to the
spirit world beyond the grave.

The dancers of Nyau are all creatures of the bush and spirit world. As
noted earlier, they are collectively referred to as wild beasts (*zilombo*), a
term that in the context of Nyau includes spirits and animals. Although
the Nyau repertoire includes numerous identifiable characters, each with
a distinctive name, form, and persona, they are subdivided into two categories. The "wild beasts of the day" are spirits of the dead, drawn to the
village by their hunger for food and beer, while the "wild beasts of the
night" are animals, such as the elephant, hare, and antelope, the vast
majority of which are game (*nyama*). Thus the Nyau repertoire is internally subdivided into two antithetical types: day and night, spirit and animal, predator and prey.

Each rite of passage represents the convergence of these separated
realms, as people, spirits, and animals enter into each other's worlds, offer
their substance to each other, and return to their own domains. The rites
of passage as a whole describe the circulation of substances among these
realms as anything given in one rite is reciprocated in the next.

This is most clearly illustrated in mortuary rites. When someone dies,
the body is placed in the house surrounded by close kin, while members
of the larger community hasten to the village for the funeral. While men
go to the graveyard, women go the village, assembling at the death hut to
assist the bereaved. The "weeping women" (*anamalira*) mourn continu-

ously until the men arrive with the spirits of the dead. Then all assemble in front of the death hut where the dancers perform their sometimes comical, sometimes threatening dances, enticing women, provoking men, and stealing food and beer. Finally, the dancers summon the bereaved from the hut and lead the assembly to the graveyard where the body is interred. Thereafter the spirits retreat further into the graveyard, while the villagers and the bereaved return to their homes.

The burial rite is fundamentally a rite of appropriation as the spirits come to claim their own. The process of appropriation continues in the weeks that follow, as the corpse is consumed by the creatures of the earth, liberating its soul (*moyo*) from the earthly realm to join other airborne ancestor spirits (*mizimu*). During this period, the deceased is in transition between human and spirit forms, while the surviving kin remain frozen in social time: widows and widowers cannot contract new marriages while the dead is between this world and the next. The transitional period lasts until the harvest when the granaries are refilled and feasts can be held. At this point, the people anticipate their reward, a return prestation for the loss they suffered.

Following the harvest, commemorative rites (*mpalo*) are held to celebrate the arrival of the deceased in the spirit realm and the release of the living from their bonds to the dead. The same Nyau spirits who attended the burial come to the commemorative rite, hoping to partake in food and beer alongside the living. But this time they bring with them the substance of the feast represented by two "beasts of the night." These are the hare and the antelope, called, respectively, "the owner of the courtyard" (*mwini wa kubwalo*) and "the end of the funeral" (*kasiyamaliro*), who as game animals are given to the village in return for the people taken from it. Thus their appearance marks the end of mourning and the beginning of feasting on meat, maize porridge, and beer, a celebration of plenty following the prior suffering of loss.

According to the ritual scenario, life and death are mutually entailed in the circulation of substance, blood for blood, meat for meat, between parallel worlds: spirits take the dead from the village so that the earth can eat them, and return game from the bush so that the survivors can feast. Thus village, bush, and spirit realm are drawn to each other by complementary urges, by the hunger for each other's flesh. This complementarity is not destructive, but regenerative, for life is replenished through the reciprocal acts of appropriation that bind them. Hence while the earth's creatures feed on the flesh of the human dead, the dead eventually return to the village, not only as guests at subsequent funerals but as souls who animate the bodies of new babies.

Similar scenarios inform puberty trites for both boys and girls: the people of the village confront the wild beasts of Nyau, as spirits take children from the village and give back meat in return. Sexual maturation, like death and rebirth, is defined by the symbiotic relation between human and extrahuman realms. The puberty rites, however, establish more complex equivalences between the world of Nyau and the world of people, transposing the iconography of the first onto the social categories of the second. Thus hunting, predation, and consumption become metaphors of sexuality, as spirits are identified with men who hunt, and animals are identified with women who are hunted by men and spirits alike. With these parallels drawn, puberty rites become more complex contests between live men and dead spirits for meat and for women, with the elders of the village, notably the chiefs and their sisters, negotiating the final outcome.

The purpose of male initiation is to turn boys into sexual men and predatory members of Nyau, a simultaneous transformation that takes place when they are led for the first time into the Nyau meeting place. At the entrance of the graveyard, they pass blindfolded through the cavernous body of the antelope, symbolizing their death as children and their rebirth as beasts. Then they are led deeper into the graveyard where each must sacrifice a chicken by impaling it, lick its blood from the stake, tear its feathers from its body, and eat its flesh. With this act, they arouse and satisfy bloodlust, becoming not just beasts but carnivores. Finally they use the feathers from the fowls to make their first Nyau masks, those of Chisudzo, a spirit of the dead. The initiates are now wild beasts in their own right, for they have consumed raw flesh and blood and fashioned their new faces as spirits.

Thereafter the initiated boys belong to two worlds: as creatures of Nyau and as adult men of the village, a dual persona as predator and hunter who perform analogous deeds in both worlds. The principle objects of their pursuit are not, however, the animals of the bush—although in earlier days they would have been—but people: as Nyau beasts they seek dead people for burial, and as adult men they seek live women for marriage. In this fashion, their initiation prepares them to act as players in all subsequent rites of passage, such as girls' initiation where both human and inhuman aspects of the male persona are required.

Female initiation is the complement of male initiation, for its purpose is to turn girls into succulent meat. This takes place at the "tree of maidenhood" (*mtengo wa namwali*), synonymous with the bush, where the girls receive instruction on the protocols of womanhood. This includes many warnings of the lurking presence of predatory creatures—of men and beasts who would eat them, of the lion who threatens to break into their sleeping hut at night. In the meantime, the girls undergo their own transformation into animals. Stripped of their clothes and their human identities, they are clothed in the insignia of Nyau. The most important insignia is the animal figurine (*chingondo*) placed on their heads, a representation of a hare, a serpent, or an elephant, the three most prestigious beasts of the night. In this guise, the girls are called "meat" (*nyama*) by their instructors who snare them, escort them back to the village, and present them to the community. Here everyone descends on the chief's courtyard to witness the climax of the ceremony.

The contest that unfolds is carefully orchestrated, its outcome a foregone conclusion: the initiates will rejoin their husbands. But for this to occur a struggle must first take place between the Nyau spirits who want the girls for their own purposes and the men who want them back. The spirits seize the initiates, drag them around the courtyard, and threaten to carry them out of the village, until the chief's sisters—the officials of the initiation—ransom the girls back, sending the spirits away with handfuls of cash. The chief then rewards the women with money and with a piece of the Nyau elephant, who passed through the village earlier in the day and was, in pantomime, trapped and killed by hunters. Accepting the gift, the women release the girls to their husbands, themselves sporting the instruments of the hunt. At last the couples retire to their homesteads where married life resumes, while the chief's sisters retire to their own homes to burn the elephant "meat" into medicine and sprinkle it on their own and the chief's relish.

Mortuary and puberty rites are similarly based on a complex model of exchange: Nyau spirits claim live boys and dead people, while the chief's people claim live girls and dead game. As such, the ritual describes the material and social reproduction of the community, enacting in the mortuary rite processes of replenishment through loss, while asserting in the puberty rites the complementarities of gender that reproduction and replenishment require. As such Nyau ritual always contains two levels of meaning. It points to the symbiotic relationship between the human world and an external world, as the creatures of each pass through the other's domain. It also inscribes that symbiotic model onto human society and the human body, as hunting and predation become metaphors for sexuality.

At every level of meaning, literal and metaphoric, the Village Headman is the center of Nyau. He sponsors the funeral commemorations and puberty initiations, dipping into his own stocks of grain and meat to feed the crowds that assemble. He pays both the Nyau officials and the women's initiation experts to perform their services in his courtyard. And he collects a fee from any man who wishes to marry one of "his" maidens. The Village Headman provides these services in his capacity as "owner of the courtyard," a role he shares with the Hare and that is conferred on him by two ritual objects given to him at his installation ceremony. One is a secret Nyau animal called a "spirit wife" (*mtsano*) which signifies his connection to the world of Nyau. The other is a cache of initiation medicines (*khundabwi*) which he keeps in his house for the duration of his chiefship and distributes to all who are initiated in his village. According to the chief's sisters and Nyau officials, the chief uses these magical instruments to ensure the fertility of his people, the return of ancestor spirits into the bodies of newborns, and the renewal and long-term continuity of his village: reproductive potency itself is transmitted from the spirit world through the chief to his subjects. In cruder sociological terms, he uses the ritual authority that these objects bestow on him to draw Nyau and village together, reproducing the ceremonial system as he creates his constituency. Symbolically and practically, the Village Headmen create through Nyau a chiefdom that is self-contained and self-renewing.

The World of Secrecy

It is easy to imagine Nyau ritual operating intelligibly in an earlier historical context. The model of reciprocity between the human world and the bush resonates with the protocols on hunting recorded in an older Malawian ethnography (Rangeley 1948; Schoffeleers 1968:174, 223; Schoffeleers and Roscoe 1985:232–33), while the model of reproduction through exchange resonates with the political logic of the centralized Maravi kingdom when kings and their subordinate chiefs were conduits through whom reproductive power moved (Langworthy 1972a). Today's realities of deforestation and decimated animal populations make any literal implications of the hunting motif implausible, while the additional realities of national politics make the life-giving powers of the Nyau chief more symbolic than real. Nevertheless, the ritual does have its resonances in its contemporary surroundings as it defines arenas of inclusion and exclusion and provides the metaphorical (or secret) language for defining their boundaries and content. Thus the logic and language of Nyau have a life of their own that extends beyond the rite of passage, imposing itself on the collective imagination and manifesting itself concretely in the social world.

Nyau ritual defines social and geographic domains that shape the whole of rural life, as initiations mark shifts in status and entries into social milieus. For men this milieu is identified with the graveyard where they convene for ritual preparations as well as the more diffuse benefits of a male fraternity. In this informal forum they congregate to discuss all manner of social and political issues, from the most commonplace and ordinary to the most timely and extraordinary. Often their discursive and ritual interests come together, as in the colonial period when Nyau was used to oppose missionary intrusion, or more recently when new Nyau characters were invented to satirize contemporary politics. On these occasions the private meeting place of the graveyard, where plans are engineered, is the complement of the public meeting place of the courtyard, where they are ultimately put into effect.

Similarly, women congregate in various locations in the village, passing many hours together in the mundane tasks of household production and in the esoteric tasks associated with sexuality and childbearing. It is in the latter context that the value of ritual expertise is most apparent, as women's initiation advisors (*anamkhungwi*) use their secret knowledge (*mwambo*) to manage women's health problems. But the more mundane occasions also provide opportunities to sort out personal issues, to discuss the social and political affairs that effect their lives, and to rehearse and revise the secret songs and dances (the *mwambo*) of their initiation rites. The political winds of Malawi sometimes breeze through these songs, expressing discontent or cynicism in the disguised form of a "traditional" chant. Thus the oft-heard refrain "the rooster crows at dawn" (*tambala walira kwacha*) is chanted publicly to proclaim freedom under Malawian indepedence, and privately to complain about men who awaken their wives for sex at the crack of dawn and then fail to perform.

If a gendered universe is the essential framework of rural life, the bodies of ritual secrets (*mwambo*) learned at Nyau are the sine qua non of that universe. This is not only because the secrets define masculinity and femininity but because secrecy reifies the boundaries between male and female, and, more generally, between those who know secrets and those who know nothing. Thus participation in the Chewa community rests on the distinction between the initiated and the uninitiated, called "the shaved" (*ometa*) and "the unshaved" (*osameta*).

The "unshaved" or uninitiated includes Chewa children and non-Chewa adults alike. But unlike outsiders, children are drawn into the world of secret domains long before they undergo initiation and become conversant in ritual language. Thus they know that they are excluded from the adult world even as they are exposed to the euphemistic ways in which adults talk about secret matters, such as sexual matters, over their not-quite-comprehending heads. Indeed, adults capitalize on the credulity of children, for they must believe that Nyau dancers are truly spirits and animals. I was warned repeatedly to keep my notes and pictures away from the young ones lest they discover truths to which they were not yet entitled.

This partial, mystifying exposure to the concerns of the adult world imbues the conventional categories of that world with psychological power long before they acquire any objective content. Hence when adolescents finally attend their own initiations, they learn not of the existence of social boundaries but the bodies of secret knowledge that enable them to transgress them and to participate in the community that they contain. Part and parcel of this is the discovery that some secrets are empty: wild beasts, they must learn, are only men in masks. Yet the discovery of false images leads children not into a world without boundaries but to a language with which the boundaries can be filled with content, fixed and fluid, real and imagined. They learn to read the drama of the rite of passage, to allude to Nyau and other secrets through circuitous paths, and to manipulate hidden meanings to create their own stories, jokes, and messages. The initiate has entered the world not simply of sex, death, and ritual, but of secret language, metaphor, and lying. It is the secret language and their secret messages that separate the inside from the outside and that make membership in the Chewa community literally imbued with meaning.

The quintessential outsider, then, is the foreigner: the European, the Ngoni and Tumbuka neighbor, the state official who, unlike Chewa children, will always be "unshaved." As the permanently excluded, not only will these people never attend Nyau ritual but they will never comprehend the messages created by its idioms. Nor will they know that they are among the many personalities represented in the Nyau courtyard, as Nyau cosmology absorbs new categories of "other," turning foreigners into Nyau beasts. Thus Nyau reclaims representational authority.

Consider, for example, the European who, in real and symbolic ways, has replaced the wild animal as the archetypal resident of an external yet imminent world. According to Chichewa linguists, the word for European, *mzungu* (pl. *azungu*), is not semantically included within the category "human being" or *munthu*; only Africans are people, while Europeans are another phenomenon altogether.[3] Linguistic coincidence or not, the etymological distinction between people and Europeans is consistent with Chewa characterizations of Europeans as radically "other," inhuman creatures who, like the wild beasts of Nyau, periodically invade the human world for nefarious, even cannibalistic purposes.

Little children, for example, are frequently told that white people eat black babies, and that their parents will feed them to white people if they do not behave. Because of this method of discipline, little children are, indeed, frightened of Europeans while older, wiser children take great pleasure in tormenting them. Much can be learned about group dynamics simply by observing how one's own presence as a resident white is used by the children one encounters. On one occasion when I encountered a group of children, the smallest of them froze dead in his tracks at the sight of me. Gathering his wits, he ran some twenty feet off the pathway and threw himself face down in the tall grass: if he couldn't see me, he obviously reasoned, I couldn't see him. Nothing could persuade him to raise his face and look at me, not even the sound of his playmates who had collapsed on the ground in gales of laughter.

This little boy probably thought that he had seen a bush spirit with his own eyes, a fate that befell many unhappy children during the course of my fieldwork. But through the inevitable process of maturation, initially terrified little children eventually realized that I would not eat them and that they had been tricked by their older, smarter playmates. This may have been their first introduction both to the dangers of the outside world and to the essential premises of joking—telling falsehoods and seeing who falls for them.

In the context of initiation, these same youngsters enter a new level of trickery. They learn that Europeans are still wild beasts—that is, members of the repertoire of Nyau characters—but they also learn that this equation is more semantic than substantive when before their eyes a spirit removes his mask and turns into a man. Still, as they get involved in the production of Nyau dances, they also discover that semantic equations have great representational value: semantics permit the incorporation of contemporary persons into the fixed structure of Nyau performance where satirical invention meshes with ritual reinvention. This is how Europeans became Nyau characters in the first place.

"Simoni" and "Maria," now well-established members of the Nyau dance troupe, are good examples of the merging of ritual paradigm with satirical invention. Representing the generic white man and white woman, their names are taken from scripture, from Simon Peter and the Virgin Mary whom missionaries are fond of evoking as exemplars of Christian virtue. But Simoni and Maria are no paragons of humanity. Simoni is a buffoon in floral pajamas who trips over himself and the spectators whenever he enters the courtyard, while Maria is a whore, whose hip gyrations and pelvic thrusts invite all manner of rude replies from the bemused spectators. Simoni and Maria can be forgiven this conduct because as beasts they are incapable of correct behavior. In the meantime, their red faces suggest that they are fundamentally predators and that flesh hunger is the real reason why they—like the other "beasts of the daytime"— never fail to show up at funerals.[4]

The adaptability of Nyau ritual to contemporary issues continues to be exploited according to the whim and the inventiveness of particular dancers. National figures follow the now familiar steps of Simoni and Maria into the courtyard, as cabinet ministers and infamous traitors from time to time appear at initiation dances. Those that take the greatest risks and depict the most problematic political figures provoke the greatest interest, but they also require the most artful submersion of political referent in cosmological metaphor. An example appeared in 1985 when a new character showed up at initiation dances. This was apparently a white man of unusual ferocity who attacked the spectators and left them alone only when given money. Several people assumed that this was a new version of Simoni, until those in the dance troupe corrected them. This was Kamuzu the Warrior, the president of Malawi, inspired by his annual tour of the countryside. As he stopped in each district to greet his subjects, he received "gifts" of gratitude from them, gifts that had been collected by local district officials. And so his Nyau counterpart descended upon Ch–Village demanding a share of the celebratory riches. Honored guest or predatory intruder? Only the man behind the mask knew for sure.

Maturation in the Chewa world is a process of incorporation into communities of storytellers, with Nyau masks providing the vehicles and Nyau cosmology the structure for puns, double entendres, and satirical commentaries. In this way the "secret society" is the entire community of Chewa adults who are conversant in the art of false images and who can read the messages embedded in the old and new dance characters. Nyau thus has enormous plasticity as a representational medium, permitting the production of new vignettes alongside the reproduction of essentially fixed ritual forms. This does not mean that the masks are always and only jokes, nor that the spirit world is assumed to be fallacious inventions. It means rather that the connection between man-made icons and invisible spirits is ambiguous and that within this gap there is enormous room for play and politicking.

Nyau and Christianity

Although Nyau encloses the Chewa world in its own "forest of symbols," members of the non-Chewa world do penetrate that forest to appear in the village on their own terms. Representatives of the state enter Chewa villages freely as tax collectors, extension workers, and party officials, while schoolteachers and village health inspectors are permanently domiciled in rural areas. That outsiders can come and go as the government dictates is evidence of the permeability of Nyau's imagined boundaries, leading one to ask what it really means to be excluded from its world. As already illustrated, it means, at least in part, to be excluded from a universe of shared secrets, a form of cultural ostracism that turns ritual esoterica into media of social criticism. But this enclosed universe exists in the immediate vicinity of another, that of Anglicized officialdom with its own discourses and symbols of cohesion. The question must arise: How do these parallel universes of meaning interpenetrate, as its members pass back and forth between them?

This problem can be drawn into focus by examining the relationship between Nyau and Christianity. While Nyau is identified with the rural Chewa community, Christianity is, to Chewa, identified with all outsiders listed above: to be part of the government—and, more generally, the urban elite—is to be Christian and vice versa. The linkage between Christianity and the state is in part pragmatic, since mission schools are the

surest pathway into the urban labor market and the civil service; certainly
it is the route by which the rural professionals cited above obtained their
own training. Yet the linkage is also semantic, emerging from the colonial
background of Chewa and missionary conflict. As a result of that conflict,
Nyau and Christianity are conjointly defined as mutually exclusive oppos-
ites, two self-enclosed societies from different worlds, wedded to each
other as self-defining "others."

Nyau and Christianity continue to exist in insulated parallel, like the
mission school that coexists with the village, for the structural opposition
has been incorporated into the conceptual language with which Chewa
understand their world and their choices: according to Chewa, you can
follow Nyau *or* Christianity, but you cannot follow both. Insofar as Nyau
and Christianity are both, at bottom, initiation systems, choosing between
them means choosing between the worlds to which each offers entry: the
world of the chief, the village, and Chewa ethnicity, or the world of the
schoolteacher, the town, and the Anglicized elite. But while the polarity
reinforces the symbolic separation of the two realms, it also provides the
means for joining them. Thus through the twin doorways of Christian and
Nyau initiation, Chewa traverse the boundaries between two worlds, creating mosaics out of the pieces of both.

These mosaics are not random or shapeless for they reveal the imprint
of rural social order, as icons of state power are selectively incorporated
into the structure of the Chewa world. That is, class strata within the
Chewa community are marked by the signs that differentiate that community from the metropole: Nyau defines the fixed frame of reference for
the Chewa world as a whole, while Christianity identifies a rural elite.
Notwithstanding the subordination of Nyau to Christianity that this hierarchical marking implies, the chiefly elite who use Christianity in this way
do not repudiate Nyau so much as proclaim themselves repositories of
foreign—that is, urban—power. This is consistent with the interior logic
of Nyau cosmology which places the chief between the village and the
invisible powers outside it.

The Traditional Authority, for example, is a typical rural Christian. Of
the many TA's I interviewed, most claimed to be Christian, though few
were regular church attendants, and none offered a theological explanation
for becoming Christian. Their choice was dictated, they said, by a sense
of appropriateness as members of civil government and as chiefs whose
authority superseded that of the Village Headmen—all Nyau chiefs—
beneath them. Christianity was, for them, a sign of superior rank claimed
from the urban aristocracy from whom they also obtained their titles of
office.

As a sign of rank, Christianity is the semantic equivalent of another

source of chiefly rank, namely, the rain-calling rites associated with territorial shrines. Several rain shrines can be found in central Malawi today,
all claiming origin in pre-colonial polities and all adorning the stature of
territorial chiefs. These Traditional Authorities also employ the services
of rain callers during periods of drought, and one provides an annual rite
of renewal to ensure the return of the rains. These were also the only TA's
I knew who were *not* Christians, not, they said, because rain shrines and
churches were mutually exclusive but because the first made the second
redundant. That is, they found their icons of rank in their inherited ritual
paraphernalia as chiefs, while those who could not found comparable icons
by declaring themselves Christian. In either case, ritual authority signified
the TA's link to an exotic source of power that was unavailable to the lesser
chiefs beneath them.

The iconography of rank is more complex at the level of the Village
Headman who, unlike the Traditional Authority, does not stand at the
juncture of rural Nyau and urban Christian worlds. Squarely located in
the rural milieu, he must solicit the resources of the metropole by distrib-
uting his key family resources—people—at various loci of economic and
political capital. These social locations are marked by religious affiliation,
as individuals join the society appropriate to their immediate circumstances and change their membership when circumstances change. Thus
the Village Headman is, by definition, a Nyau chief, and all the youngsters
in his household are initiated through Nyau to draw them into the ceremonial life of the community. But the sons and sisters' sons who show the
aptitude are sent off to mission schools where they invariably proclaim
their identity as Christians while they are groomed for employment in the
urban job market. Curiously these young Christian men are the most
likely candidates for the Village Headmanship when the post is vacated,
since their educational attainments and urban experience elevate their
stature over other villagers. But when this happens, the identification of
the chiefship with Nyau is reasserted, as he who assumes the office for-
swears church membership to claim his ritual mantle. Like a rite of passage orchestrated by Nyau, the candidate returns from the city to the
village to be claimed by his own kind, where his first act as chief is the
clearing of his own courtyard where wild beasts will dance.

As insignia of village and town, Nyau and Christianity are transposed
upon social strata within the village milieu, distinguishing Village Headmen from Traditional Authorities, and seated Village Headmen from their
heirs apparent. In this, church membership is a two-dimensional icon like
a political button that signifies linkages with an outside world, and not a
three-dimensional ritual frame which one wholly, conceptually occupies.
This means, too, that Christianity and Nyau are not structurally equiva-

lent, since the first has been subsumed within the logic of the latter. Thus there is little symbolic difference between the chief who wears a leopard skin and the chief who wears a cross, for both have appropriated icons of alien power to ornament their stature as chiefs.

Nyau cosmology determines the semantic value of Christianity because its social and symbolic forms are so naturalized that external loci of authority are inevitably interpreted through its lens. This was illustrated in the previous section by Simoni, Maria, and Kamuzu the Warrior, all of whom are Christians, all of whom are wild beasts of Nyau. But as the political uses of Christianity demonstrate, the issue is more complex and subtle than the manipulation of ritual motifs to create occasional satire. At issue is the more persistent transposition of the imagery of the spirit world upon the urban elite, evident in dance, in chiefly iconography, and in more probing inquiries about state and European power.

Many inquiries come to the fore around epitomizing symbols of urban elite culture, oddities of Western life that, in a rural mindset, resonate with the powers and proclivities of the spirit world. Europeans, for example, are famous for their gluttonous consumption of meat, a stark display of excess to those who eat meat only on ceremonial occasions. Certainly I was subject to scrutiny and speculation about the kinds and quantities of meat I required to satisfy my hunger. The issue here is not wealth per se, but appetite, that insatiable desire for animal flesh that seems more appropriate to predators than people. As linguistic categories imply, Europeans are not people anyway, so it is not altogether surprising that their behavior is animalistic. But did the postcolonial elite cultivate similar culinary habits and superhuman appetites when they ascended to the pinnacle of authority? This is implicit in state appetite for financial support, and in Kamuzu the Warrior's visits to feasting villagers.

Another evocative sign of the ruling elite is mechanized transportation. Motorcycles, cars, and lorries are all signs of superlative wealth, while airplanes are, to earthbound Chewa, the most dramatic manifestation of European technical prowess. Named after birds (*ndege*), they are identified with the creatures that convey messages between human and spiritual realms, yet they surpass birds by carrying not only messages but people. Malawi's president is the ultimate master of flight, for he owns his own jet to fly him to America and England and his own helicopters to fly him about his own country.[5]

Gluttony and flight are capacities of superhuman creatures, be they animals, spirits, or the Christian elite. But they also can become attributes of ordinary Chewa, at least on ceremonial occasions. During a Nyau performance, dancers eat and drink to excess, leap magically into the air, and occasionally carry facsimiles of cars and airplanes into the courtyard (Van Breugel, n.d.:211). And at weddings, the Christian alternative to girls' initiation, the entire community assumes the attributes of the aristocracy as they sing the following song:

We don't eat dried leaves,	Sitimadya thelele
We all eat meat.	Tidyerana nyama
Chew, chew, chew, chew.	Su, su, su, su.
Let's chew, let's chew.	Kasu, kasu.
We don't travel by foot,	Sitimayenda pasi
We travel by motorcycle.	Timayenda pa moto-saiko.
First motorcycle,	Moto-saiko,
Second minibus.	Kachiwiri minibasi.
We don't travel by minibuses,	Sitimayenda pa minibasi
We travel by airplane.	Timayenda pa ndege.
First minibuses,	Minibasi,
Second airplanes.	Kachiwiri ndege, ndege.

Although few of these celebrants are Christian, all proclaim membership in the urban aristocracy by parading its most ostentatious behavior as their own: they gorge themselves on meat and travel only by mechanized means. In reality, the revelers do eat dried leaves, do travel by foot, and never ride on airplanes, hence this celebration is a momentary, ritually prescribed, flirtation with the aristocratic persona. This is little different from the celebrations of Nyau, when all marvel at the athleticism of masked dancers and feast on the meat that the chief provides.

Virtually no aspect of Christian conduct, real or imagined, can be interpreted independent of the cultural logic of Nyau. Even the central symbol of Christianity, the death and resurrection of Christ, is understood in terms of Nyau cosmological premises. Jesus' resurrection is not about redemption from sin, nor eternal peace in heaven, but reincarnation on earth; hence the purpose of Christian baptism, like Nyau funeral dances, is to return the spirit of the dead to the world of the living. Given the marvels of European technology, some Chewa do consent to baptism just as some seek medical care in government clinics as added protection against death. But eclecticism of this sort does not imply knowledge of the cultural models with which Europeans understand either Jesus or injections. For Chewa these are simply forms of power, and like Maria and Simoni they can be incorporated into the fabric of their symbolic system without fundamentally altering its overall design.

Conclusion

I began this essay by asking how an old ritual of kingship could have relevance in the rural periphery of modern Malawi. Answers were sought in the various relations between Nyau ritual and its environment: between

the life-cycle rites and the societal structures they organize, between cosmological categories and the language of social differentiation, between
the symbolism of the bush and the conceptualization of other worlds outside the village. I argued that Nyau is implicated in the consolidation of
the rural community, the creation of boundaries between familiar and unfamiliar domains, the metaphorization of experience, and the representation of political and productive power. Through this analysis, Nyau has
become a synonym for a larger cultural order, for the signs and symbols
that define the substructure of rural Chewa consciousness.

Yet even as a totalizing frame of reference, Nyau is not the answer to
every question about Chewa ideation and cultural invention. This is apparent in the many topics untouched in this essay: in, for example, the
wedding and funeral celebrations of rural Christianity; and in the Watchtower movement which, though inoperative (or underground) during my
fieldwork, had an important history in this community. These omissions
are due in part to the limitations of space and, concomitantly, the need to
identify within the vast topic of rural ritual a domain that is most represen-
tative of the Chewa world. But this also means that omissions are motivated by a specific interpretive agenda, to define the baseline of rural
Chewa consciousness.

From the vantage point of village life, Nyau is the center of the Chewa
milieu, while alternative ritual forms are defined against this background.
That is, the rituals of rural Christians are meaningful in relation to those
of Nyau, while Watchtower must be contraposed both to the secret enclave of Nyau and to the public enclave of mainstream Christians. As such,
the emphasis on Nyau is intended not to reduce a multivocal population to
a homogeneous chorus but to elicit the cultural background against which
the diversity of the foreground is defined. In other words, I do not wish
to imply that Chewa thought cannot proceed in new directions or move
toward new conclusions, but that new directions take as their starting
point the conceptual universe that Nyau creates and the world that Nyau
represents.

Another vital issue is the relationship between the cultural orthodoxy
of the Chewa periphery and the official nationalism (Anderson 1991) of the
Malawian state. The recurring image of the bounded world of Nyau contradicts both the spirit of national unity, as the MCP represents it, and the
fact of rural penetration and peripheralization by the instruments of state
rule. And yet Chewa do think of their village community as a bounded
world, a world they consolidate through cultural signs and paradigms that
do not originate in the ideologies of the MCP. This does not mean that
Chewa do not also think of themselves as Malawian nationals. On the contrary, the republic is also institutionalized in their political economy, natu-

ralized in consciousness, hence their self-identification as Chewa melds with their self-identification as Malawians. But national identity does not override the pervasive experience of class separation, a gulf so wide that even nationality is understood in terms of a distinctly Chewa cultural order. State proclamations of national culture notwithstanding, the countryside remains its own world conceptually if not politically, while its members generate their own views of the universe they occupy.

Still, the importance of Nyau in the creation of this world and worldview is evidence less of collective resistance than of the diffuse reproduction and revaluation of available cultural forms: this is bricolage as cultural politics and history. So, too, Nyau's cosmology of opposition and appropriation can persist as structure while accommodating alternative categories of "other," because it is no more determined or determining than an algebraic formula for configuring relations with alien beings and outside worlds. This built-in flexibility makes Nyau a perfect medium for mythic models and political satire both, embodying for Chewa not only the enduring legacy of their precolonial culture but also their immediate experience on the political margins of the neocolonial state.

Notes

1. Research in Malawi (1983–86) was supported by the National Science Foundation and the Overseas Fellowship Fund of the University of Chicago.
2. My account of Nyau ritual is based on my own initiations in the men's and women's "sides," frequent attendance at rites of passage in the area around my village, and lengthy interviews with male and female ritual experts.
3. Personal communication, Drs. P. Kashindo and S. M'Chombo, Department of Chichewa, Chancellor College, University of Malawi.
4. A reader pointed out that the Chewa word, *Maria*, is the same as the Swahili word, *maliya*, which means prostitute. I did not encounter *maliya* as an alternative word for prostitute during my fieldwork, nor did I find it in Chichewa or Mang'anja dictionaries (Scott 1968; Scott and Hetherwick 1970: Zambezi Mission Inc. 1980). Nonetheless, the word may belong to the Chichewa lexicon and thus poses an intriguing coincidence: the Virgin Mary of Scripture may have been conflated with the *maliya* of the Swahili brothel. Subsequent research may confirm or refute this.
5. Some people, however, believe that the president actually travels on flying towels. Personal communication, M. Auslander.

References

Anderson, Benedict. 1991. *Imagined Communities: Reflections on the Origin and Spread of Nationalism*. New York: Verso.

Kaspin, Deborah D. 1990. Elephants and Ancestors: The Legacy of Kingship in Rural Malawi. Ph.D. diss., University of Chicago.

Langworthy, Harry W. 1969. A History of Undi's Kingdom to 1890: Aspects of Chewa History in East Central Africa. Ph.D. diss., Boston University.

——. 1972a. Chewa or Malawi Political Organization in the Precolonial Era. In *The Early History of Malawi*, ed. B. Pachai. Evanston: Northwestern University Press.

——. 1972b. *Zambia before 1890: Aspects of Precolonial History.* London: Longman.

Linden, Ian. 1974. *Catholics, Peasants and Chewa Resistance in Nyasaland 1889–1939.* Berkeley: University of California Press.

——. 1975. Chewa Initiation Rites and Nyau Societies: The Use of Religious Institutions in Local Politics at Mua. In *Themes in the Christian History of Central Africa*, ed. T. O. Ranger and J. Weller. Berkeley: University of California Press.

Pachai, Bridglal, ed. 1972. *The Early History of Malawi.* Evanston: Northwestern University Press.

Phiri, Kings M. 1975. Chewa History in Central Malawi and the Use of Oral Tradition, 1600–1920. Ph.D. diss., University of Wisconsin.

Rangeley, W. H. J. 1948. Notes on Chewa Tribal Law. *Nyasaland Journal* 1, no. 3:1–68.

Ranger, Terence O. 1986. Religious Movements and the Politics in Sub-saharan Africa. *African Studies Review* 29, no. 2:1–69.

Ranger, Terence O., and I. Kimambo, eds. 1972. *The Historical Study of African Religion.* Berkeley: University of California Press.

Ranger, Terence O., and J. Weller, eds. 1975. *Themes in the Christian History of Central Africa.* Berkeley: University of California Press.

Schoffeleers, J. Matthew. 1968. Symbolic and Social Aspects of Spirit Worship among the Mang'anja. Ph.D. diss., University of Oxford.

——. 1976. The Nyau Societies: Our Present Understanding. *Society of Malawi Journal* 29, no. 1:59–68.

Schoffeleers, J. Matthew, and Ian Linden. 1972. The Resistance of the Nyau Societies to the Roman Catholic Missions in Colonial Malawi. In *The Historical Study of African Religion*, ed. T. O. Ranger and I. Kimambo. Berkeley: University of California Press.

Schoffeleers, J. Matthew, and N. E. Lindgren. 1985. *Rock Art and Nyau Symbolism in Malawi.* Malawi Department of Antiquities Publication no. 18. Limbe: Montfort Press.

Schoffeleers, J. Matthew, and A. A. Roscoe. 1985. *Land of Fire: Oral Literature from Malawi.* Limbe and Lilongwe: Popular Publications, and Likuni Press.

Scott, David Clement. 1968. *A Cyclopaedic Dictionary of the Mang'anja Language Spoken in British Central Africa.* Farnborough, Hants.: Gregg Press.

Scott, David Clement, and Alexander Hetherwick. 1970. *Dictionary of the Chichewa Language,* London: Lowe and Brydone; Blantyre: C.L.A.I.M.

Van Breugel, J. n.d. Some Traditional Chewa Religious Beliefs and Practices: An Explanation of Evil and Suffering and Ways of Dealing with Them. Unpublished manuscript.

Zambezi Mission Inc. 1980. *The Students English/Chichewa Dictionary.* Blantyre: C.L.A.I.M.

3

Government by Seduction: History and the Tropes of "Mounting" in Oyo-Yoruba Religion

J. Lorand Matory

IN THE SAVANNAHS AND FOREST OF SOUTHWESTERN NIGERIA live approximately 15 million Yoruba, a collection of linguistically and culturally related groups, of which the speakers of Oyo dialect are the largest. Oyo speakers are descended from the subjects of a precolonial royal empire called Oyo and live mainly in the Oyo State of Nigeria. The moral and political implications of gender in the oldest and most loyal province of the extant Oyo kingdom—Oyo North—are the focus of this chapter. I will illustrate aspects of a gendered logic that has made femininity a privileged status in the delegation of politicoreligious authority (*àṣẹ*) as well as the consequences, upon that logic and its application, of a changing political economy.

That logic draws much of its authority from references to the distant imperial past. Elsewhere, I have drawn a more comprehensive portrait of the imperial system of politicoreligious delegation (in press *a*, and 1991). Here, on the other hand, we will be concerned primarily with the motives and tropic design of contemporary references to Oyo imperialism. Oyo's gendered ideology and administration are not alone among models of contemporary action. Islam, for example, had penetrated Oyo-Yoruba society by the seventeenth century and Christianity by the nineteenth. A sizable literature on Islamic and Mediterranean Christian societies documents the role of women as symbols of the community and emblems of its global moral values (e.g., Boddy 1989; Counihan 1985; Abu-Lughod 1986; Giovannini 1981). Even amid their rapid expansion in Oyo North during the nineteenth century, these evangelical religions encountered a powerful countervalent morality and iconography of gender which highlight very different dimensions of womanhood as metaphors of the local sociopolitical order. Rather than vilifying or exorcizing women's sexuality, that countervalent ideology defines women's sexual relations as a paradigmatic idiom of royal government and of production generally. In modern Oyo-Yoruba ritual and historical narration, even men's political conduct is figured in metaphors of women's sexuality. These forms of figuration invoke and legitimize forms of community leadership antithetical to the dominant religious, political, and economic forms of the contemporary Nigerian state. They declare, for rural women and transvestite men, a privileged role in the creation and distribution of the society's supreme value, namely, fertility.

Through rites of spirit possession and gender transformation, worshipers of several important *òrìṣà*, or gods, of the Oyo-Yoruba rehearse particular—and not unchallenged—visions of history and politics. Sacred body techniques, mythology, poetry, and shrine iconography—all rich in figurations of the female body—not only recall specific political orders of the past but they inform and transform modern sociopolitical relations. The ideology embedded in the possession religions emerges most clearly when we set ritual practices alongside the explicitly historical narratives propagated by leading male political actors in this society. The tropic parallels between these two communicative genres—verbal history and ritual—serve as vehicles for diverse assertions about the proper political structure of Oyo-Yoruba society and women's role in it.

On the one hand, we will consider the sense of personal and political possibilities that these historically redolent possession rites burn into the consciousness of modern rural women and men, despite the encroachment of religions and a form of government that marginalize them. On the other, we will witness some exploitative and murderous transformations of this ancient ritual technology in the postimperial age.

Igboho and Its Men: The Context and Logic of Men's Political Narratives

The town of Igboho has existed at least since the sixteenth century and was long a central hub in the political economy of the Oyo Empire. Hence, even more than most Yoruba cities, Igboho has generated multiple and contradictory accounts of its history, often in the service of intergenerational political rivalries. The narration of history by men and in male-controlled fora reveals not only the bases of conflict but also the shared understandings of the constitution of hereditary authority. Among the most fundamentally shared understandings are those that concern the central role of gender and its transformation in the project of government.

Igboho lies in the northernmost savannahs of Oyo State and in what has been, during the twentieth century, one of the most infrastructurally underdeveloped regions of Yorubaland. Only in the past three years has the Oyo North Development Project leveled and paved feeder roads to facilitate the outward transport of agricultural goods. Partly because of its

distance from the national centers of economic production and partly because of its political history, this sizable town is still without piped water.
The electrical power supply, too, remains unreliable, as in most of Nigeria.
Igboho's population is between 25,000 and 40,000, not including the inhabitants of the surrounding hamlets and the large number of its citizens
engaged in labor or commerce abroad (Agbaje-Williams 1983:161; see also
Eades 1975). Emigrants may spend months, years, or decades away from
the town. Yet they retain hereditary rights to land and titles and are considered subjects of one or more of the hereditary authorities in the town.

The town is divided into a dozen major quarters (àdúgbò), each with
a hereditary ruling family and a male chief. Each quarter hosts several
patrilineal "houses" (ilé, or idílé), each of which may have hundreds of
members. Ideally, a man lives with his wives and his children in the same
"house" as his father and brothers. Trade and labor migration has, therefore, generated culturally unexpected residential situations. Because the
young men are more likely to emigrate, the old men, divorced or widowed
daughters of the house (omo osú, or dálémosú), wives of the house (obìnrin ilé), and their minor children now make up the vast majority of house
inhabitants. Emigrant traders visit what they affectionately call "the village" on holidays and use their savings to build retirement homes and to
finance community projects, like the building of a clinic, roads, a post-
office, and houses of worship. A resident male chief monitors the disposition of land belonging to his quarter, on which resident men grow cassava,
melons, yams, tobacco, corn, and beans. Chiefs also adjudicate in civil and
minor criminal cases involving divorce and petty theft, for example. Most
importantly, chiefs act in all communal rituals as affectively potent em-
bodiments of their subjects' social and political unity. However, their role
in political affairs beyond the quarter and in the wider town is in dispute.

Through the course of the nineteenth-century wars among the Yoruba
groups and of twentieth-century British colonialism, the political relationship of male authorities to women has changed radically. In the seventeenth-
century Oyo Empire, royal wives had been the paradigmatic delegates of
kings. As a source of legitimacy, local chiefly dynasties also claimed ancient
descent from *daughters* of the Oyo palace. More recently, some Oyo
North women have held titles as market chiefs, or Ìyálòde. Since the
1950s, however, women's chieftaincy titles have disappeared.

Most women today describe themselves as traders (onísòwò), although
few in this region possess sufficient capital to support themselves in that
profession. Far more than women of southern Yoruba groups—like Egba
and Ijebu—the women of Oyo North tend to depend heavily on the financial support of male kinsmen who have access to the greatest of all local
income sources—municipal government coffers and contracts for services
to the government.

Contemporary local government is run by elected councils of men. The Ifelodun "town-improvement society"—which administers the market, funds community projects, and monitors important social developments—does not admit women. Members of the town-improvement society explain that women cannot be trusted and may betray the town on important matters. They relate legends of women who betrayed their own natal patrilineages for the benefit of their children and betrayed their husbands for the promise of marriage to a richer man. A prominent Christian member of Ifelodun told me:

> There was once a war between the king of Oyo and the king of Abeokuta . . . The king of Abeokuta had a commandant with a *jùjú* [an item of magical power] in a *koto* [a large calabash], from which he would take water and bathe himself. Then he would get on his hands and knees on four *mortars*. Thereby, he would turn into an elephant and could go to the war front and kill invincibly . . .
>
> The king of Oyo made a deal with the commandant's wife that he would *marry her* if she revealed the secret of the commandant's power. The commandant performed his magic and he went to the war front. When his wife destroyed the *jùjú*, he realized . . . that something had happened at home. He rushed back and found a bit of water, with which he changed back into a person before he died.
>
> The woman went to the king of Oyo expecting him to fulfill his promise. He took her in, and on the seventh day he invited everyone in the town to the market in front of the palace to announce the wedding plans. The king indulged her with fine food and courtesy but refused sex. He just told her every day how close the all-important day was. One day, the king sent the guards to bring her out. The king said, "You married your husband; you bore children for him. All the good things he did for you, and you would have me marry you so you can betray me? Never!" Then he had his messenger cut off her *head*. (Emphasis mine)

This Ifelodun member added, "The trouble in Igboho is caused mainly by the daughters of the house [*àwọn ọmọ ọṣú*]." This story places at the disposal of a new male political exclusivism some ancient and widespread elements of Yoruba ritual logic. A woman's betrayal of her husband is equivalent to the spoiling of his magical calabashes and mortars, of his vessels, all elements of the metaphor-based technology whereby, symbolically, male powers take control over vessel-like feminine heads. The duplicity of the Abeokuta commandant's wife is, significantly, both sexual and political, and it warrants the removal of her head. This testimony affirms the dependency of royal men on women but emphasizes the threat posed by the disloyalty of women. Despite the silencing of women in local government politics and administration, they are still blamed for the intractability among the men of the town.

Whatever the source, there are deep and numerous divisions among local male-run chieftaincies and religious organizations in Igboho. Conflicts are debated with reference to mutually contradictory histories of the town, in each of which arise seemingly extraneous and, on second thought, revealing details about gender and the Oyo-Yoruba political charter. During the period of my research—spanning the length of the 1980s—prominent Igboho men recounted and revised the town's histories in yearly court battles over which chieftaincy title is supreme—the Onigboho, the Ona-Onibode, or the Alepata.

The dispute hinges on who founded Igboho and thereby earned the right of sovereignty. Some say that Igboho was founded by the king of Oyo after Nupe armies ransacked the previous Oyo capital. Therefore, Oyo has the right to indicate which chief is locally sovereign. Others say that the first Onigboho had already lived there by the time the refugee Oyo dynasty arrived. Therefore, Onigboho is sovereign. Beyond dispute is the fact that four Oyo kings ruled from Igboho, approximately from 1555 to 1610 (Smith 1965:74). Nineteenth-century testimony from the Oyo palace bards suggests that the Ona-Onibode chief was sent there to rule in the dynasty's name after the palace returned to its earlier capital (Johnson 1921:166). Twentieth-century Oyo kings, on the other hand, have endorsed the supremacy of the Alepata.[1]

Stuck between legal contention and military history are details whose fullness seems intended more to demonstrate the speaker's expertise than to prove sovereignty. Yet, the fascination that these details continue to exercise outside the courtroom, as well as the parallels they find in royal ritual, prove their importance in the very constitution of political sovereignty in Oyo North. The debate over the implications of Oyo's exile in Igboho consistently combines elaborate details of gender relations with a sense that inappropriate and sexually conceived disjunctures brought about the present lamentable state of town politics.

The beneficiaries of Oyo's rule recall the exile of the dynasty in Igboho as an era of recovery and vast prosperity. A number of other phenomena are attributed originally or uniquely to this epoch, implying their role in generating this prosperity. Some say the second Oyo monarch who reigned in Igboho, Orompoto, was a woman; others say she was a woman who "danced in and out on the day of her coronation and then the kingmakers looked up and realized she had turned into a man." That very monarch is said to have introduced cavalry into the Oyo military, not only the means by which Oyo conquered the lands southward and became the largest empire in Yoruba history but a factor with rich implications, as we shall see, for the contemporary Oyo-Yoruba logic of gender. Up until the time of Orompoto, no woman had ever assumed the Oyo throne, and no woman has done so since. Orompoto's successor, who also reigned in Igboho, is remembered as the first Oyo king to impose castration as a condition of service upon the ranking male official of the palace (see Johnson 1921:163; see also R. and J. Lander 1832, 1:129, 169).

Whereas the political centralism and prosperity of Igboho under the Oyo dynasty are rendered in metaphors associating equestrianism with extraordinary gender transformations, the departure of the dynasty and the subsequent political disorder, with some symbolic consistency, yield sexual disjunctures and bizarre sexual mismatches. In a 1982 public inquiry over the current chieftaincy disputes, a female elder of Ona-Onibode House dictated:

> . . . after the departure of Alaafin [Oyo king] Abipa there was a bad and notorous [sic] incident in the town so that everybody in the town was not happy. The incident was that dogs were meeting [i.e., having sex with] goats, cocks were cohabiting ducks etc. It was this time that Oba [paramount ruler—sic] Ona-Onibode sent a message to Alaafin on the incident and the then Alaafin sent one of his servants bearing [the title] AARE to Oba Ona-Onibode to be leading the ayabas [Oyo royal wives] to perform the sacrifice on the tomb of four Alaafins who dies [sic] in Oyo Igboho. (Signed by Mojere Asabi, representative of the Alayabas, in Aderele 1982:163).

According to this account, the disorder created by the Oyo dynasty's departure was not only political but sexual. Not only did the local political hierarchy lose its head but the Oyo king abandoned hundreds of his wives and his predecessors' wives. Mojere Asabi tells us that this improper politicosexual order was repaired with the arrival of the Aare—a ritually prepared and usually transvestite palace delegate—who led the royal wives in the worship of the kings' graves. The Aare belongs to a class of palace delegates known as *ilàrí*, who will be described at length below. As late as 1965, the descendant of this delegate appears to have worn women's clothes to lead this annual procession (Aderele 1982; see also Smith 1965:60). Likewise, in both the imperial delegation of power and in the modern Oyo-Yoruba religion, we will discover, "wives" and male transvestites take on the power of the greatest of deceased Oyo kings—the god Shango.

The Power of the Past
The Royal Husband and His Many Brides

According to royal history, Shango was an early king of Oyo. Various accounts have it that either Shango is a Nupe or his mother was born of these powerful Northern enemies and trade partners of Oyo (see, e.g.,

Johnson 1921:149; Frobenius 1966:210; Idowu 1963:92). To many, he is now a god, the Lord of Fire. He hurls stone "thunder axes" (ọdùn àrá) from the sky to kill thieves and to punish his enemies by setting their homes on fire. As the tutelary god of the Oyo palace, he is by far the best-known god among the Oyo-speakers. His sizable priesthood is centered, ideally, on the Oyo palace and was once an instrument of imperial power. His priests acted as imperial viceroys in outlying subject kingdoms; Morton-Williams 1964:255; Biobaku 1952:40. Officials known as ìlàrí, initiated by Shango priests, and royal wives (ayaba), themselves often priestesses, played prominent roles in the projection of Oyo royal power (R. and J. Lander 1832:109–10; Clapperton 1829:21; Babayemi 1982:6–11; Babayemi 1979:15–21, 26–32, 40–46). They continued to do so until the end of British Indirect Rule in the 1950s.

The administration of Oyo royal prerogatives by wives, male transvestites, and priests appears to have followed conscious motives, which are evident in the historical record. Though these motives lapsed as the foundations of royal power changed, the contemporary initiation rites of Shango possession priests bear the unmistakable mark of those motives. These rites of spirit possession mobilize the norms of a defunct empire in the service of a rival modern order, which, unlike the modern hegemony, valorizes feminine authority.

During the seventeenth and eighteenth centuries, Oyo was the largest empire among the various groups now called Yoruba. Although it collapsed precipitously around 1830, Oyo's authority has never lapsed in Oyo North—the region that includes Igboho. The Oyo palace has long regarded the king's kinsmen as a source of not only administrative support but competition. Hence, the palace faced the problem of protecting the reigning king from these potential usurpers (see Johnson 1921:41–42, 189; Babayemi 1979:149–52). Palace bureaucrats had an interest both in protecting the throne from usurpation and in checking the influence of the king's nonroyal and, in some cases, foreign mother. The king, for his part, desired a corps of delegates of guaranteed loyalty, free from the influence of subordinate chiefs and his plebeian subjects.

In answer to these requirements, a variety of religious innovations over the course of Oyo's expansion and imperial consolidation were instituted to prepare a body of personnel as "wives" of the king and of the royal dynasty's tutelary god, Shango. Few of these palace delegates were "wives" of the king in the conventional sense. Rather, notions of the proper relation between husbands and wives were embroidered with a range of other metaphors to define and affect these delegates' absolute submission to the royal will. The image of the horse was integrated neatly among the gendered metaphors of both imperial delegation and Shango worship.

Until Oyo's collapse in the 1830s, Oyo monopolized the trade in horses from the North, enabling it to conquer virtually all the savannah kingdoms to the South. Horses (*eşin*) were Oyo's main instruments of conquest. Analogously, the king's possession priest delegates were called "mounts" (*ęlęgùn*) and "horses" (*ęşin*) of Shango. In being called "brides" (*ìyàwó*) of the god, the Shango possession priests share the symbolic nature of royal wives as well. The foremost term for spirit possession condenses several of these metaphoric predications about priests of the royal god. Not only do gods "mount" (*gùn*) possession priests, but riders "mount" horses and males "mount" females in the sexual act. These relationships at the core of the royalist order might be rendered in the following proportion:

husband	:	wife ::
god	:	possession priest ::
rider	:	horse

In royalist projects, each of these usages colors the others and illuminates a variety of otherwise opaque ritual and narrative practices.

From the beginning of the seventeenth century, the military expansion of Oyo precipitated continual shifts in the balance of power among the king of Oyo, the ranking general (Basorun), and the two Oyo councils of state (Ogboni and Oyo Misi). Royal servants and delegates called *ìlàrí*—whose very name and ritual preparation by Shango priestesses suggest some variant of "mounting," or possession, by the king's personal spirit (*orí*—lit. head)—gave a radical boost to the authority of the late-eighteenth-century Oyo king Abiodun and his successors over the nonroyal chiefs (Johnson 1921:183).[2] For generations, *ìlàrí* had served as officers of the royal *òrìşà* priesthoods, including that of Shango. Much after the manner of the Shango *ęlęgùn*'s initiation, *ìlàrí*'s initiation was focused on the head. It was conducted by the second-ranking royal wife. During the reign of King Abiodun, the *ìlàrí* not only supervised local rulers but collected tolls and policed trade routes (Johnson 1921:63; Babayemi 1979:62, 79ff). They and the palace wives made up the majority of palace delegates and functionaries.

Repeated and lengthy arguments in the scholarly literature dispute the literal meaning of the term *ayaba*, or "king's wives," and seek to specify the difference between them and the *ìlàrí* (Johnson 1921:62, 63; Oroge 1971:205; Awe 1972:269–70). All have made it clear, however, that, whether literally or figuratively, many of the women and all of the *titled* women in the service of the Oyo palace were called "king's wives." Moreover, writes Johnson, "all the ladies of rank are often spoken of as Ilaris" (1921:63). Many of the male *ìlàrí*, for their part, were horsemen (ibid., 62), and many must have cross-dressed, like their early-twentieth-century counterparts. Hence, throughout the empire, they displayed and popularized much the same symbolism of politicoreligious delegation as did the wifely and equestrian ẹlẹ́gùn, or Shango possession priests. In a sense, not only were the ìlàrí delegates, the king's wives, and the possessed ẹlẹ́gùn metonymic images of Oyo royal authority, but they were projected images of the king himself.

The Shango initiation—ìdóṣù—contains the most elaborate ritual formula of this projection. It condenses and embroiders major symbolic forms and terms of Oyo royal sovereignty, which are articulated partially in ìlàrí preparation and partially in royal marriage. Before ascending the throne, the Oyo king himself undergoes the ìdóṣù initiation. The prospective king is himself, in effect, a bride of the god. Upon coronation, he becomes Shango himself, suggesting his permanent state of possession by the god (King Adeyemi III, personal communication—17 October 1988; see also Isola 1991:97). The ìdóṣù initiation symbolized each level in a hierarchy of delegation—from the most husbandly, kingly, and ancestral Shango to the reigning king and downward through various orders of wives, delegates, and subjects. This hierarchy was not only administrative but spatial and temporal: personalities from above and from the past penetrated and thereby ruled subjects in the earthly present.

Colonial Transformations

As in much of Africa, British colonialists in the Nigerian Protectorate employed the policy of Indirect Rule. In order to avert the need to deploy large numbers of European officials, the colonial government co-opted existing political systems and used their personnel to levy taxes, organize labor, and maintain civil order. For their own cultural and strategic reason, British administrators favored the Oyo palace over the mighty plebeian generals of Ibadan to rule the Oyo-Yoruba (see Atanda 1979). In the wake of that decision, the British inadvertently revivified and expanded the effective domain of Oyo's gendered ritual politics.

In the first half of this century, not only the Oyo dynasty in itself but the ìlàrí enjoyed an unprecedented degree of authority (Asiwaju 1976:99; Atanda 1979:74, 101; 1970:216). According to various reports, even male ìlàrí during this period represented themselves as wives of the king. Tales of their extortionary and coercive behavior make comic reading (see Atanda 1979:203) but also suggest the power inherent in this wifely symbolic role, as well as the symbolic constitution of Oyo royal authority even under the British Colony. The most famous Oyo king of the colonial era and, next to Shango, the most famous of all time is Siyanbola Ladigbolu. Though backed by British firepower and the friendship of the British Resident, the unparalleled might of this king was construed in very local cultural terms. He is eulogized as having almost been able to "turn a man

into a woman," and vice versa (Atanda 1970:227), a phrase intended to
evoke the *extraordinary extent* of his political authority but also recalling
its specific *ritual foundations.* The theater of Oyo royal authority magni-
fied and amended the structure of husband/wife relations, making palace
"wives" into the public icons and agents of their husband's insuperable
authority.

Royalist historical claims and ritual enactments are not unrivaled. The
collapse of the Oyo Empire around 1830 resulted from internal dissent
and the success of Fulani jihadists from the North. Under the rule of generals, the predominantly Oyo-Yoruba city of Ibadan replaced Oyo as the
most powerful polity south of the River Niger. Although the Oyo palace
remained prestigious, its sovereignty could no longer be taken for granted.
Until the British restored the ethos of Oyo supremacy and divinity, a nonroyalist ritual complex reigned outside Oyo North. As Ibadan expanded
into the southern and eastern forests, its tsetse-smitten cavalry became
useless (see Smith 1988:101; Johnson 1921:288). As nonroyal warlords
conquered and pillaged, slaves rather than "wives" became the paradigmatic servants of sovereign power (see Akintoye 1971:72 and passim).
Concomitantly, the preeminent religious cult of the nineteenth-century
state belonged to the nonpossessing, nonroyal god of war—Ogun. Not
only are horses, "wives," and "mounting" irrelevant to that cult in Oyo
North, but women are systematically marginalized in or excluded from its
rites (see Matory, in press *a*).

Wifeliness and the hierarchy of "mounting" have not been women's
only means of achievement—a fact made colorfully evident by the lives of
several famous women during Ogun's nineteenth-century supremacy. Indeed, the most famous women in all of Yoruba history are the Iyalode—
women chiefs of the market—in towns like Ibadan, Abeokuta, and Lagos.
In the nineteenth century, the Iyalode Omosa and Efunshethan of Ibadan
and Tinubu of Abeokuta rose to prominence as traders and war financiers
in these cities created by imperial dislocation. Like the powerful men of
their age, these women enterpreneurs were mobile, militarized, and more
in control of royal institutions than under their control. Their personal
fame distinguishes them sharply from the generations of anonymous palace women and men who exercised power as the "wives" of Oyo kings and
gods. The Iyalode thrived amid the nineteenth-century marginalization of
the hierarchy of "mounting"; instead of representing the palace, they represented themselves and other women in collective action and on the
councils of state.

Yoruba historical writings about these women represent them in dramatically unwifely terms. Awe says they were without a "normal domestic
life"; Tinubu and Efunshetan are said to have been childless (Awe 1972:
271–72; Biobaku 1960:40). Efunshetan's character is represented as not

only unwifely and militaristic but legendarily antireproductive. She bore only one daughter, who died while delivering her own child. Thereafter, according to Johnson's contemporaneous account, Efunshetan submitted all of her own pregnant slaves to abortions using such cruel methods that the pregnant women usually died (Johnson 1921:393). Whether we take these accounts literally or not, what seems clear is that these women did not depend on Shango-style metaphors of marriage as conditions or parameters of power. From Johnson in particular, we draw an even clearer sense of the nineteenth-century royalist apperception of nonroyal power. Johnson's is a portrait of sociopolitical disorder drawn, again, in images of the female body.

The Past in the Present

Despite challenges in the nineteenth century and progressive marginalization in twentieth-century hereditary government, the metaphorical conjunction of horses, wives, and priests as bearers of royal authority remains highly evocative in postcolonial possession religions preoccupied outwardly with uterine fertility. These religions reiterate and recontextualize the precolonial and colonial projection of Oyo's power. The ideology of the òrìṣà religions suggests that subservience to royal authority guarantees prosperity and protection from witchcraft as well as authority over inferior personnel within the king's "cone of authority," to use Prince's term. Stepping outside that "cone," through disobedience or inattention to its internal hierarchy, makes one automatically vulnerable to misfortune. Conversely, misfortune and illness are diagnosed as signs of one's withdrawal from the "cone," and the cure entails reentry and the reinforcement of its internal hierarchical norms (Prince 1968:1172 and passim). Though the king is conventionally the nodal figure in this system of politicoreligious delegation, he occupies that position because he is a vessel and conduit of divine forces, an inferior participant in the god's "cone of authority" (see Matory 1986). There are multiple potential nodes in this system of delegation, making any given king or worldly kingship in general a dispensable intermediary. Oyo is now a town without a worldly empire. Even its administration of the Shango cult and its initiations has lapsed. Yet, the ghost of its past might remain alive and pivotal in the religion of rural Igbohoans. The memory of the Oyo Empire has replaced the modern palace as the sacred font of sociopolitical order. One suspects that, despite their metaphoric design in images of the female body, the requirements of empire distanced the priesthood from the medical problems of individual women. Today's Shango priesthood, on the other hand, focuses its public concerns and claims on those very problems, especially those related to uterine fertility. The shrinking of royal government has left rural women with fewer leadership options beyond literal motherhood, underscoring the importance of institutions that guarantee such fertility. Hence, a real and rewarded order of authority and community remains alive in the priesthood. The priestesses and priests of Oyo North administer an empire of healing and fecundation.

The chieftaincies of Oyo North have been progressively integrated into new networks of symbolic and material power. Pecuniary wealth, the profession of Christianity or Islam, Western-style education, and access to the resources of the federal state have grown in importance as qualifications for and instrumentalities of royal power. At least in the public personae of kings and chiefs, the importance of association with the possession religions and their gender transformations has decreased both proportionally and absolutely.

The graves of the Oyo kings buried in Igboho are no longer worshiped annually by the royal wives or the Ona-Onibode chief. The Aare—noble descendent of the transvestite Oyo delegate—does cast a kola nut of divination and sacrifice on some market days, but he does not cross-dress. Part of the present Alepata's coronation took place at the graves, but he does not regard his neglect of the Shango shrine in the reception hall of his palace as regrettable or harmful. He receives the parading "brides" of Shango during the various Shango festivals just as he receives Christian and Muslim groups on their various holy days. Contrary to reports elsewhere that Shango possession priests acted as political delegates from the palace, the present Alepata denies that Shango possession priests ever lorded over his predecessors, a point the present Ọyọ king echoes. King Adeyemi III says,

> Yes, *mọ́gbà* [nonpossession priests] and *ẹlẹ́gùn* [possession priests] were representatives of Oyo in the provinces. They could issue directives in the name of the *Aláàfin* [Oyo king] but only on religious matters and related to the Shango devotees—not on royal administrative matters. *Because the Oyo practiced secularism; they did not allow religion to interfere with their administration.* (Emphasis mine; King Adeyemi III, Oyo Town, interview, 17 October 1988)

The king's depoliticization and compartmentalization of "religion" contradicts various anthropological and historical accounts of the Oyo Empire (e.g., Babayemi 1979; Morton-Williams 1964; Biobaku 1952). The fact that the king acknowledges having been initiated in the Shango priesthood as a condition of his rule makes his unconventional historical revision even more ironic. This testimony evidently reflects an effort to legitimize the Oyo kingship in the light of the republican conceptions that orient Nigerian national statecraft. More concretely, it reflects the reality that the Shango priesthood has been progressively marginalized in the Oyo kingship.

Consequently, the Shango priesthood has become a center in its own right, having gained a high degree of autonomy from the Oyo palace and the local chiefly houses. Although King Adeyemi III believes that prospective Shango possession priests from Oyo North must go to the Oyo capital for their initiations, Oyo North possession priests have assured me that they did not go there and do not have to do so. The palace has lapsed as the ritual center of the Shango priesthood, and the interests of the palace have ceased to guide the priesthood's conduct. The hereditary chiefs of Oyo North—who are now all male and mostly Muslim and Christian—demonstrate a will to "secularism" much like that of King Adeyemi, although their coronations, too, link them inextricably to the gods of their respective dynasties.

Such "secularism," like its American counterpart, is sometimes zealous and imprecisely aware of its religious content (see Bellah 1968:14). The courtroom narratives of Igboho's history emerge in the fora of republican justice and negotiate the diverse political interests of Muslim and Christian men. Yet, the signs invoked in defense of those interests seem distant from any secular objectives. The links they draw among gender, history, and political hierarchy are well precedented and, nowadays, are most plainly manifest elsewhere. Elaborately invoking many of the same signs and historical sources, the rituals of women and male transvestite priests in Oyo North dramatize a politicoreligious order from which modern male chiefs and kings have tried to dissociate themselves.

As a form of personal and political assertion, the possession religions have fallen increasingly under the control of women and untitled rural men whose predecessors had been recruited as palace functionaries. The royal possession religion now represents an *alternative* historical vision and power base for the disenfranchised. It emblemizes the village sanctuary even for powerful emigres, conscious as they are of the ultimate insecurity of their status in the city and the national macrocosm (see Matory, in press *b*). Ritual and verbal claims about history wrought by the possession religions legitimize their own presence and authority in the collective life of the "village."

The processes of labor and trade migration, particularly among younger men in Igboho, accelerated during the oil boom of the 1970s and early 1980s. So did the marginalization of rural dwellers. For the women left behind, and especially those without an independent trade, the Shango cult was the most powerful image of an empire and of patrilineages no longer administratively present but emblematic, for many rural wives, of health, fertility, and familial order. Once administrative organs of the sovereign state, the possession cults have become de facto foci of rural women's organization and fertilization, in all its polysemic dimensions. If

their migrant husbands cannot "fertilize" them, young brides hope that
the children Shango gives with his healing touch will someday support
their financial liberation from both husbands and fathers. Besides offering
healing from barrenness, affliction, and dependency, initiation in the possession religions affirms women's power and centrality in their own and
other people's lives as well as their worth as active arbiters of the society's
supreme moral values. In marked contrast to local Islam, Shango-worship
valorizes women's mobility and de facto authority in sociopolitical arrangements that—in Oyo North—increasingly deny women's potentials beyond
servitude and troublemaking.

Each generation of adherents to the Near Eastern religions brings
more vocal condemnation of the "*kèfèrí*," especially from young and unmarried Muslim men.[3] On the other hand, Muslim and Christian husbands, fathers, and mothers-in-law show considerable tolerance for Muslim
and Christian women's involvement with the *òrìṣà*. Evangelical piety
could hardly nullify the Oyo-Yoruba adoration of uterine fertility. Muslim
and Christian husbands would sooner divorce a barren woman than one
who "worships sticks and palm trees" (*abọgibọpẹ̀*). Hence, the relations of
supplication, submission, and healing—the "cone of authority"—of the
òrìṣà in Oyo North increasingly cut across kin groups and public religious
identities. Òrìṣà worship promises salvation to those local communities
that rely on birth for their reproduction and challenges the monopoly of
the state medical establishment in satisfying this paramount popular demand. In the process of their indigenization and popularization, the Near
Eastern religions, too, have had to find ways of assuming and fulfilling this
promise. The Shango cult, though, more than any other, links that fulfillment to a familiar and encompassing political order, to whose history Igboho itself is a monument.

Women and Their Shango

In Oyo North, women's access to public fora for their verbal self-expression
is severely limited by their exclusion from chieftaincies, from the town
improvement society, and from local government councils. Other opportunities for leadership and for women's collective self-expression are
scarce. Igboho differs from the southern Yoruba metropolises in lacking a
vocal market women's association. Igboho's Baptist churches show no signs
of the emergence of the Christian chieftaincy titles for women that have
developed among the Egba-Yoruba, for example, to the south. Women are
featured visibly but silently among the elders on the pulpit in the services
of the Cherubim and Seraphim "spiritual" church in Igboho. On Islamic
holidays, some unmarried Muslim girls parade and sing with the mostly

male Young Muslims' League in the town, whereas adult Muslim women, as such, participate in no such gatherings.

For women of various religious convictions, occasions celebrating family gods and ancestors, therefore, furnish an unparalleled opportunity. The rites of the god Shango include both the recitation of descriptive poetry (oríkì) and the even more articulate dramas of initiation, possession, and blood sacrifice. The metaphors projected in these multimedia extravaganzas etched into the local consciousness a vivid and historically based sense of women's extant powers and possibilities. Yet, for us, the constituting visual, tactile, and verbal signs of possession ritual can yield their meanings only through close intertextual readings.

Shango's poetry, called specifically Ṣàngó pípè, is composed and sung by women priests, whose memory and apperception, therefore, become a public resource and reference. This poetry identifies Shango unmistakably with Oyo and its royalty; he is called the "King of Koso," the site of the king's main Shango shrine in the Oyo capital. Koso is also the name of a quarter of Igboho, where the dynasty left a local family to care for the Shango shrine it left behind. The mere fact of singing hyperbolic praises to the god/king asserts the value of a history that the Muslim hierarchy in this predominately Muslim region would suppress if it could. The women's poetry presents its own revision of local religious history, describing Shango as an errant Muslim, identifying him with the power of Muslims in the region and, at the same time, ridiculing Islam with allusions to Shango's blatant violation of Islamic law (see Matory, in press b). These mythic attributes suggest the religiously plural context of Shango worship and its incorporative nature as a pursuit of power.

Indeed, Shango worship embodies at its foundation both a mythic conception, a technology, and a strategy for bringing foreign power into kings and their agents. Oyo's military successes through the monopoly importation of horses from the Muslim North and the prosperity Oyo achieved through taxing the north-south trade are among its prototypical accomplishments.[4] It follows that many of the òrìṣà themselves are identified with origins in powerful political and religious centers in the North and the Near East. Odudua, an òrìṣà and the first Yoruba king, came from either Mecca or heaven (ọ̀run), depending on the tale. The Nupe Shango is the one who brings his own foreign and celestial power into the heads of his "brides" and "mounts."

The language and conduct of spirit possession, as well as the iconography of òrìṣà shrines, encode a conception of power, agency, and history deeply rooted in a shared Oyo-Yoruba past. Hence, although it is articulated most elaborately in the òrìṣà cults, it is the shared patrimony of Yoruba Muslims and Christians as well. First, as we have seen, the concept of "mounting" (*gígùn*)—which likens the priest to a royal charger and to a royal wife—also makes the possessed priest the most dramatic and visually evocative image of a past sexual-political order with which Igboho's oral historians and lawyers unfavorably compare every subsequent era. Equally evocative, pots and calabashes are used to incite the action of god upon priest, to call the past sexual-political order into contemporary action. For example, vessels filled with river water are placed on the heads of priestesses of water goddesses, like Yemoja (the goddess of the River Ògùn) in order to induce possession. Since Shango is the god of fire and lightning, a vessel containing burning coals may be placed on the head of his medium.

Indeed, heads generally are compared to pots and calabashes. Mythically, people's heads are said to have been made in heaven by the divine potter *Àjàlá*.[5] The word for "skull" in Yoruba (*akotorí*) compares it to a calabash known as *koto*, the same kind that regularly represents Yemoja in Oyo North shrines and contained the Abeokuta commandant's war medicine, according to the misogynistic cautionary tale discussed above. In shrines, calabashes and pots are permanently filled with items iconic of the god—like cowries, conch shells, river stones, and "thunder axes" (*èdùn àrá*).[6] In Igboho, most of these shrines are arranged and maintained by women.

Òrìṣà shrines are regarded by many as important repositories of dynastic power. Hence, we may read the variation in their iconic figuration as a sort of sacred dialogue concerning relations of power. For example, the presence and form of the imperial god Shango in the shrines of Onigboho House—whose claims of supremacy are undermined by Oyo imperialism—are suggestive. Yemoja is the tutelary goddess of Onigboho House. With a precedented mythic rationale, her shrines incorporate Shango's power, while apparently stripping it of the imperialist pretenses encoded in the foremost Shango shrines.

In Shango shrines, the icons of that god's power usually rest atop another type of container—the mortar. When spoken, the word for "mortar," *odó*, can also mean "You fuck." The visual/verbal pun suggests Shango's brashness and the force implicit in his relations to the world. His "brides" are also the objects of that force; they sit on the mortar in order to be "mounted" for the first time. The normal action of the pestle (*ọmọ odó*) in the mortar suggests the phallic character of Shango's penetration of the "bride." Reinforcing the parallel, an apparent pun likens the action of the pestle to that of the god: the pestle "pounds" (*gún*) and the god "mounts" (*gùn*), the two Yoruba words differing only in their tones.[7]

In leading Shango shrines—like those in Koso and Ago Igishubu Quarters of Igboho and Koso Quarter of Oyo—Shango's stones sit atop an inverted mortar or one that is not even hollowed out, suggesting Shango's impenetrability and the notion that the Shango shrine is self-sufficient in power and requires input from no higher source.[8] Shango is, in imperial principle, the paramount divine ruler: he gives power and orders rather than receiving them.

In less important Shango shrines, like those belonging to individual possession priests of the god, Shango's stones are often found in rightside-up mortars, a symbolic weakening that prefigures Shango's ultimate demotion in Yemoja shrines. Myths identify Shango as the offspring of the river goddess Yemoja, giving rise to various joint shrine arrangements that materialize a variant assertion about the relative authority of the Yemoja-worshiping Onigboho House and its Shango-worshipping overlords in the Oyo palace. In Yemoja shrines, Shango's rocks and "thunder axes" rest inside simple pots and bowls, lower in height than Yemoja's calabash. This sequence of iconographic transformations suggests both increasing distance from the source of Shango's power and diminishing interest in Shango's autocracy. Indeed, Yemoja priestesses emphatically describe the representations of Shango and the other auxiliary òrìṣà in her shrine as the goddess's "children."

The Shango cult is the foremost among several extant possession religions in Igboho. It hosts annual festivals in nine of the town's quarters. Each of those quarters boasts two or three possession priests (ẹlẹ́gùn) and several nonpossession priests (mọ́gbà), who officially head and sponsor the cult in the quarter. The chief priest of the town-wide Shango priesthood is the nonpossession priest entitled Igishubu, who is also the chief of a quarter. He is a professed Muslim, however, and attends none of the private rites as far as I know. He receives perfunctory obeisance from all other Shango priests, but he is neither expert nor active in the priesthood's regular operations.

Not only is the Shango priesthood the most populous, but the amount of time each possession priest devotes regularly to the cult recommends its priesthood as the most professional. Shango priests are present at the public rites and many of the private rites of all other òrìṣà possession religions in the town—including those of Orisa Oko (the Farm God) and Yemoja. Indeed, the Shango cult itself has possession priests of Ọya (Goddess of Wind, Storm, and the River Niger) and of Yemoja. Shango priests cooperate closely with the sizable cult of the Egungun masquerades as well. In fact, these two groups together dominate the only official organization that embraces all òrìṣà worshipers: Olórìṣà Parapọ̀, meaning "Union of Òrìṣà Worshipers." This group enlists members from all the towns of Oyo North, that is, the core of the former empire. The group appears to be of recent origin—its ecumenism, much like that of local Christian organizations, being a response to the persistent threat of Muslim aggression. Its titular head is the head of the Shango priesthood.

Though no longer officers of the Oyo imperial state, the Shango priesthood has led in the reconstitution of a supralocal politicoreligious unity. In a very nonsecular sense, the ritual cycle of the Shango cult recapitulates the imperial order. First, since Shango is a deceased king and the apotheosis of Oyo royalty, Shango altars are the most prominent in the palaces of quarter chiefs who rely most on Oyo's authorization—the Alepata and the Aare. Second, the sequence of Shango festivals culminates in the festival of Shango Koso—counterpart to the personal Shango of the Oyo king, called by the same name, in Koso Quarter of the present capital.

The leadership role of the Shango priesthood is not only organizational; it is ideological and exemplary. Shango is the paradigmatic possessing god. The term *gùn* (to mount) is associated foremost with him, whereas less emphatic terms like *dé* (to arrive) and *wá ayé* (to come to the world) are sometimes applied to other possessing gods. Shango's festivals are the most popular. Hundreds of children seeking entertainment and as many women seeking the god's healing touch attend every Shango festival in Igboho. To the peasantry and the bourgeoisie alike, Shango represents an era of Oyo-Yoruba might, an orderly royalist and noncolonial past, and an epoch when kings struck fear in witches, thieves, and other enemies of sexual and political order.

Embedded in this politically charged nostalgia are particular images of gender and health, displayed particularly in the eye-opening persona of Shango's transvestite male brides. Understanding the message of this ritual display relies on establishing the connection between the semiotics of this cross-dressing and the practical concerns that bring these hundreds of mainly Muslim and Christian women to appreciate it. The verbal and material signs of "wifeliness" and "mountedness" are shared by both male and female possession priests. When imposed on male priests, though, we are led to recognize their quality as distillates, as a signified quintessence. For not every metonym of womanhood is applied to the male priest's body.

Several discussions in the anthropological literature have interpreted male cross-dressing in Islamic societies as tropes defining womanhood *by negation*. Wikan (1977), for example, argues that male transvestites in Oman demonstrate, through their inadequacy as women, the qualities that make up proper womanhood. Boddy (1989) observes in Sudan that women's dramatization of male and foreign characters during *zar* possession rites demonstrates, again by a negative example, what qualities must be segregated from the persona of a female to make her a proper local woman. Oyo-Yoruba rituals also declare what women are not: they are not ultimately responsible for their fertility. The agent is structurally male and penetrating. Certain feminine biological and social attributes, however, are positive prerequisites to the worldly fulfillment of this agency. The male possession priest displays the *selected* feminine qualities that enable a man or a woman to be "fertile" in this sexual and political order, that enable him or her to embody the power of the royal god.

The initiatory biography of the possession priest encodes a process of essentializing the feminine state of "mountedness." New initiands are really the principal referents of the term "bride" (*ìyàwó*). This terminology follows the pattern of marriage into the patrilineal house: early in marriage, a wife is addressed simply as "Bride." Once the primary reason for her entering the affinal house is realized, through the birth of children, she remains a "bride" to the house and to all her senior co-wives, but she is far more likely to be addressed with a teknonym—"Mother of [her senior child]."

Reflecting the incompleteness of his "mountedness," the neophyte male initiate of Shango is baldheaded and wears a woman's skirt and blouse during public ceremonies. As he matures, the signs of his femininity devolve upward to the head. Ordinarily, the mature priest wears men's clothing; during ceremonies, his skirts suggest an ancestral masquerade more than they do women's clothing (Gleason 1986). The unmistakable and fixed focus of his "wifely" relation to the god is on his head. Like married women of reproductive age, elder Shango possession priests do not cut their hair; instead, as is also proper for married women, they keep it cornrowed year-round. Like rural women, they jewel their braided hair with safety pins, apply antimony (*tìróò*) to their eyes, and wear earrings.

The symbolic importance of the head in defining "wifeliness" and "mountedness" takes telling forms in worldly marriage. The defining feature of nuptial rites, which guarantees the legitimacy of any offspring's membership in his father's house, is the payment of *owó orí ìyàwó*— "money for the bride's head." Hence, the reproduction of the patrilineal house relies explicitly on the appropriation of the heads of its genetrices. The Oyo-Yoruba believe in a personal or ancestral spirit (*orí inú*—the inner head) that, once invested in the physical head (*orí òde*—the outer head), makes its bearer socially, physically, and mentally competent. Initiation in the possession religions invests another spirit in one's physical head; more or less permanently, that spirit rivals the personal or ancestral spirit for control of one's personal and lineal identity, one's body, one's consciousness, and the proceeds of one's production and reproduction— on all of which the natal or affinal house ordinarily stakes a preeminent claim.

The extensive treatments to which the heads of priests—not to mention religious supplicants, brides, and kings—are submitted appear to be acts of displacement and dispossession. For example, recruitment to the

Shango priesthood is often coercive, taking place against the will of the prospective priest's family. Priests refuse to bury a deceased priest until his or her chagrined relatives produce a replacement. The natal house—which is usually predominantly Christian and Muslim—must cede personnel and control over that personnel to the Shango priesthood. Like the family of a king, the possession priest's family loses the right to bury the priest—a fact strongly suggesting the priority of the priest's membership in the cult over his or her membership in the natal or affinal house. The requirements of kingship include some even more extreme parallels. In the past, upon installation, kings lost possession and hereditary rights over their houses and land. In Oyo, the ascending king even lost his affectively closest relative—his mother. She was killed as a condition of his installation. Whatever property the king acquired while on the throne would go not to members of his natal family but to his successor on the throne (Lloyd 1960:228: Johnson 1921:63). To varying degrees, manipulations of the heads of kings, brides, supplicants, and priests remove them from the authority of the kin group, potentiating both their liberation from one institution and their servitude to another.

The Shango initiation "makes an *òrìṣà*" (*ṣe òrìṣà*) in the neophyte's head. Secret rites include the shaving of the initiand's head, the planting of mystical substances there, and the feeding of the new *òrìṣà* in the priest with copious quantities of animal blood applied to the scalp. By circulating banknotes around the initiand's head, priests conducting initiations even mime the payment of bridewealth in order to claim the cult's legitimate control over the neophyte and his or her fertility. Possession rites that entail placing filled pots and calabashes on the priest's head mime the outcome of this ritual assertion: the filling, appropriation, and domination of the priest by a structurally male and alien power—in short, "mounting." This is not to imply that power in the palace always works in a top-down fashion. Rather, it implies that even acts of subversion by delegates and loyalists of the palace are configured ideologically in these terms.[9] Priests and especially supplicants of Shango are engaged in acts of submission, but they are acts with a potential reward of liberation from threats and exploitation outside Shango's "cone of authority."

The stereotypic desideratum of supplicants, as well as the efficacy of this hierarchy and technology of "mounting," is advertised not only in priestly clothing but in Shango shrine sculpture. Initiands, male and female, wear *òjá*, the sling used to bind an infant child to his mother's back.[10] The most common stereotype in Shango votary sculpture is a kneeling woman bearing (1) a child on her back and (2) either a vessel in her hands, a vessel on her head, or Shango's "thunder axe" embedded in her head. Her hair, like that of worldly brides and Shango priests, is usually elaborately braided. Her posture signifies both submission and birth: the female gesture of submission to superiors and the delivery of a child are both called *ikúnlẹ̀*, or kneeling." The *òrìṣà* festival, which includes the possession rites, may also be called *ikúnlẹ̀*. Thus, the human and the wooden icons of Sango's worldly presence condense images of consummated "wifeliness" upon the head and connect cerebral "mountedness" causally to women's uterine fertility.

Mounted Men: The Politics of Fertility

Personal and lineal reproduction among the Oyo Yoruba are not simply genital and uterine processes. They are religious, historical, and political. Just as "mounting" entails inextricable references beyond sexual penetration, the concept of fertility entails inextricable references beyond uterine health. When rural female supplicants face the manifest king of an ancient empire and kneel so that he might touch their heads, they themselves become icons and agents of an ancient politicoreligious order. Their intense desire for children and related desiderata leads them to endorse and reenact an imperial order whose worldly power is increasingly focused not only on rural female capacities but on their aspirations and interests as well. If, in this imperial order, wives were once mainly instruments and functionaries of kings, it is now all the more clear that they are managers and beneficiaries of the *òrìṣà*'s powers.

By what logic does the touch of a transvestite empower a woman to bear and rear good children? On the one hand, he concentrates within himself the feminine feature associated with proper social reproduction—a properly controlled "head" (*orí*). Though that reproduction finds its most prominent instance in childbearing, the reproduction of the Union of *Orìṣà* Worshipers, of the Shango priesthood, and of an empowering vision of history equally manifest the fertility wrought by the *òrìṣà*, even against the forceful resistance of Islam, Christianity, and a "secularism" afforded by new sources of power in the merchant capitalist state. Igboho's royalist symbolic order codifies the reign of these nonroyalist forces in the same terms as barrenness. Hence, the healing wrought by Shango's modern brides concerns the postpartum world of mother and child as well. A child made possible by Shango belongs to Shango; the child is born into a world and into a ritual practice conducive to his own and his mother's prosperity and to safety from the malevolence of witches and thieves, big and small.

Hence, a woman's submission to this order of fecundity is also an acquiescence to a historical vision and a plea for a specific modern politicoreligious order. That order explicitly classifies proper female authority as wifely—renouncing, as a source of illness and infertility, the female powers that function independently of marriage, "mounting," and the royalist hierarchy—namely, witchcraft (*àjẹ́*), which is commonly associated with the market. Shango rites declare a legitimate order of female authority by direct reference to the hegemonic prototype of political order and legitimacy in Oyo North—the Oyo Empire. This form of rural women's and transvestite men's resistance to their modern disenfranchisement is, to adapt Fernandez's (1982) felicitous phrase, an "argument of historical images."

Unmounted Women: Infertility and Political Chaos

In modern Oyo North, uterine fertility is a moral, economic, and political issue. It is the sine qua non of the survival of the "house" and the parents' posthumous reincarnation, the foremost index of social wealth, and a major determinant of a parent's status within the patrilineal house and in the town. Certain vivid ritual idioms promising to restore a threatened fertility and its analogs, as noted above, are linked closely in the shared historical memory of the Oyo Yoruba to royalist political formations. Those idioms, therefore, potentiate both an escape from and a critical vision of the current hegemony. They also inform frightening alternative modes of action in the postimperial metropolis.

The ritual and mythic critique of the contemporary order illustrates itself in images of female infertility and antifertility. The alleged antireproductive and antisocial malevolence of some women finds one precedent in the image of the female market chiefs of the last century—the Iyalode. In the late twentieth century, market women attract greater suspicion and opprobrium than any other visible group of men or women in Nigeria. Although it is easy to find men and women who will testify to their mothers' generosity and its source in the market, most Yoruba are equally quick to blame market women in general for an unlikely range of social ills. For example, in the late 1980s women traders took the blame for the spiraling inflation and market shortages created by years of federal mismanagement, the ebb of oil wealth, and the government's efforts to secure IMF loans.

In some respects, witches (àjẹ́) seem the nocturnal personae of market women. When they gather in conference, it is in the market. They fly about at night in the form of birds, devouring children in the womb and draining blood from their victims. Much lore attributes these women's evil powers to the pots and calabashes they keep (see Morton-Williams 1956: 318ff). Detractors of the postcolonial "big men" allege that these nonroyal businessmen and politicians have women with pots behind them—implicitly witches—guiding their greedy acquisition and providing the mystical means of their enemies' undoing. In tabloid comics, their diurnal personae are enormously fat women who stand alongside overfed men in flowing *agbádá* gowns. The *Alágbádá*—"Wearers of *Agbádá*"—are the stereotypic embezzlers of government funds and receivers of kickbacks. Thus,

modern political changes have generated new images of gender and recon-
textualized old ones.

Women have been all but invisible in both the military and the civilian
regimes of postcolonial government. Although Yoruba women have the
vote, elected and appointed government councils, judicial benches, and
legislatures are invariably overwhelmingly male in their membership.
Women are a minority in the civil service as well. The richest and most
influential women, stereotypically, are those who secure government contracts by sleeping with well-placed men. Though, like "mounting," it is
cast in a sexual idiom, modern women's so-called "bottom power" is fleeting; it has the longevity of a well-placed man's desire, and it elicits little
more respect than prostitution. It is barren sexuality.

The paradigmatic vessels of power under the Oyo Empire, women are
less and less recognized for any potential to hold legitimate power in the
twentieth-century bourgeois state. Where women's normatively authorized options for achievement have diminished, accomplished women may
be classified as men. In small towns, one might hear a woman driver
praised as obìnrin bíi ọkùnrin (a woman like a man)! A ranking priestess
in Igboho distinguished herself from the subordinate priestesses of the
goddess Yemoja by saying, "I am the warrior; they are the brides" (Èmi ni
jagun; àwọn ni iyàwó). In the former national capital, Lagos, a vastly
wealthy market woman once summarized for me the significance of her
accomplishment. She declared simply, Ọkùnrin ni mi (I am a man)!

Neither where the ritual idiom of "mounting" is marginalized in royalist institutions nor when royalism in general is devalued does that idiom
necessarily become obsolete. The bourgeois condemns erratic or imperi-
ous behavior by asking, Kí ló ń gùn ọ́? (What is mounting you?) He or she
might suggest that the money of the overbearing rich man is mounting
him, or that the beauty of the harlot is mounting her. Insofar as "mounting" still represents proper sociopolitical corder in the urban context,
it is reputedly under the constant and immediate threat of women's self-
interested disloyalty. The core of the urban migrant family—partially
detached as it is from the rural house—is the conjugal pair. Popular conversation and the urban press detail the effects of a "medicine" called
Mágùn, meaning "Don't mount." Once a suspicious man fixes it on his
wife or girlfriend, any other man who penetrates her will die. On the other
hand, if she proves innocent of the suspected betrayal, she herself will
die. In the urban world, "mounting" is fraught with sometimes curious
and sometimes frightening potentials.

The highly popular independent African churches cultivate rites akin
to "mounting." Here, prophets under possession by the Holy Spirit protect supplicants from witches, heal them from disease, and enable them
to bear children. Like the Shango cult, these churches confront the most

prominent worshipers with the question of who owns their persons and who controls their consciousness—themselves, or a supernal being? Yet, all these processes of shifting identity, consciousness, and control recognize the integrity of the human vessel, the irreducible humanity of the "bride" or "mount" in the execution of social re-design.

Somewhere between the glorification of female fertility and the vilification or exclusion of women lies a ritual complex, reported by respected Nigerian newspapers and television stations, in which women are murdered and their excised vulvas, breasts, and heads are used in money-making magic (*lùkúdì* and *èdà*). One instance occurred in Igboho, between 1969 and 1970. In such rites, as in marriage and the possession religions, those female body parts likened in *òrìṣà* liturgy and iconography to pots and associated with fertility are used by ritual entrepreneurs as instruments of power. In the present case, however, those parts—breasts, "lower parts," and head—are regarded as alienable. An alternative technology requires the juxtaposition of the victim's head with a calabash, much as Yemoja possession ritual does. Hypnotized people, typically children, have calabashes containing special soap put on their heads. When the descriptive poetry (*oríkì*) of money or of the victim is spoken, money comes out of the calabash or the victims' mouth. When the victim dies, the body must be kept indefinitely. Some rural people believe these atrocities to be common among urban elites—"the rich Alhajis, Alhajiyas, and ministers," whose mansions are full of bodies.

Like labor, women's body parts and families appear to be alienable in the distant logic of capitalist exchange and accumulation—whose nefarious forms are particularly identified with Islam, the federal government, and the magical production of money. Unlike those who have exploited marriage and spirit possession for their own empowerment, the *gbómọgbómọ* (kidnappers) can get power and wealth without acquiring a living dependent. Like marriage and *idóṣù* initiation, the rituals of the *gbómọgbómọ* transfer the productive ownership of a person's head from one social group to another.

Women's bodies above all are metonyms of the social relations they produce through marriage, procreation, and nurture; they are also metaphors of the integrity of the social body. Their physical dismemberment and the kidnapping of their children are homologous images of an ambiguous social process. The state's protection of individual rights, including liberal divorce legislation, and the commodification of labor undermine the hierarchical and collectivist premises of Oyo-Yoruba royalism. Yet, urban ethnic pluralism, widening income gaps, and rising urban crime rates in the postcolonial age reinforce royalist nostalgia. The values inherent in Western economic individualism and the right (or obligation) of individuals to sell their labor are at odds with the ideology of "mounting," which nullifies individual identity and responsibility. For the critics of modern Nigerian capitalism and individualism, the *lùkúdì* victim is proof of the villainy of the new ideology, of its alienating and both socially and bodily divisive effects. For the opponents of royalism, the proverbial fury of the possessed Shango priest is an equally frightening apparition.

Conclusion

Prominent among the shared themes of men's political histories and the rites of the possession religions in Igbòho are gender transformation, marriage, equestrianism, the filling of vessels, and the manipulation of heads—all depicted as conditions of or means to extraordinary politicoreligious power (àṣẹ). These motifs offer a view of the conditions and efficacious strategies of Oyo royal sovereignty. Such strategies faced identifiable opposition during the nineteenth-century reign of Ibadan, the early twentieth-century reign of Great Britain, and the late twentieth-century reign of Nigerian soldiers and businessmen. In both the oral histories and the rituals of Igboho, a wide range of political and moral trends, moments of royalist supremacy and resistance, have been interpreted and manipulated through the idiom of "mounting."

The hegemonic forms of the Oyo Empire have come to articulate a new configuration of interests—largely female and marginal to the mercantile capitalist state. The tropes of "mounting" have contributed a liberating apperception and technology to rural counterassertions. Yet, the gravity of the empire and its village altars extends to the metropolis as well. These metaphoric modes of thought and action structure city people's sense of belonging in and alienation from their native villages, rural and proletarian critiques of politicians and the comprador bourgeoisie, unscrupulous entrepreneurs' magical pursuit of wealth, and rural women's efforts to achieve fertility, in its broadest sense. No less than the narrative recitations that charter Igboho men's political claims, local women's rituals of spirit possession assert a theory of history and political order. Indeed, they dramatize that theory in a play of seduction: credulity entails the promise of penetration and fecundation by the most virile of lords.

Notes

I wish to thank Jean Comaroff for her multiple readings and many invaluable suggestions during the preparation of this chapter. Any errors and oversights, however, are my own.

1. See, e.g., "Report to Support Recommendations for a Subordinate Native Authority and a Sub-Treasury for the Village Areas of Igboho, Kishi and Igbẹtti,"

p. 4, in Oyo Prof II, file 4162, undated (printed between 1940 and 1944), National Archives, Ibadan (Nigeria).

2. While recent etymologies of the word *ìlàrí* vary, Johnson's nineteenth-century account of the etymology presumably given in the palace specifies that the male *ìlàrí* were the "keepers of [the king's] head," translatable as *ì lí orí* (Johnson 1921:62). This apparent folk etymology interpolates the same grammatical formula that is used to identify Shango possession priests as "keepers [or owners] of Shango"—*Onísàngó*. *Oní-* and *ilí-* are variants on the same inflectional particle. See Babayẹmi (1979:56–64) on Abiọdun's revolution.

3. *Kèfèrí* comes from the Arabic *kafír*, meaning "infidel."

4. Oyo was an intermediary in the trade in natron, swords and knives, leather, beads, unwrought silk, and Saharan salt from the north, as well as kola nuts, pepper, cloth, and salt from the south (Smith 1988:38).

5. He is praised as *Ajàlá alámọ tó mọ orí* (Ajala, the Potter Who Mold Heads) and *Ajàlá Amọ̀nkòkò* (Ajala, Molder of Pots).

6. Even gifts from pilgrims to Mecca—a cowry necklace in one case—make it into *òrìṣà* altars. As proof of access to goods from distant places, these are representations par excellence of power in both the Oyo kingdom and the present mercantile state.

7. In quotidian situations, a woman sitting on an upright mortar might provoke Shango's unwelcomed penetration—that is, the striking of the woman by lightning, which is conceived of as penetration by a "thunder axe." Hence, women are cautioned against sitting on mortars during rainstorms.

8. These shrines belong to the nonpossession priests (*mọ́gbà*), who are the official heads of the cult and who are responsible for initiating possession priests.

9. E.g., the sacred poetry Yemoja priests chant to the chief of Onigboho House suggest that he, too, is subject to "mounting" and that his own will is subject to limits (see Matory 1991:343–44).

10. Even senior possession priestesses beyond childbearing age do so in other possession cults, like that of Yemoja.

References

Abu-Lughod, Lila. 1986. *Veiled Sentiments*. Berkeley: University of California Press.

Aderele, T. A. 1982. Report of Public Inquiry into the Headship Tussle among Alepata, Onigboho, and Ona-Onibode. All in the Irepo South Local Government Area. Held on 1–3 June 1982. Compiled by T. A. Aderele, Zonal Local Government Inspector, Oyo Zone, Oyo State of Nigeria.

Agbaje-Williams, Babtunde. 1983. A Contribution to the Archaeology of Old Oyo. Ph.D. dissertation, Department of Archaeology, University of Ibadan.

Akintoye, S. A. 1971. *Revolution and Power Politics and Yorubaland, 1840–1893*. New York: Humanities Press.

Asiwaju, A. I. 1976. *Western Yorubaland under European Rule, 1889–1945.*
London: Longman.

Atanda, J. A. 1979. *The New Oyo Empire.* London: Longman.

————. 1970. The Changing Status of the Alafin of Oyo under Colonial Rule and
Independence. In *West African Chiefs,* ed. Michael Crowder and Obaro
Ikime. Ile-Ife, Nigeria: University of Ife Press.

Awe, Bolanle. 1972. The Economic Role of Women in Traditional African Society:
The Yoruba Example. In La Civilisation de la Femme dans la tradition africaine. Colloquium in Abidjan, Ivory Coast, 3–8 July.

Babayẹmi, S. O. 1979. The Fall and Rise of Oyo c. 1760–1905. Ph.D. diss., University of Birmingham, U.K.

Babayẹmi, S. O. 1982. Oyo Palace Organisation. Paper presented at the Institute
of African Studies Seminar, University of Ibadan, 16 June.

————. 1971. Upper Ogun: An Historical Sketch. *African Notes* 6, no. 2:72–83.

Barber, Karin. 1990. *Oriki,* Women and the Proliferation and Merging of *Orişa.*
Africa 60, no. 3:466–537.

Bellah, Robert N. 1968. Civil Religion in America. In *Religion in America,* ed.
William G. McLoughlin and Robert N. Bellah. Boston: Houghton Mifflin.

Biobaku, Saburi. 1952. An Historical Sketch of the Ẹgbá Traditional Authorities.
Africa 22, no. 1:35–49.

Biobaku, Saburi. 1960. Madame Tinubu. In Eminent Nigerians of the Nineteenth Century. A series of studies originally broadcast by the Nigerian
Broadcasting Corporation. Cambridge: Cambridge University Press.

Boddy, Janice. 1989. *Wombs and Alien Spirits.* Madison: University of Wisconsin
Press.

Clapperton, Hugh. 1829. Journal of a Second Expedition into the Interior of Africa, from the Bight of Benin to Soccatoo. London: John Murray.

Clarke, William H. 1972. *Travels and Explorations in Yorubaland, 1854–1858.*
Ibadan: Ibadan University Press. From a manuscript completed in 1871.

Counihan, Carole M. 1985. Transvestitism and Gender in a Sardinian Carnival.
Anthropology 9, nos. 1 and 2:11–24.

Eades, J. S. 1975. The Growth of a Migrant Community: The Yoruba of Northern
Ghana. In *Changing Social Structure in Ghana,* ed. J. R. Goody. London:
International African Institute.

Fadipẹ, N. A. 1970. *The Sociology of the Yoruba.* Ibadan: Ibadan University
Press. Originally a 1939 Ph.D. diss., University of London.

Fernandez, James W. 1982. *Bwiti.* Princeton: Princeton University Press.

Foucault, Michel. 1980. *Power/Knowledge.* New York: Pantheon.

Frobenius, Leo. 1968 [1913]. The Voice of Africa, vol. 1. New York: Benjamin
Blom.

Giovannini, Maureen. 1981. Woman: A Dominant Symbol within the Cultural
System of a Sicilian Town. *Man,* n.s. 16, n. 3:408–26.

Gleason, Judith. 1986. *Oya: In Praise of the Goddess*. Draft of a book by the same title, published in 1987 by Shambala, Boston.

Idowu. E. Bolaji. 1963. Olodumare: God in Yoruba Belief. New York: Praeger.

Isola, Akinwumi. 1991. Religious Politics and the Myth of Shango. In *African Traditional Religions in Contemporary Society*, ed. Jacob K. Olupona. New York: Paragon House.

Johnson, Rev. Samuel. 1921. *The History of the Yorubas*. Lagos: C.S.S. Bookshops.

Lander, R., and J. Lander. 1832. Journal of an Expedition to Explore the Course and Termination of the Niger, three volumes. London: John Murray.

Lloyd, P. C. 1960. Sacred Kingship and Government among the Yoruba. *Africa* 30, no. 3:221–37.

Matory, J. Lorand. In press *a*. "Turn a Man Into a Woman": Gender in the Contestation of Political Order in Oyo. In *Queens, Queen Mothers, Priestesses and Power*, ed. Flora Kaplan. Carbondale: Southern Illinois University Press.

———. In press *b*. Rival Empires: Islam and the Religions of Spirit Possession among the Oyo-Yoruba. *American Ethnologist*.

———. 1991. Sex and the Empire That Is No More: A Ritual History of Women's Power Among the Oyo-Yoruba. Ph.D. diss., University of Chicago.

Morton-Williams, Peter. 1964. An Outline of the Cosmology and Cult Organization of the Oyo Yoruba. *Africa* 34, no. 3:243–61.

———. 1956. The Atinga Cult among the South-Western Yoruba: A Sociological Analysis of a Witch-Finding Movement. *Bulletin de l'I.F.A.N.*, series B, 18, nos. 3–4:315–34.

Oroge, E. Adeniyi. 1971. The Institution of Slavery in Yorubaland with Particular Reference to the 19th Century. Ph.D. dissertation, University of Birmingham, U.K.

Prince, Raymond et al. 1968. The Therapeutic Process in Cross-Cultural Perspective—a Symposium. *American Journal of Psychiatry* 124, no. 9:1171–77.

Smith, Robert S. 1988 [1969]. *Kingdoms of the Yoruba*, 3d ed. Madison: University of Wisconsin Press.

Smith, Robert. 1965. The Alafin in Exile. *Journal of African History* 6, no. 1:57–77.

Wikan, Unni. 1977. Man Becomes Woman: Transsexualism in Oman as a Key to Gender Roles. *Man*, n.s. 12:304–19.

PART 2

Moral Economics, Modern Politics, Mystical Struggles

4

The Moral Economy of Witchcraft: An Essay in Comparative History

Ralph A. Austen[1]

IN A RECENT STUDY OF SLAVE TRADING, the Beninois historian Abiola Felix Iroko (1988:199) notes with some embarrassment an oral tradition about the provenance of cowry shells, a major currency in this commerce. According to indigenous informants, cowries were obtained by killing slaves, floating their bodies in the Atlantic Ocean, and pulling them back after cowries had adhered to the corpses.[2]

Such local knowledge not only clashes with our empirical information on the origin of cowry shells—Iroko reminds us that they were imported to West Africa from the Indian Ocean via Europe—but also contradicts the entire body of analysis built around recent economic studies of the slave trade. Precisely by focusing on a commodity like cowries, these studies have argued for the relevance of market principles in understanding African development. First of all, it can be demonstrated that the movements of cowries and slaves across a complex international market operated according to predictable patterns of supply and demand; second, in the interior of West Africa, large-scale imports of shell currency allowed the monetization (and thus market expansion) of transactions in foodstuffs and other local consumer items (Hogendorn and Johnson 1986).

The equation of cowries with slave corpses derives from a very different view of what such commerce meant both within Africa and in African relations with the wider world. It does not take much imagination to understand why death should be the metaphor for a traffic built upon the removal of human beings from their home continent, many to a literal death but virtually all to "a bourn from which no traveller returns." The more challenging task is to consider how fully the perception embodied in such terms represents an alternative to the concept of market rationality and its encompassing discourse of modernization.

This task will be pursued here through the discussion of two well-established ideas in academic literature: moral economy and witchcraft. The first is a pure abstraction purporting to explain the response to capitalism of various communities who, like Africans in the slave trade era and afterward, insist that considerations other than those of the market should and do govern the production and distribution of material goods. The middle portion of this essay will review critically the debate over moral economy to consider how useful it may be for understanding African history.

Witchcraft, as used here, is also an abstraction, but one intended to represent directly the terms used by African and other societies to describe their own beliefs and practices. The introductory section of this chapter will attempt to identify an African witchcraft idiom which gives broader meaning to texts such as the Beninois oral account of slave-cowry transactions. The concluding section of this chapter will examine the early modern European "witch craze" in order to consider how the elaboration of common elements in European and African culture both reflects and mediates differing trajectories into the modern world.

African Witchcraft Idiom as a Discourse of History and Power

The various issues surrounding witchcraft, including the comparison of African and European cases, have long been a staple of Africanist anthropological research.[3] All these discussions share a general definition of witchcraft as the use of preternatural power by one person to damage others. Almost all have focused on beliefs about such practices and the means used to counter them rather than on the practices themselves. All assume that beliefs of this kind have important social consequences and reflect the manner in which the peoples concerned understand their broader historical experience.

For purposes of the present analysis, two issues in African witchcraft studies are to be emphasized: (1) the kinds of social relationships involved in witchcraft accusations; and (2) the role of reproduction, sexuality, and gender in these beliefs.

Virtually all existing work, at least in rural Africa, indicates that witchcraft efficacy is held to be a direct function of the intimacy between witch and victim. Thus the vast majority of accusations and rituals involve relations between peers, kin, and co-wives; the corollary being that, with greater social distance, such accusations would decline (Douglas 1970, xxx–xxxi; Marwick 1982:377ff.). Recent research, however, shows African urban elites to be afraid that those left behind in their villages are bewitching either them or the state projects with which they identify (Geschiere 1988; Ciekawy 1990; Bastian, Chap. 6 this vol.). Also, while formal witchcraft accusations against the powerful and wealthy are rare, it has "become a commonplace observation in African studies" (Rowlands and Warnier 1988:121) that such ascendent individuals are perceived to be witches.

Commonplace as it may be, the equation of witchcraft with the attainment of power and wealth has been neglected in the anthropological literature, which has mainly focused on the sociology of formal witchcraft accusations. However, it is witchcraft beliefs that cross hierarchical boundaries that enter most directly into the concerns of this chapter: the contemplation of historical change by Africans, the competition of witchcraft idioms with the discourses of markets and modernization, and their comparison with early modern European antiwitchcraft beliefs.[4]

For this purpose, Binsbergen (1981:141–142) provides a very useful distinction between "impersonal" and "anti-personal" witchcraft. The latter consists of misfortunes attributed to the ill will of peers with whom some identifiable tension already exists. It is this category which Marwick (1982:330) probably had in mind when he asserted that "increased tensions attendant upon urbanization are not necessarily expressed in the idiom of witchcraft." Impersonal witchcraft, on the other hand is defined by Binsbergen (1981:163) in terms all too easily linked to modern situations as "the reckless manipulation of human material for strictly individual purposes."

In rural Africa the human material manipulated by witchcraft is frequently identified with control over the forces constituting the reproduction of everyday life. In the most unproblematic circumstances, these forces are contained within the domestic sphere of conjugal sexuality and food cultivation and consumption. Congenital witches are almost always described as insatiably hungry: they seek to "eat" others by imbibing their reproductive powers in the form of corpses, children, sexual fluids, and so on.

A number of studies (Goody 1970; Gottlieb 1989) have noted a distinction between female witches, who are totally stigmatized, and males who are recognized as both witches and legitimate figures of political and ritual authority. The distinctions do not lie in the activities or immediate relationships to reproduction and production which identify each category as witches: all may be guilty of killing and consuming close relatives, and the males may procure wealth only by predation upon surrounding societies. Rather it is the *public* positions held by the men in question that makes their witchcraft somehow more tolerable and even, in some cases, celebrated. This acceptance of "official" witchcraft is generally explained as a form of resignation: antiwitchcraft measures are ineffective against such concentrations of power (Rowlands and Warnier 1988:121). But it is also recognized that many Africans take the existence of witchcraft to be inevitable and ubiquitous; there is thus positive value in the fact that some figures of authority have the mystical power to ward off the malignancy of others. This need is particularly strong when the dangers come from outside the community and can only be combated by kings and diviners of one's own (Goody 1970; Austen 1986).

The conception of witchcraft as an ambiguous attribute of power within Africa is often presented in ahistorical terms, as a timeless reflection of the tension between communal values and selfish individualism and anxieties about natural threats to subsistence. Our data on witch beliefs, however, are all relatively recent; with little exception they are drawn from societies that had long been involved with either the Islamic or European outside world. It is striking that several West Central African cosmologies link witchcraft with the deployment of victims in a nocturnal and/or distant "second universe," echoing, in more or less explicit terms, the experience of the Atlantic slave trade (Hagenburcher-Sacripanti 1973:143–63; Rosny 1985:58–63; McGaffey 1986; Miller 1988:4–5).

The Beninois explanation of cowry imports should now appear more familiar, not only as a metaphorical account of the slave trade but also as the expression of a discourse equating the acquisition of wealth and power with (1) the consumption of human life and (2) links to a more powerful outside world. But if we are to assert the relevance of this discourse for understanding the wider African experience of historical change, we need to consider it in more general terms. The witchcraft idiom in Africa echoes perceptions elsewhere in the world of relationships between communal norms and externally centered market economies. The comparison of these perceptions and relationships by social scientists has produced its own metadiscourse around the concept of moral economy.

The Moral Economy Debate: Microeconomics and Culture

The central trope of the various efforts to define moral economy has been an opposition between, on the one hand, the maximizing individual and everexpanding market of classical political economy and, on the other, a community governed by norms of collective survival and believing in a zero-sum universe—that is, a world where all profit is gained at someone else's loss. The communal/zero-sum side of this equation is broadly consistent with African beliefs identifying capitalism and witchcraft as the dangerous appropriation of limited reproductive resources by selfish individuals. The great danger of such a set of dichotomies is that it may remain trapped where it first originated, within the discourse of capitalism itself. Exotic economies thus become constructed around either a market/nonmarket opposition or a subsistence-based variant of market rationality. In analyzing the history of societies confronting capitalism, even from the outside of the bottom one cannot reject out of hand all references to capitalist terms. But a cultural account proceeding entirely on this basis represents a concession to the very hegemony moral economy is supposed to be contesting.

The term "moral economy" actually came into wide scholarly use through the study of early capitalist Europe, specifically with E. P. Thompson's writings on eighteenth-century Britain (Thompson 1968:225–26, 1971); its application to the Third World awaited the somewhat later book of James Scott (1976). Scott, according to his references, was indeed inspired by Thompson; yet Thompson had predecessors who were more concerned than he with non-Western economies and remain more directly relevant to the genesis of moral economy theory and its role in studying Africa.

It was the substantivist economics of Karl Polanyi[5] and his associates (1957) that initiated a sophisticated argument among anthropologists and historians about the relevance of market models to the study of economies outside of the modern West (LeClair and Schneider 1968; Hopkins 1973; Dalton 1974). The substantivists, who questioned those models ultimately lost most of the arguments. On an abstract level, their "non-market" terms (derived from a somewhat naive reading of structural-functionalist anthropology) were easily converted into "collective utilities"; more concretely, what substantivists defined as uniquely Western market behavior could be documented in large portions of "primitive" and "archaic" Africa. Polanyi's explicitly Aristotelian critique of profit seeking is a perfect example of what Parry and Bloch (1989:2–3) identify as a fatal ethnocentrism in interpreting "the morality of exchange" in societies outside Europe. Nonetheless, the concept of how markets may be "embedded" in other systems of hierarchy, distribution, and value remains—when understood less rigidly than Polanyi did—a useful tool for analyzing the relationships between individual acquisitiveness and witchcraft (see below, this chap.).

The more robust notion of a zero-sum universe as the basis for "traditional" economic behavior derives from the ethnographic work of George Foster (1965). Foster argued that peasants everywhere experience a world of "the limited good,"[6] but he regarded such attitudes as obstacles to both progress and true communal cohesion, much as did the more acerbic Edward Banfield (1958). Foster and Banfield are rarely cited in moral economy literature because their developmentalist outlook fits ill with the ideological stance in most of this writing; however, their vision of negative utilitarianism states most clearly its underlying premises.

Thus, in his original formulation of moral economy, Scott attributes to Third World (and even European) peasants a formal economic logic far more akin to the approach of the unnamed Foster than to the acknowledged Thompson and Polanyi. Having decided that these cultivators maintain a "subsistence ethic," Scott undertakes what he considers a sympathetic analysis of their actions by replacing the motive of profit maximization with one of risk aversion (Scott 1976:4ff.). It was thus possible for Popkin (1979) to produce a work ostensibly criticizing Scott for neglecting evidence of profit-oriented entrepreneurship in peasant communities, while actually providing a very similar picture of the calculations underlying rural Southeast Asian responses to colonial capitalism (Hunt 1988).

Scott (1985) has recognized that his earlier formulations were overly abstract and too focused on explaining the relatively rare occurrence of peasant revolt; his newer work thus contributes to a version of the moral economy argument revised in both method and vision (see Roeder 1984; Berry 1985; Magagna 1991). The basis for these more recent studies is a combination of intensive village fieldwork (even by Scott, a political scientist) and detailed historical research. No longer is the "essential" need of the premodern rural small holder seen to be subsistence; it is now security, sought by contesting the dominant order through complex processes of patronage-clientage, small-scale (often hidden) rebellion or resistance, and the claim to overlapping rights in vital property. Thompson's early (1971) formulation of moral economy fits this model well; the British crowds he describes appeal against unregulated market prices both to abstract principles of communal needs and to established paternalist norms and practices.

In its more nuanced versions, the moral economy perspective is less open to empirical criticism from rational choice advocates and can provide rich accounts of the devices by which communities reproduce complex relations of dependency (Berry 1985). But the ability to bring cultural analysis into these efforts remains limited; Scott's *Weapons of the Weak* (1985) depicts peasants whose poverty extends to their inability to offer any compelling description of the larger world in which they are encompassed, and Berry sees the commitments of Yoruba entrepreneurs to village investments mainly in terms of her own norms of productivity. Perhaps the most successful treatment of culture is found in Magagna's discussion (1991) of protoindustrial England, where the values expressed in village charivari and "alehouse discourse" are successfully incorporated into the rural negotiations of such capitalist incursions as enclosure. Missing in this argument, however, is any serious attention to witchcraft, the very feature of the cultural landscape in early capitalist Europe most open to comparison with Africa.

The concept of moral economy thus has serious shortcomings; even in Europe, where it has proven most useful, it leaves unexamined the cultural dimensions of capitalism and its opponents. Nonetheless, the moral economy school has a good deal to teach those more seriously concerned with culture. Most obviously, it demands that attention be paid to the conditions of access to material resources that determine, with some degree of autonomy, the understandings of capitalism possible within any community. Furthermore, in the revised versions it provides detailed, socially sensitive accounts of political and economic strategies that illuminate any discussion of ideology.

Marxian Moral Economy

Although most of the moral economy theorists discussed so far are critics of historical capitalism, few of them are Marxists. Indeed, whether stressing market rationalism or communal norms, they refuse (often explicitly) to discuss peasant society in class terms (see especially Magagna 1991). Marxist analyses of the peasantry, along with "peasant studies" in general may indeed be out of fashion (Roseberry 1989). Nonetheless, it is Marxists who continue to search for the cultural components of Third World responses to capitalism—including witchcraft beliefs. The results may be problematic, but they nonetheless point to paths of inquiry not opened by the individualist and functionalist approaches of other moral economy theories.

Much of the Marxist effort to date consists of criticism and self-criticism about claims "to have discovered peasant ideology in academic discourse" (Kahn 1985:71). Not surprisingly, a favorite vehicle for approaching those ideologies is Gramsci, who can be read as setting out terms for applying Marxist concepts to popular consciousness of various kinds (Arnold 1984a). Gramsci himself, however, held disparaging views of Italian peasant *senso comune*, and his own cultural theory stressed the hegemony of the exploiters rather than the class consciousness of the exploited. The difficulties are illustrated by comparing David Arnold's (1984a) sensitive account of the theoretical and historiographic issues in a Gramscian approach to the peasantry with the same author's study (Arnold 1984b) of peasant consciousness in nineteenth-century India. Despite some references to religious beliefs and a critique of moral economy theory, Arnold's empirical effort very closely resembles *Weapons of the Weak* (Scott 1985). One seeks in vain for any fuller theory or practice of cultural analysis in the Subaltern Studies school to which Arnold adheres.[7]

The most ambitious Marxist attempt at defining countercapitalist culture, and the one most relevant to studies of African witchcraft, is Michael Taussig's *The Devil and Commodity Fetishism in South America* (1980). Taussig provides us with very vivid and detailed accounts of a Colombian and Bolivian peasant "cosmogenesis" of capitalism in which the acquisition of commodities for the purpose of producing extraordinary wealth is intimately linked to the expropriation of the reproductive powers of both land and people.

The Marxist inspiration of Taussig's work is responsible for his sensitivity to indigenous conceptualizations of relations of production and reproduction, as opposed to the exchange models that inform most of the moral economy literature. However, the situations Taussig describes involve more direct capitalist exploitation (estate agriculture and tin mines) than is commonly found in tropical Africa. Even in this context, Taussig makes interpretive leaps that are highly questionable in both theoretical and empirical terms. For example, he insists on an identity between his ethnographic data and orthodox Marxist theories of "commodity fetishism" and use/exchange value dichotomies. He further conjures up an implausible precapitalist "peasant/village" society with no markets, individual competition, or ecological deterioration.

The critique of Taussig's argument as applied to Bolivian miners has inspired the participants in a recent symposium to rethink both Marxist and substantivist notions of moral economy (Parry and Bloch 1989). Far from seeing capitalism as an intrusion upon the values of the precolonial Andean economy, Sallnow (1989:227) insists that the "supernatural perils of gold mining are a consequence, not of the ultimate commoditization of the product, but of the cultural logic within which it is imbedded." This logic, as further explicated by Harris (1989), identifies mining with the hierarchies of mountain gods and state authority (whether Inka or modern), which, like African "legitimate" witches, protect and maintain local reproduction in return for their periodic destruction of individual human life.

Parry and Bloch (1989:23–30) have abstracted from these insights a concept of "two transactional orders" involving, respectively, short-term individual acquisitiveness and the long-term reproduction of the social and cosmic order. The value of their model is that it overcomes the simplistic market/community dichotomies of both moral economy and Taussig's Marxism, while preserving the understanding that vital issues of reproduction may be at stake in engagements with capitalism.

The cultural logic evoked by Sallnow and Harris is specific to the historically continuous identity in the Andes of relationships between reproduction, the production of wealth, state authority, and a mountain ecology. We may still question whether the witchcraft/devil concepts used by Taussig are entirely irrelevant to this mining complex and speculate that they are more so for Colombian cultivators.

In Africa, the cosmologies built around the slave trade and later colonial and postcolonial experiences imply confrontations with a source of wealth and misfortune much more alien than the mining hierarchy of the world of Sallnow and Harris. As already suggested, it is possible in some African situations to equate even the most destructive effects of capitalism with local "legitimate" authorities, who have often been its collaborators. But precisely as capitalist culture has moved more directly into the African landscape, the gap has widened between hegemonic values of productivity (the equivalent of Parry and Bloch's term "long-term reproduction") and the African experience of individual acquisition. A capitalism that kills ✓ less individuals than do the Andean mines but also fails to imbed itself in recognized systems of order may thus be perceived in more horrific, anti-reproductive terms.

The common denominator of all the work discussed so far is that it does focus upon capitalism from outside its core and below its commanding heights. A different kind of insight into the cultural issues surrounding capitalism may be gained by transposing the discussion to a new register of ethnocentricity and considering how Europeans themselves moved from a moral economy of witchcraft to the more orthodox discourses of capitalism.

The Moral Economy of the European Witch Craze

Almost at the same time as students of Third World economies were debating questions of moral economy, a large group of social and cultural historians undertook studies of the extended outbreak of witchcraft persecution in early modern Europe.[8] The fact that the moral economy literature has paid virtually no attention to European witchcraft is understandable; the panic over alleged witches had ended by the beginning of the eighteenth century and was thus absent from the phases of capitalism leading directly to the industrial revolution. The appearance and disappearance of witchcraft concerns during the fifteenth through seventeenth centuries are, however, relevant to understanding the cultural contestations of capitalism in both European and comparative terms.

The comparison of African and European witchcraft studies is complicated by the fact that the former are mainly based on ethnographies of contemporary village culture, while the latter focus on the written records of now-vanished urban elites who imposed themselves upon rural society. Nonetheless, the two sets of cases share a base of rural beliefs in interpersonal witchcraft as well as a confrontation with capitalist modernization. The comparison can thus, at the very least, help to historicize further our understanding of African witchcraft and add cultural context to our understanding of European capitalism. In pursuit of these goals, my discussion ✓ of European witch-hunting will focus on three issues: the relationship between urban/elite and rural/popular culture in defining witchcraft, the role of reproduction and female sexuality within these definitions, and the process by which European witchcraft beliefs gave way to both capitalist utilitarianism and various forms of moral economy/socialist anticapitalism.

The early modern European persecutions allow us, far more easily than do the African cases, to identify two socially distinct sets of beliefs about witchcraft and the vectors of its operation. Corresponding to the Africanist notion of interpersonal witchcraft was the European term *mal-*

eficium, literally referring to the use of preternatural powers as an expression of malice among village neighbors. At the center of the formal witch trials which resulted in the tens of thousands of public executions for witchcraft lay the elite concept of the *sabbat*, an orgiastic sacrificial ritual presided over by Satan.

Although the difference between these definitions of mystical evil is critical to understanding the persecutions in early modern Europe, it is also necessary, particularly for purposes of comparison of Africa, to recognize the ideological and practical links between them. *Maleficium* accusations, from what we know of them, seem remarkably similar to local witchcraft allegations in Africa. What we cannot easily see through existing records is the larger systems of popular beliefs within which such ideas functioned.[9]

The *sabbat*, on the other hand has no real parallel in African witchcraft belief or even "syncretistic" Christianity, because it was imagined as a specifically counter-Christian cult. Undoubtedly the content of this putative ritual, if not its structure, derived from European folk culture. Moreover, the condemnation of individuals as participants in a witches' sabbath required that they (or at least their immediate accusers) first be charged by neighbors with *maleficium*. Confessions of congress with the devil usually depended upon suggestions from the prosecutors, reinforced by torture. But there are significant cases in which villagers provided such statements spontaneously, indicating that they, too, had come to believe in the *sabbat*. As will be seen below (this chap.), this belief may have rested upon European understandings of sexuality which turn out to be critical for comparison with Africa.

The attribution of European witchcraft persecution to the rise of capitalism emerged from the study of trials in England, where both torture and *sabbat* beliefs were largely absent (Macfarlane 1970: 195–97; Thomas 1971:553–67, 581–82). The argument here is that the direction of *maleficium* accusations from wealthier members toward more impoverished members of the community reflected a shift from a redistributive to an accumulative (i.e., capitalist) mode of property control. This thesis has recently been called into question: it seems not to explain the scale and timing of accusations found throughout Europe in the early modern period.[10]

However, comparison with recent African material (Geschiere 1988; Bastian, Chap 6 this vol.) suggests that such fears by newly emergent elites—And even the use of witchcraft threats by their rural neighbors or ex-neighbors—are indeed a common phenomenon in times of economic transition. But, in any case, if our aim is to understand the cultural content rather than the behavioral patterns of witchcraft accusations in these circumstances, we must give more attention to the *sabbat* than to *maleficium*.

In the *sabbat*, as in African ideas of "official" witchcraft, the deployment of preternatural malignancy against individuals is equated with concentrations of power in the public arena. The European *sabbat*, however, was formulated mainly by elites among the clergy and judiciary who accused poor and marginal individuals of allying themselves with Satan, the unambiguous antithesis of all legitimate temporal and spiritual authority. Before spelling out the contrasts with Africa, it is useful to consider the interpretations by historians of what, for them, is a puzzling similarity between early modern Europe and primitive society. How could some of the most educated of our post-Renaissance ancestors, on the verge of the Enlightenment and the industrial revolution, have subscribed to, and worse still, acted violently upon, such "primitive superstitions"?

For Trevor-Roper (1968:90–192), who poses the question in just these terms, the answer lay in some irreducible substratum of irrational human hatred which, during the period in question, was inspired by the religious rivalries of the Reformation and counter-Reformation. Reformed religion is certainly critical to understanding the witch persecutions, but its role must be understood through a more serious social and cultural analysis than Trevor-Roper even begins to envisage. Muchembled (1987) and Ginzburg (1983) attempt such analyses by presenting the *sabbat* as a device by which the newly emerging centers of urban power stigmatized the autonomous culture of the countryside, thus promoting the establishment of a single hierarchy within each European state. This last argument, with its populist and Foucaultian overtones, has more contemporary appeal than the intellectualist approach of Trevor-Roper. But it suffers from an indifference to the content of elite witchcraft beliefs and their contradictory relationship to the rationalizing project they were apparently serving. An Africanist might further ask why in Africa, by contrast, neither indigenous intelligentsias (e.g., Iroko), mission-based churches, nor the colonial or postcolonial state have ever been very comfortable with recognizing the entire concept of witchcraft.[11] If witchcraft persecution was merely an unfortunate detour or an opportunistic strategy on the route to modernization, perhaps such discomfort is justified. But if it has some more intimate relationship with the genesis of capitalism in Europe, further questions need to be asked. One line of inquiry emerges from the obvious and discomforting links between witchcraft, gender, and sexuality.

In both Europe and Africa accusations of *maleficium* or its equivalent fall most heavily upon women. In Africa, however, the more elaborate beliefs about the use of witchcraft to attain material power tend to focus upon males or women active in the public sphere of the market place (Apter, Chapt. 5 this vol.). In Europe, on the other hand, women—usually with little power—still constitute the vast majority of those implicated in the most complex allegations of *sabbat* practice.

There has been no shortage of explanations for this misogynistic aspect of the European witch craze. Most commentators have stressed the vulnerability of women, particularly the older ones without husbands who were frequently charged. Yet, this is a universal condition that tells us little about the distinct situation of Europe in the sixteenth and seventeenth centuries. Muchembled (1987:67–69) provides a more historical argument that connects the rising modernism of this period with a "devalorization" of women who functioned as the main bearers of embattled rural/popular culture through their roles as healers, midwives, and purveyors of established norms and oral learning. There is much to be said for this last claim, as it suggests why specific aspects of rural culture should be so much under attack; it also helps us understand their later relegation to the realm of folklore with its gendered aura of "old wives' tales" and the nostalgic infantilization of the rural "motherland." However, even here Muchembled (to say nothing of less nuanced feminist versions of this interpretation) reduces the specific *sabbat* charges under which women were convicted of witchcraft to mere devices of the learned urban elite for subjugating a competing source of power. The intensity with which *sabbat* ideas were apparently believed, and their high load of sexual content, suggests that they have to be taken more seriously if we want to explain the relationships between gender, witchcraft accusations, and the emergence of a modern capitalist order in Europe.[12]

From an Africanist perspective, the connection that immediately suggests itself is that of reproduction. For cases within Africa, it must be recalled, a central trope of witchcraft beliefs is the misappropriation of scarce reproductive resources from households or communities for the selfish use of accumulating individuals. Similar themes are found in European *maleficium* accusations, which frequently involve attacks on the fertility of fields, livestock, and other human beings (Briggs 1989:91; Le Roy Ladurie 1981). Such actions were sometimes attributed to the demands of Satan, and the rites of the *sabbat* regularly included the consumption of babies and fetuses. At a more abstract level, it also seems possible to identify, in both European and African representations of the sexuality of witches, a common concern with the escape of female reproductive power from the enclosed domestic space in which it serves male-dominated communal norms to the open nocturnal realms of self-contained female power (Levack 1987:126ff.).

A comparison of these representations and their historical contexts suggests, however, some important distinctions precisely around the issues of reproduction, gender politics, and accumulation. In rural Africa, reproduction (whether sexual or agricultural) and its potential misappropriation, that is, the zero-sum economy, remains a central cultural issue right through contemporary times. "Modernization" has not solved these problems; rather it has created a new category of witches in the urbanized "femmes libres," witches who literally use market control over their domestic reproductive capacities (sex, food, and even baths) for individualized accumulation (White 1990*b*). In the early modern European *sabbat* accounts, on the other hand, female sexuality seems to be severed from the issue of reproduction; these nightmare women are less independent of male authority than submissive to an alternative vision of masculine power, a vision opposed to the accumulative process with which the persecutors themselves identified. In short, European antiwitchcraft beliefs represent a moral economy *of,* and not opposed to, capitalism.

The frequent references to antireproductive acts in *maleficium* accusations suggest that European rural communities had concerns over maintaining the basic forces of life similar to those of Africa. As historians have regularly noted, however, the witch craze occurred in a period when population and food production capacities had recovered from earlier crises. Moreover, even in the more spontaneous rural European accounts, there is little echo of the classical African equations of witchcraft with eating and insatiable hunger. Moreover, the women accused were usually beyond reproductive age, and the striking feature of their sexuality was its continuation at this point in their lives. The many contemporary woodcut illustrations of the *sabbat*—itself a kind of licensed pornography for this era—focus on the sexual power of female witches; here they are often depicted as far younger than in the statistics of accusations, but in almost all cases they display firm breasts and buttocks, frequently being fondled in foreplay with the devil.[13]

The central role of Satan in the *sabbat* contrasts sharply with the modern African vision of witchcraft as a realm of autonomous female power. Women in the European accounts subject themselves to an alternative male authority through a conscious inversion of Christian ritual. The killing of children is a sacrificial act parodying communion (and recalling "blood libels" against Jews and other heretics) in which it is not the female witches who are nourished but rather the male anti-Christ. The sexual acts portrayed or reported sometimes include women cavorting among themselves, but more commonly concentrate on submission to Satan in acts that give no real pleasure; the devil's penis is always described as cold and pain inducing, and often it is his buttocks that are embraced.

With reference to broader social processes then, we may interpret the *sabbat* fantasy as a vision less of female reproductive power escaping male control than of male control in a mode diametrically opposed to the self-image of a reformed Christian elite. The terms of this opposition seem better understood through the categories of Max Weber than those of Muchembled. The question is not whether female sexuality, as a surrogate for rural culture, should be autonomous or subdued to an absolutist hierarchy but is, instead, whether the ethos of this subjugation should be one of orgiastic consumption or worldly asceticism. The issue of accumulation is not addressed directly in the discourse of witchcraft; however, the construction of female sexuality as a force liberated from reproductive imperatives implies a nonzero-sum universe in which both accumulation and reckless consumption of vital resources are now historical and equally "rational" possibilities. In the long-run development of European capitalism, the limitation of consumption was a critical choice, but no one could think in such terms at the time. Hence, we have the "non-rational" obsession with salvation in the afterlife—linked by Weber to capitalist accumulation—and the even more irrational premise of a satanic witch cult connected here with the repression of alternatives to such accumulation.

Unlike in Africa, therefore, the European witch in her most powerful form was the antithesis of the accumulator. If we look for a popular moral economy to oppose the reformed religious ethos of the witch hunts, we do not find it in rural witchcraft beliefs, which only fed the repression. Instead, such a counterculture expressed itself in the organizations and carnivals of misrule used during the early modern period to maintain traditional domestic order, mock the rich, and play publicly and often quite joyously with issues of sexuality and gender (Davis 1975:97–187). These practices, unlike the movements of Thompson's eighteenth century, did not directly address capitalism and could even, as Natalie Zemon Davis has noted, be channeled into the violent service of reformed religious intolerance. But in the rampant quality of even their religiosity they gave vent to energies that were culturally articulated along lines of community, reproduction, and the festive consumption of accumulated resources—thereby providing an antithesis to the spirit of witchcraft persecution.[14]

Historians of the European witch craze, who have differed so much over the analysis of its meaning and causes, disagree far less in their explanations of its demise in the late 1600s. Most scholars concur that the procedural rationality of witch-hunting finally overwhelmed the antirational premises upon which it had been based. For Trevor-Roper it was the combined destructiveness of religious warfare and the alternative worldview of the scientific revolution—previously committed to its own Neoplatonist demonology—that brought the shift. For Muchembled and some of his critics, the key was the successful erection of the absolutist state whose agents provided both a new, external enemy to rural populations and a self-critique of judicial operations based upon torture and rural folk beliefs. But again, it is Weber who provides the most useful insight into the political economy of the shift through his contention that the decline of ascetic capitalism was inevitable once its own success had made the abundance of goods so evident (Weber 1930:174ff.).

To develop this last point we must go well beyond Weber, who never himself either explicitly addressed the issue of witchcraft or explored the culture of the early eighteenth-century "consumer revolution" (McKendrick et al. 1982) which linked the era of the Protestant ethic to that of industrialization. However, if we accept the equation made above between the witch craze and the anticonsumption ethos of early capitalism, we can similarly associate the abandonment of witchcraft beliefs with Enlightenment liberalism's attacks upon European versions of zero-sum economics. The latter were expressed not through the idiom of witchcraft but rather by mercantilist trade policies, sumptuary-law restrictions on who could purchase what, and assumptions that increased wages would decrease labor incentives. From an Africanist perspective, it is more than ironic that this emergence of classical market ideology in eighteenth-century Europe depended upon the low-cost import from the Third World of commodities previously seen as luxuries—not least among them sugar produced by black slaves (Austen and Smith 1990). In Africa, it should be recalled, the export of those same slaves provides the major historical reference for the equation of capital accumulation, zero-sum economics, and witchcraft.

The decline of European witchcraft beliefs in the eighteenth century becomes more complicated if we contemplate the connections between the construction of women in witch-hunting doctrine and the cult of domesticity that accompanied nineteenth-century capitalism. The latter transformed woman from the devil's mate of the *sabbat*, a sexual force threatening both religious orthodoxy and productive enterprise, to the angel of the house, a desexualized guardian and reproducer of values endangered by the amorality of the surrounding marketplace (Cott 1977). Recent studies of rural women spinners in the protoindustrial textile industry (Medick 1984; Schneider 1989; Stone-Ferrier 1989) suggest an interesting transitional phase of revalorized female production and reproduction. Capitalists of this era explicitly calculated the benefits of women's labor both to their own factor costs and to the marriage opportunities of their employees. For their part the women, gathered together in semi-public spaces, spun not only flax but also rich and ambivalent narratives which used the idiom of witches and other preternatural forces to define the moral economy of their new situation.

This is not the place to trace such developments any further or to explore the dialectics of self-conscious domesticity in the transition to female activism in the modern public sphere. The important point for Africanists is to recognize that the middle-class domestic ideal—so heavily promoted by colonial missionaries—has its own history and moral economy; one that is not totally alien to the African idioms of reproduction and sexuality along with concerns over their relationship to market commerce.

The elite preemption and then exhaustion of the idiom of witchcraft in Europe did not—anymore than the very imperfect functioning of the eighteenth-century grain markets—break down all barriers between capitalist political economy and popular moral economy. However, the latter now developed along the lines laid out by Thompson and Magagna, either negotiating the terms of capitalist expansion on the basis of existing contractual rights and obligations or converting to some version of modern socialist doctrine. In short, moral economy doctrine in Europe, even at a relatively early stage in the development of capitalism, constituted an opposing (and not always ineffectual) voice within the larger discourse that produced capitalism itself.

African efforts at socialism, on the other hand, have both aroused and deployed a continuing witchcraft idiom. To the extent that this socialism draws upon its colonial heritage and Eastern European models rather than local popular discourses, it has inspired an image of "l'état sorcier" in which public authorities exercise arbitrary control over such vital resources as medicine (Hours 1985). In one of the few tropical African cases where capitalism, both local and international, rather than the state is seen as the dominant force, the Kenyan novelist Ngugi wa Thiongo (1982) has produced a socialist vision which draws heavily upon an equation of individual wealth with the appropriation and exportation of indigenous life forces. However problematic may be Ngugi's prescriptions for cultural authenticity and socialism, his view of foreign capitalism thriving on African blood not only resembles the Beninois view of the slave trade but also draws upon long-standing Kenyan popular beliefs concerning vampirous collaboration between European technology and indigenous urban prostitutes (White 1990a).

Conclusion

This essay offers two rather opposing arguments about the relationship between culture and capitalism in Africa and Europe. On the one hand, it insists that, in both cases, there is a shared embeddedness of market rationality in a much wider discourse on moral economy, a discourse most dramatically demonstrated by the concern with witchcraft. In so doing, it seeks to subvert the hegemonic Western dichotomies between self/rational/modern and other/irrational/primitive and evoke greater empathy with African struggles to make sense of their contemporary predicament.

On the other hand, the comparison of Africa and Europe within the common terms of moral economy and witchcraft suggests some very profound differences. The African conception of the witch is tied to various forms of belief in a world where the apparent production of new wealth depends upon appropriating the scarce reproductive resources of others while collaborating with an arbitrary and destructive external power. The European vision of witchcraft is no less frightening, but it assumes an abundance rather than scarcity of the sexual energies required for reproduction. It could be, and eventually was, transcended and transformed by the same political and economic forces responsible for domestic witch hunts, industrialization, and overseas imperialism. In short, the innovative common road though witchcraft branches off into the conventional separate destinations of capitalist modernization and hegemony for Europe and marginalized domination for Africa. It is difficult, despite an Ngugi, even to depict African witchcraft idioms as a weapon of African resistance. Their immediate moral targets are other Africans while they leave the European bases of power mystified to a point where they can only be avoided, not effectively invaded.

What, finally, can be said to rescue the African vision from its subordinate position? Above all else, it represents a telling, truthful insight into the modern experience of the continent, especially at a moment when European concern for Africa becomes ever more remote and AIDS threatens local populations precisely in the realms of sexuality and reproduction. If this kind of truth is valid only for Africa, then it remains a badge of subordination. But it also may provoke a self-critique of the capitalist West (and neocapitalist Asia and Eastern Europe) in an era of massive ecological decay, of increasingly unclear links between production and the accumulation of wealth through the manipulation of stock markets, banks, and electronic media. Comparative history of this kind thus may show us not only how capitalism emerged from the unique circumstances of Europe but also how the self-proclaimed universal logic of capitalist discourse may have to subject itself to the moral and cultural interrogations of a new genre of witch finders.

Notes

1. John Comaroff and Peter Geschiere provided very helpful comments on earlier versions of this essay.

2. Following the initial presentation of this essay, colleagues have reported similar traditions from various parts of the West African coast.

3. See the essays in this collection by Apter, Auslander, Bastian, Masquelier, Schmoll. For older accounts, see Douglas 1970; Marwick 1982 [1970]. For more recent ones, Rowlands and Warnier 1988; Geschiere 1988.

4. For a comparison of African and European witchcraft concepts that stress the distinction between "primitive" and "complex" societies on the basis of what sort of malevolent behavior individuals actually confessed to, see Rowland 1990.

5. Cited by Scott (1976:6n) as "formative for my own work."

6. "Limited good" was translated into the more economistic "zero-sum" by one of Foster's commentators, but Foster accepted the term (Bennett 1966; Foster 1966).

7. Compare the work of this school and the various methodological essays by

its leader, Ranajit Guha, with the dense deconstructionist gloss of their efforts by Gayatri Chakravorty Spivak (Guha and Spivak 1988:3–43 and passim).

8. Their work is best summarized, for the moment, in Cohn 1975; Klaits 1985; and Levak 1987. See also the annotated (from a partisan perspective) bibliography in Muchembled 1987:249–61.

9. I do not wish here to pursue the debate among either radical feminists (see Muchembled 1987 bibliography) or the more sober (but not entirely convincing) Carlo Ginzburg (1990, 1991) on the reconstruction of such a residual "pagan" culture.

10. Nonetheless, Muchembled (1987:175ff.), a critic of the Macfarlane/Thomas thesis relies on similar functionalist arguments (about disintegrating communal bonds) to explain the increase of *maleficium* accusations among Cambresis villagers.

11. Fiisy and Geschiere (1991) have examined recent efforts by the Cameroonian state to involve itself in witchcraft accusations, but the practice seems restricted to one region of the country and resembles the classic British cases of alleged *maleficium* by the poor and marginal against relatively wealthy fellow villagers.

12. What follows is perhaps the most speculative argument in this paper and can ultimately be defended only by far more empirical work than I have yet undertaken. The argument is supported, however, by the sharp contrast drawn in the work of, among others, Martin (1989) between the kinds of charges laid against witches by the Italian and Spanish Inquisition and Northern European accusations of *maleficium* and *sabbat* participation. This geographical and institutional distinction does not touch upon issues of elite control over popular culture as represented in largely female activities; however, it does suggest a connection between the perceived sexuality of witchcraft and the centers of early modern capitalist development. On the other hand, Macfarlane (1987) argues that the precocious success of English capitalism rests precisely upon the absence of extreme witch persecution and its accompanying beliefs.

13. See examples of this iconography in Klaits (1985:54–65, 75); and Levack (1987:between 132–33).

14. Ginzburg and Muchembled have both (Le Goff and Schmitt 1981:131–40, 229–36) attempted to assimilate the history of these youth organizations to their respective arguments on witchcraft; this is not the place to pursue the debate any further.

References

Ankarloo, Bengt, and Gustav Henningsen, eds. 1990. *Early Modern Witchcraft: Centres and Peripheries*. Oxford: Clarendon.

Arnold, David. 1984a. Gramsci and Peasant Subalternity in India. *Journal of Peasant Studies* 11:155–77.

————. 1984*b*. Famine in Peasant Consciousness and Peasant Action: Madras 1876–78. In *Subaltern Studies, III*, ed. R. Guha. Delhi: Oxford University Press.

Austen, Ralph A. 1986. The Criminal and the African Cultural Imagination: Normative and Deviant Heroism in Precolonial and Modern Narratives. *Africa* 56:385–98.

Austen, Ralph A., and Woodruff Smith. 1990. Private Tooth Decay as Public Economic Virtue: The Atlantic Slave-Sugar Triangle, Consumerism and European Industrialization. *Social Science History* 14:95–115.

Banfield, Edward C. 1958. *The Moral Basis of a Backward Society.* New York: Free Press.

Bennett, John W. 1966. Further Remarks on Foster's "Image of the Limited Good." *American Anthropologist* 68:206–10.

Berry, Sara. 1985. *Fathers Work for Their Sons: Accumulation, Mobility and Class Formation in an Extended Yoruba Community.* Berkeley: University of California Press.

Briggs, Robin. 1989. *Communities of Belief: Cultural and Social Tensions in Early Modern France.* Oxford: Clarendon Press.

Ciekaway, Diane. 1990. Utsai and the State: The Politics of Witchcraft Eradication in Coastal Kenya. Unpublished paper, African Studies Workshop, University of Chicago.

Cohn, Norman. 1975. *Europe's Inner Demons: an Enquiry Inspired by the Great Witch Hunt.* New York: Basic Books.

Cott, Nancy F. 1977. *The Bonds of Womanhood: Woman's Sphere in New England, 1780–1835.* New Haven: Yale University Press.

Dalton, George. 1974. Review of Hopkins (1973), *African Economic History* 1:51–101.

Davis, Natalie Zemon. 1975. *Society and Culture in Early Modern France: Eight Essays.* Stanford: Stanford University Press.

Douglas, Mary, ed. 1970. *Witchcraft Confessions and Accusations.* London: Tavistock.

Fiisy, Cyprian S., and Peter Geschiere. 1991. Judges and Witches, or How Is the State to Deal with Witchcraft? Examples from Southeastern Cameroon. *Cahiers d'Etudes Africaines* 31:135–56.

Foster, George M. 1965. Peasant Society and the Image of the Limited Good. *American Anthropologist* 67:293–315.

————. 1966. Reply to . . . Bennett. *American Anthropologist* 68:210–14.

Geschiere, Peter. 1988. Sorcery and the State: Popular Modes of Action among the Maka of Southeast Cameroon. *Critique of Anthropology* 8:35–63.

Ginzburg, Carlo. 1983. *The Night Battles: Witchcraft and Agrarian Cults in the Sixteenth and Seventeenth Centuries.* Translated by John and Anne Tedeschi. Harmondsworth: Penguin.

————. 1990. Deciphering the Sabbath. In Ankarloo and Henningsen.

————. 1991. *Ecstacies: Deciphering the Witches Sabbath.* Translated by Raymond Rosenthal. New York: Pantheon.

Goody, Esther. 1970. Legitimate and Illegitimate Aggression in a West African State. In Douglas.

Gottlieb, Alma. 1989. Witches, Kings and the Sacrifice of Identity among the Beng of Ivory Coast. In *Creativity of Power: Cosmology and Art in African Societies.* ed. W. Aren and I. Karp. Washington, D.C.: Smithsonian Institution.

Guha, Ranajit, and Gayatri Chakravorty Spivak, eds. 1988. *Selected Subaltern Studies,* New York: Oxford University Press.

Hagenburcher-Sacripanti, Frank. 1973. *Les fondements spirituels du pouvoir au royaume de Loango, republique populaire du Congo.* Paris: ORSTOM.

Harris, Olivia. 1989. The Earth and the State: The . . . Meanings of Money in North Potosi, Bolivia. In Parry and Bloch.

Hogendorn, Jan, and Marion Johnson. 1986. *The Shell Money of the Slave Trade.* Cambridge: Cambridge University Press.

Hopkins, A. G. 1973. *An Economic History of West Africa.* New York: Columbia University Press.

Hours, Bernard. 1985. *L'état sorcier: Sante publique et societe au Cameroun.* Paris: L'Harmattan.

Hunt, David. 1988. From the Millennial to the Everyday: James Scott's Search for the Essence of Peasant Politics. *Radical History Review* 42:155–72.

Iroko, Abiola Felix. 1988. Cauris et esclaves en Afrique occidentale entre le XVe et le XIXe siecles. In *De la traite a l'esclavage, tome I: Ve-XVIIIe siecles.* ed. Serge Daget. Nantes: Centre de Recherche sur l'Histoire du Monde Atlantique.

Kahn, Joel. 1985. Peasant Ideologies in the Third World. *Annual Review of Anthropology* 14:49–75.

Klaits, Joseph. 1985. *Servants of Satan: The Age of the Witch Hunts.* Bloomington: Indiana University Press.

LeClaire, Edward E. Jr., and Harold Schneider, eds. 1968. *Economic Anthropology.* New York: Holt, Rinehart.

Le Goff, Jacques, and Jean-Claude Schmitt, eds. 1981. *Le charivari: Actes de la table ronde organisee a Paris (25–27 avril 1977).* Paris: Ecole des Hautes Etudes en Science Sociale.

Le Roy Ladurie, Emmanuel. 1981. L'Aiguillelle: Castration by Magic. In *The Mind and Method of the Historian,* by Emmanuel Le Roy Ladurie. Translated by Ben and Sian Reynolds. Chicago: University of Chicago Press.

Levack, Brian P. 1987. *The Witch-Hunt in Early Modern Europe.* London: Longman.

Macfarlane, Alan. 1970. *Witchcraft in Tudor and Stuart England.* London: Routledge & Kegan Paul.

————. 1987. *The Culture of Capitalism*. Oxford: Blackwell.

McGaffey, Wyatt. 1986. *Religion and Society in Central Africa: The Bakongo of Lower Zaire*. Chicago: University of Chicago Press.

McKendrick, N., et al. 1982. *The Birth of a Consumer Society: The Commercialization of Eighteenth Century England*. London: Europa.

Magagna, Victor V. 1991. *Communities of Grain: Rural Rebellion in Comparative Perspective*. Ithaca: Cornell University Press.

Martin, Ruth. 1989. *Witchcraft and the Inquisition in Venice*. Oxford: Blackwell.

Marwick, Max, ed. 1982 [1970]. *Witchcraft and Sorcery: Selected Readings*. Harmondsworth: Penguin.

Medick, Hans. 1984. Village Spinning Bees: Sexual Culture and Free Time among Rural Youth in Early Modern Germany. In *Interest and Emotion: Essays on the Study of Family and Kinship*. ed. H. Medick and D. Sabean. Cambridge: Cambridge University Press.

Miller, Joseph C. 1988. *Way of Death: Merchant Capitalism and the Angolan Slave Trade, 1730–1830*. Madison: Wisconsin University Press.

Muchembled, Robert. 1987. *Sorcieres: Justice et societe aux 16e et 17e siecles*. Paris: Imago.

Ngugi wa Thiongo. 1982. *Devil on the Cross*. London: Heinemann.

Parry, J., and M. Bloch, eds. 1989. *Money and the Morality of Exchange*. Cambridge: Cambridge University Press.

Polanyi, Karl, et al. 1957. *Trade and Market in the Early Empires*. Glencoe: Free Press.

Popkin, Samuel L. 1979. *The Rational Peasant: The Political Economy of Rural Society in Vietnam*. Berkeley: University of California Press.

Roeder, Philip G. 1984. Legitimacy and Peasant Revolution: An Alternative to Moral Economy. *Peasant Studies* 12:149–68.

Roseberry, William. 1989. Review of second edition of Teodor Shanin, *Peasants and Peasant Societies*. *Journal of Peasant Studies* 16:631–33.

Rosny, Eric de. 1985. *Healers in the Night*. Maryknoll, N.Y.: Orbis.

Rowland, Robert. 1990. "Fantasticall and Develishe Persons": European Witchbeliefs in Comparative Perspective. In Ankarloo and Henningsen.

Rowlands, Michael, and Jean-Pierre Warnier. 1988. Sorcery, Power and the Modern State in Cameroon. *Man* 23:118–32.

Sallnow, M. J. 1989. Precious Metals in the Andean Moral Economy. In Parry and Bloch.

Schneider, Jane. 1989. Rumpelstiltskin's Bargain: Folklore and the Intensification of Linen Manufacture in Early Modern Europe. In Weiner and Schneider.

Scott, James C. 1976. *The Moral Economy of the Peasant: Rebellion and Subsistence in Southeast Asia*. New Haven: Yale University Press.

————. 1985. *Weapons of the Weak: Everyday Forms of Peasant Resistance*. New Haven: Yale University Press.

Stone-Ferrier, Linda. 1989. Spun Virtue: The World Wound Upside Down:

Seventeenth-Century Dutch Depictions of Female Handiwork. In Weiner and Schneider.

Taussig, Michael T. 1980. *The Devil and Commodity Fetishism in South America.* Chapel Hill: University of North Carolina Press.

Thomas, Keith. 1971. *Religion and the Decline of Magic.* New York: Charles Scribner's Sons.

Thompson, E. P. 1968. *The Making of the English Working Class.* Harmondsworth: Penguin.

———. 1971. The Moral Economy of the Crowd in the Eighteenth Century. *Past and Present* 50:76–136.

Trevor-Roper, H. R. 1968. *The European Witch-Craze of the Sixteenth and Seventeenth Centuries and Other Essays.* New York: Harper & Row.

van Binsbergen, Wim M. J. 1981. Religions and the Problem of Evil in Western Zambia. In *Religious Change in Zambia: Exploratory Studies,* by van Binsbergen. London: Kegan Paul.

Weber, Max. 1930. *The Protestant Ethic and the Spirit of Capitalism.* Trans. Talcott Parsons. New York: Charles Scribner's Sons.

Weiner, Annette B., and Jane Schneider, eds. 1989. *Cloth and Human Experience.* Washington, D.C.: Smithsonian Institution.

White, Luise. 1990a. Bodily Fluids and Usufruct: Controlling Property in Nairobi, 1917–1939. *Canadian Journal of African Studies* 24:418–38.

———. 1990b. *The Comforts of Home: Prostitution in Colonial Nairobi.* Chicago: University of Chicago Press.

5

Atinga Revisited:
Yoruba Witchcraft and the Cocoa
Economy, 1950–1951

Andrew Apter

CRITICAL APPROACHES TO AFRICANIST ETHNOGRAPHY question its methods, categories, and epistemological claims as inventions of a colonial mentality, or what Mudimbe (1988:69) calls "a philosophy of conquest." The critique is pitched directly against the classic ethnographies that were produced as much for district officers as for growing numbers of anthropologists, but it implicates the very possibility of ethnography itself. To be sure, British functionalism incorporated the practical units of administrative overrule into its theoretical lexicon. Tribes, chiefdoms, lineage heads, and elders represented the "patterns of authority" that were officially sanctioned—even as they were revised—by the British Crown. Moreover, ethnographic fictions occluded the politics of the colonial situation, since societies were conventionally depicted as ethnically "pure," located in a timeless world of the ethnographic present which generally excluded the colonial state.[1] But even as this ethnographic vision expanded to embrace history, change, and imperial intervention, the "colonial gaze" endured. And, as the more radical argument goes, it still endures, implicitly, in any ethnography that treats Africans as objects, symbols, or even victims of change rather than as agents of their own histories and sociocultural transformations.

It is against this general interpretive problem that I will reanalyze the Atinga witch-finding movement among the Yoruba of Southwestern Nigeria. The case is interesting for several reasons. Historically, it captures a dialectical moment when local communities, regional economies, state structures, and global markets dramatically collided and dynamically realigned; a moment precipitated by a sudden increase in cocoa prices from 1945–50 (see fig. 1). Ethnographically, it represents an unusual event, when an antiwitchcraft cult from the (then) Southern Gold Coast spread east, and crossed the (then) Dahomean border into Western Yorubaland, where it persecuted thousands of women in many Egba and Egbado Yoruba towns (cf. Matory 1991:183–91). And historiographically, the

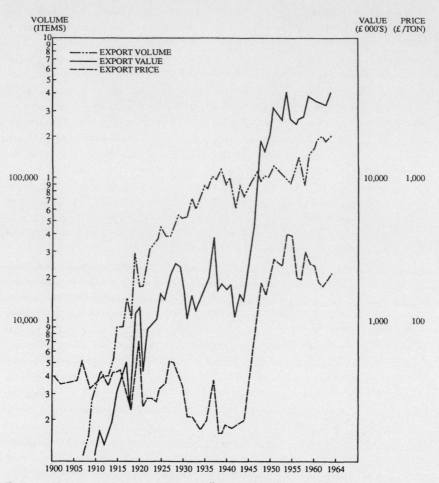

Figure 1. Nigerian cocoa exports. (From Helleiner 1966:80)

text that first documented this movement is a classic of functionalist anthropology, revealing both the acuity of a finely trained fieldworker and the methodological limitations this training imposed. The point of revising the original ethnographic interpretation is not to take potshots at functionalism—an exercise which is as unnecessary as it is uninteresting—but to extract the rational kernal from its ideological shell. Motivating this interpretive strategy is the recognition that a more critical anthropology should not reject its history but should build upon it by taking it into account.

My basic thesis is that the Atinga antiwitchcraft movement responded with alarming vitality to contradictions generated by the cocoa economy. This response is not proposed in terms of a simple cause and effect but as the complex mediation of competing interests and claims, articulated by the logic of Yoruba witchcraft. Moreover, the contradictions themselves were complex, since their levels of "articulation" were ultimately local, regional, national, and even global, given fluctuating cocoa prices on the world market. What I hope to illuminate is the view from "below"; how Atinga made sense at a local periphery, not merely as a critique of capital accumulation but as a strategy of political and economic empowerment by a rising commercial elite. The success or failure of this strategy remains an open question, since some of those who stood to gain from the movement may well have achieved their goals. If they did, however, it was at the expense of many people, especially the women who were involved.

An empirical question this study addresses is why witchcraft as such— and "borrowed" techniques of eradication—provided salient idioms of hidden power and collective action within Egba and Egbado villages and towns. The answer, ventured more as a hypothesis than a final solution, is that the cocoa economy intensified structural contradictions that were already articulated by the logic of witchcraft, creating a witchcraft epidemic of extraordinary proportions which demanded extraordinary redressive measures. As such, the epidemic created new opportunities for various groups and actors to compete for power and resources, or simply assert control over their lives. Clearly, the Atinga cult configured a multiplicity of motives which cannot be reduced to a simple socioeconomic formula. To see the Atinga movement as a "symptom" of social upheaval does not illuminate the forms of its violence or the logic of its practice. To understand why women were sought out in such unprecedented numbers, as imputed—and at times self-professed—agents of death and destruction, we must understand how they came to embody the contradictions of a larger world in the southwestern corner of Yorubaland. From this dialectical perspective, both internally derived and externally informed, we can see the Atinga movement for what it was—a complicitous assault on female power in its social, economic, and ritual domains.[2]

The Atinga Cult

Like many powers of the Yoruba cosmos, the Atinga cult came from the "outside," crossing ethnic, regional, and colonial state boundaries. Although its genesis as a witch-finding movement remains obscure, it swept eastward through the Southern Gold Coast in the mid-1940s, across Dahomey, and by 1950 into Nigeria, entering Southwest Yorubaland when cocoa prices boomed on the world market (Berry 1985:55). The cult was clearly of foreign provenence, renamed "Atinga" from "Tingere," and linguistically "appropriated" as in *Al + atinga*, or "owners of Atinga." The cult itself thus represents a foreign power which its members brought to different Egba and Egbado Yoruba towns, and even sold to enterprising Yoruba witchfinders. The leaders of the cult claimed that "they did not visit a settlement unless invited by its chiefs, who would send a 'small present' with the invitation" which could be as much as 200 pounds, a considerable sum at that time (Morton-Williams 1956:316). Upon arrival, cult members would prepare antiwitchcraft medicine in a large pot by combining kola nuts, animal blood, and water and uttering incantations. The pieces of kola were then extracted, dried, and sold as antiwitchcraft medicine to individual buyers, who were subsequently marked with a chalk disc on their foreheads to signify witchcraft immunity and association with the cult. It was claimed that Atinga would kill anybody who tried to practice witchcraft after eating the kola.

The cult then organized a public dance in which young men and women, augmented by local youths and adolescents, were possessed by the Atinga spirit and thus empowered to detect witches. One branch of the Atinga cult was known as the "Glass" because its "leading dancers would look at women indirectly, reflecting their faces in a small hand-mirror, before declaring whether or not they were witches" (Morton-Williams 1956:324). Accused witches who maintained their innocence were tested by cutting a chicken's throat and flinging it on the ground. If the chicken died on its back "facing heaven," the woman was innocent; if it died in any other position, she was a witch. Confirmed witches were required to confess; to pay a cleansing fee (thirty shillings); to surrender their witchcraft materials (including divining beads or objects from altars to their òrìṣà [deity]); to be washed in water from the sacrificial pot; and to eat the medicinal kola, so that Atinga would kill them if they attempted to practice witchcraft again.

In the Egbado town of Aiyetoro, a "new" town with a population of about 10,000 in 1950, 483 women were recorded by the king's scribe as confessed witches within the first week of Atinga's activity.[3] Many confessed to cannibalism, to killing agnates and children, to joining the witches' ẹgbẹ́ coven, and to killing enemies and rivals with evil thoughts. One woman told how she sacrificed a goat to cure her sick child on the advice of another woman. The other woman packed the goat's entrails into a calabash, which she placed at the base of an apá (African mahogany) tree. The mother was told not to eat any of the goat, but at night her "soul" left her body, went to the tree, and ate from the calabash. Her child then died, because the goat was its alibi, "and in the calabash were really the child's entrails" (Morton-Williams 1956:324). It was then that she knew that she was in the witch society. Notions that witches consume children and cause infertility take many forms. When the Atinga cult was proscribed by the administration, the Olóbì of Ilobi, an educated king, complained to the divisional council that the cult was useful, citing as evidence a woman who, after eating the medicinal kola, delivered a child who had been blocked by witchcraft in her womb for three years.

After its official prohibition by the colonial authorities, the Atinga cult turned to felling trees (particularly the *irokò* tree) inhabited by witches, and destroying *òrìṣà* cult shrines and altars, although the conventionally male antiwitchcraft cults of Gelede, Egungun, Ogun, and Oro were spared (Morton-Williams 1956:326). By March of 1951, the Alatinga had amassed considerable wealth and, dodging police harassment and prosecution, returned to Dassa in Dahomey. Local interest turned away from Atinga and toward the heavy farm labor the season demanded.

How can we account for this unusual antiwitchcraft movement in recent Yoruba history? For Morton-Williams, the "sociological meaning" of the Atinga cult derives from the relative decline of traditional religious institutions and the rise of a commercial elite. In brief, his argument runs like this:

1. Yoruba witchcraft is the cultural and psychological expression of contradictions generated by affinity. Witches are "wives and mothers," and hence both "strangers" and "members" of the husband's compound and patrilineage. What is more, they are never fully accepted until they bear children, preferably sons. Thus witchcraft, born of jealousies, emotional strains, and feelings of ambivalence, is practiced between co-wives and close kin, resulting in infertility, early death, and contested accusations.

2. With the decline of traditional rituals to placate witchcraft, the Atinga cult provided a convenient substitute, particularly since it could [and did] embrace Christians and Muslims as well as "pagans."

3. The final phase of Atinga—the attacks on *òrìṣà* cults— represented "an assertion by youth that their world was triumphant over that of a backward-looking age"; it also promised increasing independence from the "forces of nature" which the *òrìṣà* controlled. (Morton-Williams 1956:327).

Almost as an afterthought, Morton-Williams (1956:333) mentions that the sponsors of the Alatinga were "wealthy and influential men," many of whom "had achieved status through utilizing wealth obtained in commerce, and whose interest in the Alatinga was largely speculative." What is so clearly missing in his functional explanation, despite this tantalizing glimpse, is how new forms of production and exchange were transforming social and political relations at the time; and how Atinga was implicated in the process. The "general shift" thesis—that this antiwitchcraft cult represents a rite of passage from tradition to modernity—can be recast in more complex forms: as a series of encounters between local and global worlds, encounters that intensified the contradictions of everyday Yoruba life. Let us begin to analyze the encounter by looking, albeit schematically, at the material conditions of precolonial witchcraft beliefs and accusations.

Production and Reproduction in Precolonial Polities

In the so-called traditional Yoruba polity, according to canonical accounts, witchcraft beliefs and practices expressed "structural contradictions" between basic principles of social organization. In a more or less agnatic lineage system (Schwab 1955; Lloyd 1955, 1962, 1970; Bender 1970; Bascom 1969:42; Forde 1951:10–15; Fadipe 1970:97–146), virilocal polygyny generated jealousies and rivalries between co-wives—who often accused each other of witchcraft—as well as more general tensions between agnates and affines. Since a new wife was not fully incorporated into her husband's household until she bore her first child, preferably a son, childless wives accused co-wives, particularly senior wives, of using witchcraft against them. When wives did bear children, these tensions acquired a matrifilial dimension. Within a polygynous household, children of one mother (ọmọìyá) were taught never to eat food prepared by co-wives, for fear of being poisoned. If a successful child would attract the witchcraft of the household's jealous co-wives, the child's misfortune, sickness, or death confirmed it. Hence the proverb: Àjẹ́ ké lánàá, ọmọ kú lóòní (The witch cried yesterday, the child died today) (Bamgbose 1968:75). These suspicions and hostilities were further fueled by inheritance patterns, which devolved property of the deceased male head between different sets of ọmọìyá, precipitating competition between "half-siblings" for property (Lloyd 1962:279–307). Corporately held lineage rights—such as access to land and political titles—generally devolved through agnatic kin, but occasionally passed through women, introducing a "cognatic" element to the lineage system. Thus powerful women connected with political and economic resources could even precipitate lineage "optation" by drawing sons away from the father's patrilineage and into the mother's patrilineage.[4] Even in the absence of such lineage optation, tensions between different sets of full siblings (ọmọìyá) defined salient points of lineage segmentation and fission. United by paternity but divided by different matrilines, lineage segments would (as they still do) trace back to half-brothers (ọmọkùnrin bàbákan) who fought and separated at some time in the past.

This orthodox functionalist perspective accounts for several basic features of Yoruba witchcraft.[5] First, the high proportion of accusations between co-wives expressed relations of competition and vulnerability. The wife's dependence on her children for full incorporation into her husband's household underscored the significance of "infertility" as a sign of witchcraft victimization. And the cannibalistic aspects of witches' appetites— the eating of men, particularly husbands and their children—echoed the potential ability of mothers to "snatch" sons away from their patrilineages, draining them of their strength, or of precipitating fission to achieve a similar effect. The matrifilial impact of mothers on the male household and lineage was further expressed by ideas of transmission of witchcraft between women, largely between mothers and daughters, and appears in the Yoruba belief that all women, particularly mothers, are potential witches. *Ìyá wa* (our Mothers) is in fact the most common way of referring to witches. But the "principles" of polygyny, inheritance, lineage optation, segmentation, and fission do not exist as isolated structural postulates. They articulate with production, exchange, and the sexual division of labor.

In addition to their domestic roles as wives and mothers, Yoruba women have historically sold their husbands' produce and engaged in trade in local markets (Sudarkasa 1973). There they organized into trading associations (*ęgbę́*) in which they pooled resources, rotated credit (Bascom 1952), regulated market activities and their wider communal affairs. Represented by a formal female head, the *Ìyálòde*, who aggrandized considerable political clout, market women controlled the exchange of goods, set collective guidelines, fixed minimum prices, accumulated merchant capital of their own, and maximized personal profits. Nor were these relations of production and exchange restricted within kingdoms; they were extended between them through regional market networks. By attending "periodic" markets in other towns—some quite far away—market women mediated between them, taking their goods to other areas and bringing back wealth from beyond the local kingdom.[6] These economic roles and opportunities conflicted with the domestic obligations of cooking (including chopping firewood and grinding pepper and onions), cleaning house, feeding children, and humoring the husband and his agnates (Fadipe 1970:887–90)—indeed, they *subverted* the ideology of household labor and reproduction. Market activity took mothers out of their homes and away from their children, undermining the domestic values of fertility and procreation while empowering these women with public responsibilities. Furthermore, economic success in the market could threaten male authority in the household and lineage. A wealthy wife could precipitate the divisive conflicts of polygyny, inheritance, lineage fission, and optation by gaining strength, power, and considerable independence as a member of the market womens' *ęgbę́* association.

This economic dimension of female power in precolonial Yoruba society fits Nadel's model of Nupe witchcraft in both "base" and "superstructure."[7] According to Nadel (1970:174), "the witch is accused of doing mystically precisely what the women, in virtue of their economic power, are accused of doing in real life." As with the Yoruba, these female activities included indebting husbands to wives; accumulating more liquidity and capital than their menfolk, with which mothers "influenced" their children; and neglecting domestic and reproductive obligations to pursue profit further afield, where women figured as "prostitutes." For Nadel, it was the contradiction between domestic and economic roles, between domestic "purity" and the worldly "corruption" of female wealth, that challenged male authority and transformed mothers into witches.

The Yoruba situation appeared nearly identical. A basic contradiction between the roles of mother and merchant pitted female power against male authority in both private and public domains. Privately, the witch afflicted the household by striking husbands, co-wives, and children; that is, both the witch's children and those of her rivals. She did this by allegedly drinking the blood of her victims, consuming their vital essences, and in the case of female victims, by consuming their fetuses and blocking their reproductive fluids. From a "phallocentric" perspective, female economic power and its dangerous consequences were embodied in menstrual blood, both in its periodicity and its capacity to undermine male potency and power.[8] For example, it is still maintained that a man's most powerful *jùjú* medicines are immediately neutralized by contact with menstrual blood. In addition, witches could cause male impotence by "borrowing" a man's penis to have sex with his wife or another woman (Prince 1961:798), thereby consuming his sexual powers.

Publically, witchcraft sabotaged political relations between men, even to the extent of weakening kings. It is still averted by sacrifices at the "crossroads" (*orìta*) of chiefly jurisdictions, which converge upon the marketplace itself. For it is there, at the bases of baobab and *ìrokò* trees, that witches form "covens" that are modeled on womens' market associations and are designated by the same term (*ẹgbẹ́*). Note that, in addition to inheriting it from one's mother, witchcraft could be acquired by donating a child or other family member to a coven, which divided and consumed its body as an "entry" fee.[9] Women "tricked" by other witches to consume human flesh and blood could also become unwitting witches and thereby join a coven.

These diverse aspects of Yoruba witchcraft had one thing in common: they sabotaged the reproduction of bodies human and social. The Yoruba cannibal-witch profited at the expense of her family, lineage, and community by taking without returning. She profited in the marketplace by acquiring more than she spent, and by hoarding capital to block the flow of productive resources (Belasco 1980:27, 30, 102). As one proverb states, the wife "threatens the husband in the marketplace with a cutlass" (Drewal and Drewal 1983:54), this being an allusion to Shango's troublesome abduction of the goddess Oya, encoding the "castrating" potentialities of female wealth in a master symbol—the cutlass (*agada*)—of inheritance. Indeed, the accumulation of trading capital and the organization of female power "eats away" at male potency and political hegemony at all levels of corporate organization. In the precolonial polity, this included the house-hold, lineage, quarter, town, and kingdom at large. Today, the invisible organization of witchcraft associations recapitulates the administrative structure of the Nigerian state. According to Idowu (1970:10):

> Witches are well organized: they choose their local, regional and inter-regional heads. A head of a local guild may be the head of all women in the community (very often such is the one chosen, if she passes the test, in consequence of her exalted, commanding position). Often the head may be the chief priestess of a particular cult.

And mirroring the male-dominated Pan-Yoruba Ogboni Society, which binds its members in total secrecy, fights witchcraft, and formerly ordered human executions, witches administer their consuming powers through hidden chains and languages of command (Idowu 1970:13):

> Witches maintain a chain of contacts through their local, regional and inter-regional systems. They have a subtle means of contacts which consist in part of signs, symbols, telepathy and their own peculiar language . . . Thus, a person who is marked down in Ibadan for punishment or destruction may be dealt with through the local cult of Lagos or Ilorin. The Ibadan or Ilorin cult is only a tool and may be under an obligation not to reveal the source of the operations.[10]

But this expansive vision of covens in modern Nigeria is not merely the conceptual reflex of a growing economy and state bureaucracy. Grounded in material relations of production and exchange, the "immoral economy" of Yoruba witchcraft mediated the very contradictions such developments entailed.

Atinga and the Colonial Economy

The impact of Islam, Christianity, the colonial state, and the cash economy on precolonial productive activities and ideologies was complex and profound. Here I can only highlight the most basic transformations. Although Islam and Christianity have never displaced local òrìṣà worship (as their more dogmatic followers claim), but in fact were reconfigured within local cosmological horizons (Apter 1992:174–77), they did introduce "foreign" sources of spiritual and economic capital. Both religions of the book, first Islam powered by northern *jihad*, then Christianity motivated by coastal trade and further encouraged by British overrule, established regional and transethnic networks and associations which widened the Yoruba universe of discourse and commerce. By 1914, Lord Lugard's amalgamation of the Nigerian Protectorate transformed the content of political offices and roles by incorporating them within the colonial administration. Yoruba kings lost certain powers of prosecution (e.g., they could no longer authorize the death penalty) and decision making, but gained the Crown's protection against traditional mechanisms of disaffection and deposition. What subordinate chiefs gained in status as government civil servants, they lost in real power, being subject to administrative demands and directives—such as tax collection—from above. If the new government provided schools, roads, piped water, and health clinics, it also taxed male household heads, appropriated political power, and recruited a new generation of literate youth into local and regional administrative structures and positions.

This political transformation was largely funded by foreign markets and local wage labor. The introduction of cash cropping, mainly cocoa for export in the Western (i.e., Yoruba) Region, provided profits which farmers often invested in their children's education to prepare them for elite professions (Berry 1985). The many consequences of this dramatic shift in production on local economies, social structures, and political strategies have been explored in detail (Berry 1975, 1985). The most salient include (1) a general breakup and "nucleation" of the patrilocal compound (*agbo ilé*) with rising cocoa profits; (2) a proliferation of independent women traders as the prosperity of the agricultural sector rose; (3) an increase in polygynous households among farmers who traded in cocoa, with their wives as managers; (4) an increase in the provision of petty trading capital by mothers for daughters, contravening the "customary" pattern of husbands providing it for their wives; (5) the migration of farmers and their immediate kin away from natal towns to cocoa villages, where "family" labor combined with migrant (nonkin) wage labor; (6) a rise of profits in the distributive sector; (7) the development of cooperative marketing schemes among farmers to compete with the state-formed Marketing Board which exploited producers in the name of price protection; as well as (8) the formation of a new educated elite that sought greater participation in local affairs.

It is in this historical context that the Atinga witch-finding movement should be reanalyzed; not as a "symptom" of structural change but as a drama which sought to comprehend and control it. First, I would argue that the development of a cocoa economy *intensified* the existing etiology of witchcraft. Competition between co-wives and their children, inheritance disputes, lineage optation, segmentation and fission, and, most important, the tug of war between women's economic autonomy in the marketplace and subordination at home were fueled by prevailing trends—notably, the proliferation of independent petty traders, the nucleation of patrilocal compounds, increased migration, the rise of polygyny among cocoa farmers and traders, and a general increase of profits in the distributive sector. Indeed, trading capital, like the power of witchcraft itself, was now transmitted from mother to daughter. Under these conditions, the symptoms of mystical affliction might have been expected to reach "epidemic" proportions, justifying unprecedented and unorthodox placations and persecutions.

Second, it appears that the Atinga cult had strategic value for the rising commercial elite. By financing the Atinga cult from profits in trade, these "new men" could (a) bypass the traditional authority of elders to force an alliance with "traditional" chiefs, who became indebted to them for antiwitchcraft protection; and (b) persecute women traders, either directly as witches, or indirectly through general intimidation, into whose traditional sphere of commercial activity the "new men" were intruding. In this respect, the fate of the traditional cults represents a direct assault on female power. The decline and rejection of Yoruba religion asserted (if overstated) by Morton-Williams (1956) does not explain why the predominantly female òrìṣà cults were attacked while the male Oro styled antiwitchcraft cults were left alone.[11] Clearly, a gendered opposition was taking shape, asserting the ascendancy of male over female power in ritual, social, and economic spheres.

Finally, in order to explain, as Morton-Williams cannot, why a "foreign" antiwitchcraft cult enjoyed higher prestige than its local counterparts, we must consider the Atinga cult in relation to the rise of the commodity economy. Both were of foreign provenance, the former establishing a medium in which the contradictions wrought by the latter might be addressed.

This final point highlights the emergent relationship between witchcraft and the state. For if the colonial administration encouraged cocoa production, it also sought to regulate it. In the early days, cocoa became the object of struggle between farmers, traders, and British companies, each seeking to maximize their share of the earnings. In 1939, the government established Marketing Boards (reorganized in 1947) with a monopsony on the purchase of cocoa for export, and increased control over the domestic terms of trade. The state thus became a powerful broker between Yoruba producers and regional distributors, intervening in the prices commanded by export markets. Poised between local and global arenas, the Marketing Boards set up a chain of buyers and sellers which, if cost-effective for the state, siphoned profits away from the farmers and appropriated the surplus value of their labor. Before fetching its world market price, cocoa passed through many intermediaries—from "pan buyers" who purchased it directly and resold it to "scalers," who then retailed it to Licensed Buying Agents (LBAs), who in turn resold to the Marketing Board at a fixed commission (Berry 1985:90).

In theory, the Board guaranteed farmers a fixed return on their cocoa, promising to "cushion" the impact of world price fluctuations. In practice, it acquired enormous reserves: during the boom years of 1947–54 these totaled over 46 million pounds sterling (Helleiner 1966:161), which were invested in British securities and used to finance general development projects. Helleiner (1966:162) estimates that this amount was 39% of "potential producer income"; that is, income that *could* have been distributed to farmers. But if the state extracted profits from afar, local purchasers incurred additional costs in more visible and concrete forms. Just as the government eventually bought the cocoa, it also extended credit, again through its chain of contracted (and contracting) agents: LBAs and their subsidiaries paid advances to farmers in return for cocoa purchased below the guaranteed board price. To complicate matters, many of the unlicensed middlemen and women at the lower end of the distributive chain were members of cocoa farmers' households (Berry 1985:87)—brothers, sons, affines, and collateral kin. Under these conditions, as kinsmen and affines turned debtors and creditors on an unprecedented scale, it is hardly surprising that the "traditionally" gendered tensions attendant upon agricultural production and exchange would be invested with new conflicts of economic interest.

The period of Atinga in Southwest Yorubaland coincided with an indisputable period of cocoa production and economic growth. But this growth exacted its costs and generated its own local paradoxes. For cocoa farmers, increased values meant greater appropriation of their profits as their wealth was sucked away by the state and its intermediaries. If cocoa production stimulated greater commerce and trade, it pitted men against women, literate youth against elders, in a market held hostage to world price fluctuations and an evermore powerful political center. The "witchcraft" of the cocoa economy meant different things to different people. For farmers, it meant the extraction of surplus value ("potential producer income") by the invisible appetites of an encroaching state, and the inflation of exchange values by unlicensed and licensed buying agents. Within lineages, it meant increased competition for wealth and merchant capital, intensifying segmentation, fission, and nucleation of households, while bolstering the power and autonomy of market women. If the logic of witchcraft illuminated these developments, it also prescribed remedial measures. The Atinga movement objectified the contradictions of cocoa production in the nefarious forces of female power, and offered new techniques of eradication that would be equal to the task. In so doing, it provided opportunities for a rising literate and commercial elite to bypass their elders and secure access to merchant capital and state resources. More generally, it enabled local communities of an emerging periphery to assert control over the forces that were transforming daily life.

A complex dramaturgy of resistance and opportunism, of competing agendas and emerging interests, Atinga attacked the female body as icon

Plate 1. Women identified as witches during an Atinga dance. (From Morton-William 1956:318)

and agent of commodity value; of false representation, of unbridled circulation, and of hidden accumulation. As soul eater, the witch profited at the expense of her kin and affines, consuming their productive and reproductive powers while appearing to cater to their needs. In her coven, she occupied two "places" at once; the private sphere of her domicile and the public arena of the marketplace itself, where as a disembodied witch bird she aggregated with her soul-eating sisters to conduct nocturnal business. As Atinga attacked the sites and signs of women's corporate power—their *òrìṣà* cults, ritual paraphernalia, their market and mystical *ẹgbẹ́* associations—it *immobilized* their bodies in public tribunals, where they sat "fastened" to the ground beneath the burning sun (plate 1) until they received the oracle's verdict (see Matory 1991:189–91). Women thus accused were not killed but cleansed, spending heavily to divest their bodies of accumulated witchcraft and to invest in the economy of collective purification. Whether we see its efforts as maliciously misguided or symbolically displaced, the Atinga movement's popularity need not be taken as a measure of its success in solving the problems of the growing cocoa economy but of the growing recognition that something had to be done.

INASMUCH AS THE ATINGA MOVEMENT represents a particular interpenetration of Yoruba, Nigerian, and global worlds, a turning inward against hidden enemies to confront the dislocations of socioeconomic change, it entered more generally into popular discourse. Omoyajowo (1965:23–24) recalls a song praising Atinga which he heard on a Yoruba gramophone record:

Ajeji mefa kan wo'lu Eko,
Mo bere oruko won, won l'Atinga ni.
Iru ise wo l'e nse, won l' aje l' awon nmu.
Iya b'o l'o l' eiye, ofo l'omi efo nse,
Wa ba sigidi n'ile, wa ba Baba wa l'oke.
E ba wa ko won lo o.
Agbere aje poju, Atinga ko aje lo.

Six strange people entered Lagos town,
Asking their identity, I was told they were Atinga.
I asked of their mission, they said they were witch hunters
You madam, dare you deny possessing a bird-familiar?
You will be got rid of like dirty water.
You will encounter spirits on earth and face our Father above.
Wipe witches away.
Their wickedness is immeasurable, Atinga, wipe witches away.

It is a song which Omoyajowo "loved to sing in those days," for it celebrated the spirit of a crusade against evil, a march toward progress and purification which captured the popular imagination. "Great was the disappointment of many Yoruba people," he writes, "when the group was banned by the government in 1951, for they had expected them to help wipe out once for all the institution of witchcraft" (1965:23).

Atinga might have been suppressed by government intervention, as its supporters complained, yet witchcraft remains alive and well in Nigeria today. To be sure, it is still largely a family affair, with kinsmen and affines afflicted and accused. But family life has been strained and further reshaped by the growing power of the Nigerian state. The witchcraft generated by the cocoa economy was a mere whisper compared to the calamitous consequences of the 1970s oil boom, which built a new Nigeria on rhetorical foundations. The sudden government infusion of new wealth, the rise of contractors, luxury hotels, hospitals, and schools swelled the salaried class of professionals empowered by their access to state structures and resources. As intensified class divisions crosscut lineage and family sodalities, the witch's work became more devastating than ever.[12]

Today witchcraft thrives among the Yoruba elites as well as the masses, a relational calculus of resentment, fear, and envy measuring the costs of "alienated production" in the consumption of human powers and souls.[13] Witchcraft persists as a practical discourse of hidden agency because economic "development" in the larger sense has failed. Rising fortunes, costs, and expectations have run up against bitter economic realities. Seen historically and dialectically, from the periphery and the center, witchcraft and "development" have converged. As Taussig (1987) might say, Yoruba witchcraft in Nigeria has become the *terror* of development—the subversion of order (from "above," the "outside") apprehended and refashioned by implicit social knowledge (from "below," the "inside"). If Atinga signaled the beginning of this totalizing experience, there are no indications that it is coming to an end.

Notes

1. These ideological limitations were transcended by the 1950s in studies of urbanization, monetization, and sociopolitical change inspired largely by Max Gluckman and associated with his "Manchester school." See also Smith (1960) for a diachronic framework of political change which incorporated British overrule into its analysis of Hausa government.

2. The methodological lead for this approach is established in J. L. Comaroff (1982) and elaborated in J. Comaroff (1985).

3. We know from Forde (1951:45) that Aiyetoro became wealthy by marketing and exporting cocoa to Abeokuta.

4. The concept of "optation" comes from Barnes (1962:7) who, invoking Firth, uses the term to designate descent systems that permit (in his case a male) ego to "opt" into his mother's patrilineage. Among the Yoruba, a man can opt into his mother's patrilineage to inherit chieftaincy titles and other property which is vested in her descent group, although by doing so he forfeits full membership in his father's patrilineage. The multiple affiliations optation permits has caused considerable debate over the precise principles of Yoruba descent. See Lloyd (1955, 1962, 1970), Bender (1970), and Eades (1980:49–55).

5. It is of course reminiscent of many classical Africanist accounts of witchcraft; e.g., Wilson (1951), Marwick (1965), Middleton and Winter (1963), Mair (1973).

6. In 1976 I encountered three Yoruba market women trading in the Rome market, in Italy, selling "African" goods and buying cloth and foreign "imports" for resale at home. This particular case may be exceptional, but it represents the expansive scope of Yoruba trading networks.

7. The Nupe are located just northeast of Yorubaland and raided Yoruba towns for slaves throughout the nineteenth century. They are called Tapa in Yoruba colloquial discourse.

8. It is possible that the "periodicity" of menstruation—at once a general condition of female fertility and a specific sign of nonconception during its flow—is associated with the periodicity of market women's "monthly" meetings (as well as with the meetings of òrìṣà cult priestesses, which in Ayede-Ekiti were calibrated in alternating two-week periods). This association might connect the power of menstrual blood to the collective power of market women and priestesses. Postmenopausal witches, whose bodies consume without reproducing, would seem to

represent the "other side" of female potency (see Apter 1991). For comparable observations, see Gottlieb and Buckley (1988).

9. The division of sacrificial meat between members of a corporate group— e.g., a lineage, an association of diviners (*babaláwo*), an age-set organization, or a hunters' guild—is a standard ritual of corporate solidarity. Similarly, the fission of such a group is often attributed to "fighting" over the meat. The division and consumption of a human victim by a witch's coven evokes the antisocial character of organized female power in opposition to the jural authority of Yoruba men.

10. These descriptions of Yoruba witchcraft organizations are provided as statements of fact, not belief, by a Yoruba Methodist minister and university professor well known for his work on Yoruba religion (Idowu:1962). As such, they support the conclusion of this paper.

11. It must be emphasized that witchcraft is not a purely negative power but can be channeled toward more positive ends, such as empowering the king and community against rivals, enemies, and imminent disasters (including the deadly appetites of witches themselves). The birds perched atop Oshun and Osanyin staffs, as well as on royal beaded crowns, represent the protective powers of witchcraft. Similarly, *òrìṣà* cult priestesses are feared and respected as witches since they can see into the future and preempt malefactors. Since witchcraft is immanent in women, it can never be fully eradicated. One of the ostensible goals of *òrìṣà* cult ritual is to placate witches' appetites and channel their destructive powers into communal gain (Drewal and Drewal 1983). In the Atinga movement, the identification of witchcraft with *òrìṣà* vessels was cosmologically coherent but revalued these "positive" dimensions of witchcraft in negative terms.

12. See Barber (1982) for a rich exegesis of popular Yoruba reactions to petronaira, including themes of nefarious money making which permute the general logic of witchcraft—i.e., gaining illegitimate wealth from the bodies and blood of others—into the figure of "the child-stealer who uses his victims to conjure up boundless riches" (438).

13. I use the term "alienated production" to emphasize the peculiar character of the Nigerian political economy, based less on the exploitation of wage labor and more on the exploitation of state power, wealth, and resources. As Berry (1985:13–14) emphasizes, the Nigerian ruling class is in reality a "state class" which has internalized the dynamics of class formation at its own expense. In a sense the state has become the ultimate witch, appearing to grow rich at the expense of its "children."

References

Apter, A. 1991. The Embodiment of Paradox: Yoruba Kingship and Female Power. *Cultural Anthropology* 6, no. 2:212–29.

———. 1992. *Black Critics and Kings: The Hermeneutics of Power in Yoruba Society.* Chicago: University of Chicago Press.

Bamgbose, A. 1968. The Form of Yoruba Proverbs. *Odu* 4, no. 2:74–86.

Barber, Karin. 1982. Popular Reactions to the Petro-naira. *Journal of Modern African Studies* 20, no. 3:431–50.

Barnes, J. A. 1962. African Models in the New Guinea Highlands. *Man* 62:5–9.

Bascom, William. 1969. *The Yoruba of Southwestern Nigeria*. Holt, Rhinehart & Winston.

———. 1952. The *esusu:* A Credit Institution of the Yoruba. *Journal of the Royal Anthropological Institute* 82, no. 1:63–9.

Belasco, B. 1980. *The Entrepreneur as Culture Hero: Preadaptations in Nigerian Economic Development*. New York: Praeger.

Bender, Donald. 1970. Agnatic or Cognatic? A Re-evaluation of Ondo Descent. *Man,* n.s. 5, no. 1:71–87.

Berry, Sara S. 1985. *Fathers Work for Their Sons: Accumulation, Mobility and Class Formation in an Extended Yoruba Community*. Berkeley: University of California Press.

———. 1975. *Cocoa, Custom and Socio-Economic Change in Rural Western Nigeria*. Oxford: Clarendon Press.

Comaroff, J. 1985. *Body of Power, Spirit of Resistance: The Culture and History of a South African People*. Chicago: University of Chicago Press.

Comaroff, J. L. 1982. Dialectical Systems, History and Anthropology: Units of Study and Questions of Theory. *Journal of Southern African Studies.* 8, no. 2:143–72.

Drewal, H., and Drewal, M. 1983. *Gẹlẹdẹ: Art and Female Power among the Yoruba*. Bloomington: Indiana University Press.

Eades, J. S. 1980. *The Yoruba Today*. Cambridge: Cambridge University Press.

Fadipe, N. A. 1970. *The Sociology of the Yoruba*. Ibadan: University of Ibadan Press.

Forde, D. 1951. *The Yoruba-Speaking Peoples of South-Western Nigeria*. London: International African Institute.

Gottlieb and Buckley, eds. 1988. *Blood Magic: The Anthropology of Menstruation*. Berkeley: University of California Press.

Helleiner, G. 1966. *Peasant Agriculture, Government, and Economic Growth in Nigeria*. Homewood, Ill.: Richard D. Irwin.

Idowu, B. 1962. *Olodumare: God in Yoruba Belief*. London: Longmans, Green and Co.

———. 1970. The Challenge of Witchcraft. *Orita* 4, no. 1:3–16.

Lloyd, P. C. 1970. Ondo descent. *Man,* 5, no. 2:310–12.

———. 1962. *Yoruba Land Law*. London: Oxford University Press.

———. 1955. The Yoruba Lineage. *Africa* 25, no. 3:235–51.

Mair, L. 1973. *Witchcraft*. London: World University Library.

Marwick, M. G., ed. 1965. *Sorcery in Its Social Setting*. Manchester: University of Manchester Press.

Matory, James L. 1991. Sex and the Empire That Is No More: A Ritual History of

Women's Power among the Oyo-Yoruba. 2 vols. Ph.D. diss., University of Chicago.

Middleton, J., and Winter, E., eds. 1963. *Witchcraft and Sorcery in East Africa.* London: Routledge & Kegan Paul.

Morton-Williams, Peter. 1956. The Atinga Cult among the South-Western Yoruba: A Sociological Analysis of a Witch-Finding Movement. *Bulletin de l'IFAN* 18, nos. 3–4:315–34.

Mudimbe, V. Y. 1988. *The Invention of Africa: Gnosis, Philosophy and the Order of Knowledge.* Bloomington: Indiana University Press.

Nadel, S. 1970 [1954]. *Nupe Religion: Traditional Beliefs and the Influence of Islam in a West African Chiefdom.* New York: Schocken Books.

Omoyajowo, A. 1965. *Witches? A Study of the Belief in Witchcraft and Its Future in Modern African Society.* Ibadan: Daystar Press.

Prince, R. 1961. The Yoruba Image of the Witch. *Journal of Mental Science* 107:795–805.

Schwab, W. 1955. Kinship and Lineage among the Yoruba. *Africa* 25, no. 4:352–74.

Smith, M. G. 1960. *Government in Zazzau, 1800–1950.* London: Oxford University Press, for the International African Institute.

Sudarkasa, N. 1973. *Where Women Work: A Study of Yoruba Women in the Marketplace and in the Home.* Ann Arbor: University of Michigan.

Taussig, Michael. 1987. *Shamanism, Colonialism and the Wild Man: A Study in Terror and Healing.* Chicago: University of Chicago Press.

Wilson, Monica. 1951. Witchbeliefs and Social Structure. *American Journal of Sociology* 56:307–13.

6

"Bloodhounds Who Have No Friends": Witchcraft and Locality in the Nigerian Popular Press[1]

Misty L. Bastian

Witches are predators, bloodhounds who have no friends. As predators, greed is their hallmark; an abiding zest for destroying the successful, the healthy, and the "lucky" in the community.

The witch is propelled by an uncanny obsession with self; every other person is an object to be victimized. Familiarity with the witch is essentially superficial, and once entranced by the inner urge to hurt, the frontiers of its operation can only be circumscribed by the satisfaction of its thirst.

Darkness, that aweful [sic] period of intense gloom is the witch's finest hour. Stealthily and unobtrusively, it makes its way into its victim's abode and strikes decidedly at its target. If caught in the act, the witch instantly feigns remorse, only to revert to the same old habit once it is let off the hooks. Which doesn't surprise anybody either. Or don't they say that "old habits die hard"?

Grafted unto Nigeria's political scene, the "eaglet" politicians on who much hope has been placed for the establishment of a new political culture and political order, have also demonstrated a striking resemblance with witches.

The modest hope that the political greenhorns, who were perceived to have been uncontaminated by the filthy habits of their banned predecessors, would abide by the canons of civilized conduct and fair competition is again collapsing like a bad dream. And like witches, most of the "political upstarts" imbibed the political chicanery and gerrymandering of the old foxes.

However the greater danger is not that they represent a chip of the old block but that they might in fact out-wit them in new stratagems of political brigandage. Take for instance how, suddenly, the word residence *has been invested with a new definition which has turned it into the undoing of many candidates.*

Until recently, the typical Nigerian, unless he is a civil servant, resides in at least two places at the same time. In other words, a businessman from say Afikpo could have another home in Calabar and shuttle between the two points evenly during the week.

Such a person, if he is a community leader at home, would attend village meetings in both places, despense [sic] largesse and patronage to endless hordes of favour-seekers at home, and even serve as the community's spokesman in matters that require well-connected individuals and financial muzzle [sic]. In a word, they are the "best" in the community.

Encouraged by such enhanced status and role recognition, many of them, leaders of thought and beacons of hope in their respective communities, all rolled out their political machines. Time had come, so they thought, not to put their popularity to test but to legitimize their traditional roles and formalise the informal positions they had occupied.

But they were naive, and did not reckon with the vagaries of man's unpredictable nature. They did not reckon with the witch's malice, and the danger of betrayal. And before they knew it the erstwhile beneficiaries of their goodwill had put together "cast-iron" evidence portraying them as foreigners whose abode can only be located elsewhere. The witch's malice, which knows neither friend nor bounds has put faggots in the political sauce of some candidates.

But the moral of the situation contains a sickening revelation: our stubborn resistance to change. Down here we have learnt nothing and forgotten nothing. The Igbo man, whether in Nigeria or abroad, is permanently resident at home and we must resolve to stop the dis-ingenuous habit of using, and throwing our best away.

Since the end of the civil war, most Igbo men whose sources of livelihood rest outside their villages maintain two homes, one at the source and another in the village. Between these two, the line of distinction as to which constitutes his residence is a tenuous one and the mischief makers who have suddenly started labelling their brothers "nonresident indigenes" are nothing but traitors. A word is enough for the wise.

—Emma Agu, "Politics and the Witch's Malice," in the "Forum" column of the *Sunday Statesman* (December 13, 1987).

The Popular Press in Nigeria

DURING MY FIELD STUDIES ON ONITSHA MARKETS in 1987–88, I became fascinated with the lively Nigerian popular press.[2] All of my literate informants read *Lagos Weekend* and *Lagos Life*, two of the most popular tabloids, passing their copies on to others until the papers were rendered back into pulp. Nonliterate informants wanted to hear the latest stories from the papers, and it was not uncommon to see a literate trader in Onitsha's Main Market surrounded on Fridays by nonliterate, non-English-speaking colleagues, for whom he would translate (with embel-

lishments) the most exciting tabloid tales into Igbo. Stories that appeared
in the tabloids one week might very well make their way back to me as
choice Onitsha gossip the next—with names and situations altered to suit
the local taste. It soon became obvious that these stories were striking
deep chords with the Igbo people I knew, that they felt a resonance to
their own situations in the themes expressed by the tabloid writers, especially in those stories about witchcraft and other supernatural encounters.
I began to collect and sort through these stories, keeping copies of those
that caused the greatest comment. This chapter comprises an attempt to
discuss a single editorial concerning witchcraft thus collected in light of a
number of pervasive themes, notably those of identity, economic stratification, and an emerging consciousness of the liminal character of urban
Nigerian life.

Before turning to these themes, however, a few things ought to be
said about the nature of the popular press itself. For present purposes, I
am defining the popular press in Nigeria as those newspapers and magazines that target the widest audience literate in English. This excludes
newspapers like *Ndoka,* an Igbo-language publication with a relatively
small circulation,[3] the major news magazines *National Concord* and the
African Guardian, or the "elite" newspaper the *Guardian.* These publications are either in languages unintelligible to the majority of the Nigerian population or use an elevated style of English that most readers find
almost as difficult. Within the popular press there are weekly or monthly
magazines like *Prime People,* which self-consciously attempt to emulate
the "lifestyle" forums of the West, emphasizing human interest stories,
photography, health, fashion, society news, and advice column features.
There are also daily newspapers, both local and national, that divide their
column space between "hard" news and the same type of features found
in *Prime People.* Last, there are two weekly tabloids, *Lagos Weekend* and
Lagos Life, that print scandals (mostly taken from divorce court proceedings in Lagos and around the country), humorous pieces in Pidgin and
standard English, soft-core pornographic stories, and supernatural stories,
along with the types of features mentioned above. The Western counterpart of these tabloids can be found in supermarket checkout lanes and are
generally called something like the *Sun* or the *Star.* The Nigerian versions
are more explicit than most mass-market Western tabloids would dare to
be, however, and their popularity may be measured accordingly.

It is not easy to find out circulation figures for Nigerian newspapers,
but I did get some sense of the tabloids' market share by measuring the
number of times Onitsha news vendors reported themselves to be out of
stock. Trying to buy a copy of *Lagos Weekend,* the more popular and most
explicit of the tabloids, in Onitsha generally required me to be at my regular vendor's stand prior to 9 A.M. on Fridays; after this time, I would have

to hope the vendor put aside a couple of copies for his regular customers, because his ordinary stock would be depleted. There was rarely any difficulty in finding a selection of other newspapers and magazines at any time of the day. Because of the rise in newspaper prices from thirty *kobo* to fifty *kobo*[4] just prior to my arrival in Nigeria, few people I knew bought more than one or two newspapers a day and one news magazine (prices ranging from 2 to 2.50 *naira* per issue) or tabloid (fifty *kobo*) a week. As I quickly learned, those people affluent enough to buy newspapers and magazines were expected to share their stock with all literate comers. All periodicals, and any other reading material for that matter, seemed to have great pass-around value, but the tabloids and magazines were chosen first and passed the greatest distance from their original buyers.[5]

One reason for this extreme popularity was the steady diet of reports about witchcraft and other supernatural activities that was a mainstay of Nigerian tabloid writing. Except for articles about flagrant sexual misconduct, the first reports read were invariably those dealing with witches, *ogbaanje*, ghosts or "medicine." *Ogbaanje*, a term with no English equivalent, are Igbo spiritual forces who choose to incarnate as sickly, willful children ("children who will not stay"), mainly to cause mischief against their human parents. *Ogbaanje* are of central concern throughout the Igbo-speaking areas because there appear to be few families who can claim to be exempt from their malevolent influence. The Yorùbá version of this type of spirit, the *emere*, was also discussed in the tabloids, but *ogbaanje* was more often used, almost as a generic term, to describe the phenomenon. "Medicine" or *jùjú* was another tabloid topic popular with my informants. Local charms or shrines were read about with great affection but very little reverence. The greatest interest was evinced in *jùjú* from outside the Southeast, particularly if the charm was said to originate in Bendel State, across the Niger.[6] Very little skepticism was expressed about the existence of any of these supernatural agents, once people were assured that I was not there to judge them superstitious or to scoff. Rather, serious discussions about the state of Nigeria, and, more particularly, about Onitsha itself, would sometimes be elicited by tabloid articles concerning familiar supernatural activities. Emma Agu's editorial, entitled "Politics and the Witch's Malice," was one of the articles that seemed to speak most richly to my Igbo informants.

"Bloodhounds Who Have No Friends": Whose Village Is It?

Agu's column includes a number of themes found throughout the articles about witchcraft published in the Nigerian popular press. This column itself, however, was not from the tabloid press. It was found in a "serious" local newspaper, *The Statesman*. There seems to me to be a great deal of significance in the introduction of the topic of witchcraft into the editorial page of a Nigerian Sunday paper. In this particular case, the author is using the idea of witchcraft, not for satire or to show his sophistication in the face of "superstition" but to make a point about local politics.[7] Agu knows that witchcraft is seen as a major source of evil in Nigerian society. He also knows that his potential readership is in agreement with him as to the objective reality of this evil.[8] At times, Nigerian (and specifically Igbo) witchcraft takes the form of stereotypical afflictions, like a wasting sickness or a loss of ability to "progress," but at others it may manifest itself as a criminal lack of fairness in Local Government elections. In the former case, witchcraft afflicts the human body. In the latter, it is "the body politic" which is at risk. What remains constant is the intent of the putative witch or witches, the "uncanny obsession with self," and the witchly belief that "every other person is an object to be victimized."

The argument I would like to make in this chapter is that the idiom of witchcraft retains its value and continues to give meaning to certain West African life experiences, rather than withering away in the face of contemporary problems in favor of, say, the idiom of class. Witchcraft is not seen in Nigeria as the sole province of the "traditional" (or of "the" village). Witchcraft happens in urban contexts; it may even gain new meanings and power from the urban situation. Witchcraft themes dominate popular cultural discourse of all sorts, marking their importance in the everyday urban as well as rural experience. Agu's text shows very clearly how witchcraft becomes a medium for describing the complexities of Nigerian urban and rural relations for Nigerians themselves.

There have always been people who did not wholeheartedly take part in Igbo sociality, murderers and criminals among them. One class of such people, although not dangerous to the social order or to others, at least not physically dangerous, are characterized as being too close to the world of spiritual forces.[9] Witches are not of the same order as these "living ancestors" or "human spirits," but neither are they involved in human, criminal behavior. If anything, Igbo-speaking peoples see the *amoosu* (witch) as more like an animal than a human being. Agu makes this point when he calls witches "predators." The "human spirit" cannot be properly social on a human scale because he/she has commerce with dangerous spiritual forces on a regular basis, and those spirits do not recognize the same values or norms found in human society.[10] The spirits and their nominally human allies are amoral in human terms.

The *amoosu* is immoral, in a profound way, because she was once human and has now taken the path of animality.[11] She no longer regards the bonds of sociality, of community, and she is especially contemptuous of family and lineage. She becomes a psychic cannibal, worse than a murderer, because she treats other human beings as though they were meat and her prey. Among Igbo groups, murder is generally thought of as a public act, motivated by normal human emotions (notably dislike or envy) gone out of control. The fear of poison, for example, is prevalent in Onitsha. Whenever the motive for an alleged poisoning is talked about, the deed is said to have begun through the envy of the poisoner. If murder is proved, the murderer and his/her entire lineage will be punished.[12] Murderers are caught because they lack control. They make their grievances, and often their murders, known to the public. If anything, witches are overly controlled. They keep their wrongs inside until those wrongs and wrongful deeds reshape their very persons. Wickedness (*njo*, which also means ugliness or wrongful action) becomes a necessary condition for the witch's continued life.

In previous discussions of Igbo witchcraft, the witch is said to prey upon her closest relations, especially her immediate family or the families of her siblings, most often the families of her brothers.[13] Metuh (1981 : 102) quotes a relevant proverb: *Amusu adaghi ebu n'iro*, literally, "a witch does not sting in the open spaces." A witch does not attack people from outside—that is, beyond her village, her lineage, or her immediate family. Witchcraft is an intimate act. Nonetheless, Metuh suggests that an impersonal quality is creeping into Nigerian witchcraft. This quality seems to come from a widening recognition of social relations among the many communities of Nigeria—in effect, the recognition that "community" is now a larger and even more complicated entity, encompassing social barriers like language and historical antagonisms. Among other things, this new community is built up through the dissemination of knowledge(s) in the popular Nigerian media. "News" is mixed with regional opinions in an attempt to create what we might call a Nigerian common knowledge, or common-sense approach, to the predicaments Nigerian people find themselves in. In Agu's editorial, we can see this process in action.

Agu draws a parallel between Igbo "common knowledge" about how witches act and what they are, and how some towns acted toward their nonresident populations during the Local Government elections of late 1987. There have long been problems in Nigeria's growing urban areas between the indigenous populations of the cities and their immigrant neighbors. Although these problems are not the specific focus of Agu's editorial, it will be helpful for us to understand how they manifest themselves. The indigene/immigrant model of Igbo social relations is similar in some ways to the emerging resident/nonresident indigene pattern. Onitsha's own indigene/nonindigene situation is an excellent example of what difficulties arise when "sons of the soil" find themselves forced to live with "outsiders."

In Onitsha, *ndi onicha* (indigenes) express severe reservations about traders in the market system. These traders are usually referred to, slightingly, as *ndigbo* by Onitsha people. (As Leith-Ross noted as early as 1936, "Igbo" people always seem to be others, those living in a town or village other than that of the informant.) The so-called *ndigbo* work in a majority of the stalls in the two major marketplaces. According to Onitsha indigenes, non-Onitsha traders have come to the city to take its wealth without having to return anything in compensation. It is true that most of the non-Onitsha traders' earnings either go into the expansion of their trade or back into their town of origin in the form of house building, title taking, sponsorship of students, etc. But it is also true that Onitsha Local Government collects tax revenues from these traders (although they may pay other, larger taxes in their town of record), and some of that revenue goes into public works, like road construction or the upkeep of Onitsha's markets. Onitsha indigene landlords very often reap rich rewards in rent from the resident nonindigenous population; they are also usually the owners of hotels, bars, and gambling places where *ndigbo* spend much of their recreational money.

Non-Onitsha residents of the city have only recently attempted to express their perceived "rights" in Onitsha through Local Government agencies, and, by and large, their attempts have failed.[14] This indigene/nonindigene story, however, might be taken for granted by Agu as a case of natural community self-interest. Rumors of sorcery undertaken by indigenes to rid themselves of nonindigenes abound. This type of sorcery is almost to be expected, since the latter is perceived to be encroaching upon the former's autochthonous rights. Agu is mapping out a new brand of antagonism in the contemporary situation: that between people sharing spiritual territory (or locale) and disputing spiritual rights.

Uchendu (1965), the Ottenbergs (1962), and other ethnographers of the late twentieth-century Igbo scene have remarked upon the propensity of Igbo people to maintain close ties to their natal villages and towns. The literature on town associations and "improvement unions" in West Africa classically cites the Igbo as an example to make its case.[15] This literature generally does not address the issues brought up by Agu's column on witchcraft, however, because the Igbo were still recent emigrants when these associations were first studied. Although tensions were present between the urban-based and rural indigenes, even in the early 1960s, ties continued to be strong and relations continued to be immediate between the two groups. Perhaps more important, there was not yet a sense of the permanency of the urban-dwellers' residence in the city, nor of how natal village life (and, along with this, its values) might become secondary in the eyes of nonresident indigenes and their children.

As Agu's editorial suggests, the two groups have developed differing perspectives on the issue of residency over the past two or three decades. Nonresident indigenes continue to consider themselves full members of their patrilineages or patriclans, retaining the same rights in town affairs as their resident "brothers."[16] Meanwhile, resident townsmen have begun to see the nonresident indigenes as collateral members of the community—still related, but no longer directly involved in the daily town business that grants real rights in community decision making.[17] This distinction between what the nonresidents and residents believe about their relative statuses is absolutely crucial for comprehending the rationale behind Agu's witchcraft accusation.

Agu, writing for an urban-based audience, literate in English and presumably tied into the Western workweek, uses the notion of witchcraft to express the feelings and fears of the nonresident indigene.[18] In the densely populated Igbo areas of Southeastern Nigeria, economic or scholastic opportunities often are perceived as existing more in the urban areas, particularly in commercially oriented cities like Aba or Onitsha. This perception has been borne out in many instances, although the majority of urban nonindigenes live a difficult, even a marginal, existence in town. They are forced to take the meanest jobs offered, for very little pay, and have to spend most of that for relatively expensive lodgings and food. Access to cash, however small the amount may seem to the town dweller, breeds its own expectations among lineage mates.

Even unsuccessful urban residents are thought "wicked" if they do not send money back to village relations or invite those relations to stay in the city. A moderately successful urban resident is expected to build a house for himself in his hometown, to take titles and give elaborate ceremonies for his townspeople, to sponsor "brothers" by sending them to school or by giving them start-up capital for business. He must also support local improvement projects with monetary contributions, labor, and materials from the urban area. The corresponding expectation of these nonresident indigenes is an eventual retirement to their home, hopefully to enjoy the fruits of their labor in the peace of their natal compounds or, more likely, a recently constructed concrete "bungalow." This retirement is generally expected to be crowned with the great respect of their rural "brothers" and the pleasurable prospect of power in local affairs.

In reality, urban dwellers often find it difficult to leave the city—even when the time has supposedly come for their retirement. Nonindigene residents in Onitsha usually cited "the reluctance of [their] children to return to the 'bush'" or the demands of a thriving business as the reasons why they could not go back to the village at age fifty, or sixty, or sixty-five. One of these people, a prominent medical doctor originally from Atani, found his Onitsha house more comfortable and much more convenient for his younger children's schooling than his Atani home. He also told me that his practice would be greatly lessened in Atani, although he could easily set up a clinic in the area. This doctor did own a very fine "storey" house in his natal town and had taken *ozo* title there.[19]

His children, however, very rarely visited their hometown and evinced no interest at all in living there.[20] Their interests and actions remain oriented toward a continuing urban lifestyle: two of the daughters of the family are now living and working in Lagos, one considering marriage to a man she met in Onitsha (who is himself a nonindigenous Onitsha resident, but with maternal kin ties in the town). Nonetheless, the doctor did participate in the Atani area Local Government elections and was considered a possible candidate from the region for the coming national elections, because of his knowledge of the urban milieu and his Western education. It was also suggested that he would have to return to his hometown and take up residence there if he wanted to be considered a "serious" candidate. It remains to be seen whether the doctor will actually leave Onitsha to pursue these somewhat nebulous political goals rather than to maintain his immediate family in their present location and in the style which they expect.[21]

Agu's article is speaking to just such an audience as the Atani doctor and his family and is warning them that their jural rights are slipping away—while, at the same time, they remain open to a particular type of attack. As out-migrants, they may become wealthy in a Western sense of the word and may even be celebrated as "sons of the soil," but this no longer means they may expect to be treated as equals in their natal towns. A premium is being placed on local power, particularly in the face of rural perceptions of a more general powerlessness brought about by Nigeria's current economic and political difficulties. Cities are seen as taking up more and more of the very limited public good as well as swallowing the best people (the most intelligent and industrious) from the rural areas. In the older "wealth-in-people" system of the villages, this is tantamount to robbery—which, for Igbo-speaking peoples, is one step below murder. Initially out-migration was supposed to be a temporary thing; the emigrants were to learn Western skills and bring them back to the town to help it "get up" (Uchendu 1965:34–39). Instead, the out-migrants did not return at all, or have made token returns, and the towns find themselves so much poorer, in terms of wealth-in-people, than before.

In Agu's view, the village residents have begun to act like witches toward their unsuspecting, nonresident "brothers." The residents hold on jealously to the little power they have over village affairs, while accepting monetary assistance from the outsider indigenes. Residents no longer intend to share so equitably what, in Igbo, one would call the "good" (*mma*) of the town with these nonresidents. From the nonresident point of view, this is the same as being treated like meat or an animal by their nearest

kinsmen. In biblical terms—the terms one often hears in the highly chris-
tianized Igbo region—the nonresidents have ceased to be seen as the
prodigal sons of their town and, instead, have begun to feel like fatted
calves. This ties directly into the discussion of Igbo notions of witchcraft
noted above.

To understand more fully the complex set of ideas behind Agu's charge
of witchcraft, it is necessary to say something about the connection between an Igbo person's life, his or her productiveness, and the communal
"good." *Mma* is arguably the most important, single Igbo cosmological
term. It contains a complex bundle of meanings: not only "good" but
wealth, health, and beauty are also implied. The key to following the discussion below is that the reader must keep all of these meanings in mind,
since the values expressed by the use of *mma* are central to Igbo thought,
particularly Igbo thought about human worth.

For the Igbo, personal *mma* is both a reflection on the *mma* of the
community and a positive statement about, or a continuation through time
and space of, that good. "Goodness" is thus an active property in the life
of an individual as well as in the life of a group. In practical terms, this
means that a productive person is a person who manifests "goodness"
through his/her actions, by working hard and creatively, by having children and by teaching those children proper values, by accumulating
wealth and by redistributing that wealth to the community through participation in title taking, town and local credit associations, and the establishment of patron-client relations with the less fortunate.

One of the most important signs of "goodness' for the Igbo is children.
Children are, on one hand, the visible continuation of the lineage into the
future, but they also represent material and spiritual wealth in the present. This is why murder and robbery are so closely linked in Igbo thought.
The death of any person implies the loss of his/her productive and reproductive potential for the community at large. As the Igbo person goes
through the life cycle, he/she is expected to accumulate material wealth,
first, then to accumulate spiritual wealth through material redistribution
and through the dissemination of equally valuable life experience to the
community. This spiritual accumulation and redistribution is necessary for
the successful transformation of a living human being into the more powerful but still human form of the (dead) ancestor. Premature death disrupts
this life process, robbing the community of both the present, material
contribution of the individual and the potentially more important future
ancestral intervention.

The witch is an improper accumulator, an eater of blood instead of a
redistributor of wealth. One might say that she has substituted "food" for
"good." Instead of producing children for the lineage, she destroys them.
She takes their potential into herself and keeps it from circulating through-

out the community; she attempts to gain control over what should be communal wealth in order to enrich and prolong her individual life. This, among other things, is a statement about the separateness of the witch from her community. Not only does she refuse to participate in communal activity but she actively subverts the communal good. Agu suggests that resident townsmen are beginning to act like witches—are beginning to think they are separate from their nonresident "brothers"—while becoming avid for the consumption of those "brothers'" substance. I would argue that it is this separateness that activates the hunger for other people's blood in the Igbo models of witchcraft with which I am familiar; it is a necessary precondition for the pathology. People who have a well-developed sense of community and solidarity with their fellow human beings do not turn toward predation. Their needs for communion are met through the "eating of words," not the eating of hearts/centers (*obi*). Where wealth is literally health and beauty, a person's money becomes an outward manifestation of his/her inner progression through the life cycle.

In the ideal system of the Igbo individual in his/her community briefly described above, redistribution should be matched with expressions of spiritual wealth. One does not only take a title but he/she takes on the importance of an acknowledged accumulator of spiritual wealth, or experience. He/she becomes an elder, a person of consensus-based power and influence, who must be respected. Disruption of the proper respect to elders is tantamount to a spiritual dispossession. The witch is able to feed on her victims so handily because she has access to them and to a knowledge of them that only an intimate could have, while lacking the proper respect for their essential beings, for their humanity. Her lack of respect and its implied refusal of consent enables her to treat human beings as meat.

The resident townspeople, says Agu, benefit from a system that doubly dispossesses its most productive members. Nonresident indigenes are bereft of the comfort and understanding of "home," trying to better themselves and, by extension, their towns. They are also bereft of the respect and acknowledgment that their achievements ought to elicit in those same towns. The rural towns are pictured by Agu and his fellows as increasingly turned inward, accumulating the spiritual "good" but not allowing it to circulate freely to all members of the community. In a society that values openness and the free circulation of cosmological forces, this sort of accumulation equates to social suicide—where the accumulated, trapped *mma* is transformed by its improper stasis into *nso* (abomination or danger, an affront to cosmological order). Good that does not benefit all members of a community is no longer *mma*. The Igbo model of human action that best describes this type of behavior is witchcraft.

Other anthropological theorists, notably James Ferguson, have recently begun a reconsideration of witchcraft models and how those models effect the mutual perceptions of rural and urban African peoples. Ferguson suggests that rural people in Zambia are enjoying a sort of revenge against the formerly privileged Zambian urban dwellers. (Ferguson 1988:6–7) That also seems to be the case in Agu's editorial. What he does not discuss, however, is the whole question of what constitutes privilege. What I would like to argue here is that Western consumer culture does not constitute the only form of privilege that is of interest to Igbo traders, outmigrant workers, and their rural-based kin. The flourishing institution of title taking and concerns over the building of village houses throughout Nigeria point to a different set of (rural/village) privileges considered to be of equal or greater importance in the popular consciousness. There is more to this than style, "localist" or "cosmopolitan" (Ferguson 1987:1–2), and it can only be explored by trying to learn more about indigenous systems of value.

Rural and urban Igbo systems of value are very much at stake in Emma Agu's editorial. A close community of human beings, in Agu's estimation, has been transformed into a pack of blood-scenting animals, seeking their prey from the spoor they are most familiar with, their relatives without rights. Yet they are able to rationalize this hunt to themselves by the construction of an idea of otherness: the nonresident is reclassified as somehow alien, not really of the community, and therefore "meat." Murder is only murder if the humanity of the victim is acknowledged.

The problems with the Local Government elections thus become, for Agu and his audience, a representation of a deeper-seated anxiety. There is a very real fear that the choices the nonresidents have made about their livelihood and lives have put them into an untenable position: expectations of urban business success and rural social success turn out to be contradictory in practice. The nonresident villager apprehends that he or she will not be able to fully participate in *any* community, including the larger community of ancestral forces.[22] Although the nonresident has access to cash and to opportunities unavailable to his or her resident counterpart, this is only half the Igbo equation as it is represented to us by Agu. Without real access to the spiritual wealth inherent in communal recognition and appreciation, the nonresident cannot complete the normal process of his or her life. It is as if a witch had eaten his or her heart.

There is another side to this story of witchcraft in the rural areas—the side of the resident townspeople themselves. If they were to write in the popular press (which, by and large, they do not), they might well (re)pose the question of who, or what, these witches are. As mentioned briefly above, there is a feeling of great powerlessness about the national condition in the rural areas, a sense that the Nigerian discourse of politics and power is being carried on without rural people. Along with that perception of power lying elsewhere, sometimes there is a sense of outrage toward those young people of two or more decades ago who were sent to secondary school and to university, often at great hardship to the town as a whole, and who now seem to have forgotten their roots while "enjoying" in the cities.[23]

In some cases the cities themselves are blamed, as if they had a personality or a character of their own. For instance, Onitsha was always characterized to me, by people who did not live there (and sometimes by people who did), as "too hot." After I had settled in and started working, I was asked if I should not take a periodic break from Onitsha, to "cool down." The intense commercial activity in Onitsha, and most particularly my constant attendance in the markets, were being measured and were considered to have taken their toll on my (nonmaterial) temperature. It seems to be a pan-Igbo notion that the accumulation of wealth, without its subsequent redistribution, generates an unhealthy psychic heat. Large-scale accumulation blocks the circulation of those dangerous forces that develop around and through excessive and unregulated productivity.

This idea of an unhealthy heat, noted by anthropologists and other social scientists throughout Africa, is relevant to Igbo models of witchcraft, which in turn are relevant to our understanding of Agu's editorial.[24] Unhealthy psychic heat is manufactured in the cities, with their unregulated forms of accumulation, and it is in the cities that Agu's audience lives and works. The immoderate accumulation of the witch (or the political-economic exploiter) constricts the normal circulation of forces in the community, leading to death and disaster, and ultimately to a widespread abomination.[25] Metuh says that a witch is *"Onye n'ebu ihe n'obi,"* which he glosses with great simplicity as meaning an "introvert." (Metuh 1981: 101) In a more literal translation, this seems to mean "a person who keeps a stinging thing inside his/her heart." Note the reference to enclosure or constriction here. Instead of letting go of the "stinging thing," the witch embraces it and keeps it in. The witch accumulates her pain and is goaded by it to seek solace in the pain and the exploitation of the life force of others, even to their death.

For many Igbo-speaking people, large commercial towns in the Southeast have come to resemble the person of the witch. Nigerian urban areas stand somewhat separate from their own village, historical backgrounds: by which I mean that these towns have become involved in a wider, national and even international set of relationships that alienate them, to some extent, from their "close kin," the neighboring small towns and villages. With almost magical ease, the commercial centers have made themselves the most visible members of the national community, drawing off the best in government services and attention. They act as a force of attraction within their local vicinity as well: often taking the most ambitious, the most intelligent, and the wealthiest people from the rural areas—and only rarely returning them in an enhanced condition. And it is quite obvious, at least to rural townspeople with whom I spoke, that the cities must continue in this cycle of the exploitation and expropriation of their rural neighbors if they are to survive.

We can turn again to Onitsha to provide us with an example of the witch-like nature of the urban Nigerian system, as seen from both the perspective of Onitsha indigenes and of outsiders. Onitsha's dangerous heat and its "unhealthy" environment are warning signs of both its accumulative and seductive nature, of its witch-like being in the eyes of indigenes, other residents, and even of people who know it mostly by reputation. Onitsha indigenes watch with dismay while "their" town attracts larger and larger numbers of *ndigbo*, unsure of how to regain control over its runaway economic potential or of its increasingly unruly population. Outsiders view Onitsha as a potentially deadly locale, beyond the control of its proper "owners"—something like a wild beast, or maybe the "evil bush," where lost human spirits dwell.

From inside, Onitsha looks like an incredibly dense mass, kept together mainly by the call of its markets, and constantly on the verge of explosion. From outside, Onitsha looks opaque: always ready to absorb people, goods, and money into itself, without returning equal value for this trade. It hides a sting in its heart, as one might say, potentially dangerous both to those who inhabit it and to those within the reach of its influence. Onitsha indigenes are rumored by outsiders to be the most notorious witches in all of the Igbo-speaking Southeast, and, even inside Inland Town, *ndi onicha* agree that there is abomination in the land which must be eradicated. It becomes a matter of perspective as to who the witches are in this instance: the commercial townspeople, members of the outsider community, lineage mates from one's own natal village, or even the town itself. The transformation of all relations of town life into witch-like relations of expropriation and selfishness may be read as the material sign of a community of entrenched witchcraft, something like a child fed witchcraft substance by his or her mother. Small wonder (Agu's protestations notwithstanding) rural village residents are inclined to distrust the relatives who live and work in such a place.

After all, from the viewpoint of the resident village population, those persons who readily partake of commercial, urban life, without a stringent course of return and revitalization through the practice of communal, village, and lineage relations, have begun to look like witches themselves. They cannot readily understand local issues and are certainly not able to make informed judgments about their deposition. In a sense, they have taken the first step toward separation from the community they claim to be a part of. Yet these same nonresidents, by virtue of wealth gained in unobserved, unregulated, virtually unknown urban activity, wish to become recognized as elders—that is, to take on power from a community in which they cannot fully participate.[26] What seems like common sense to Agu and his audience, is not necessarily common sense to the rural villager, who has his own and the town's spiritual well-being to look after.

The dangers inherent in the encroachment of the nonresident villagers are represented by what they actually do in the village. They are easily able to build houses on communal land that contain such wonders as electric generators, air conditioners, televisions, even satellite dishes to pull in television programming from across the world (when average rural dwellers consider themselves fortunate if they can listen to radio broadcasts in Igbo).[27] These houses remain largely untenanted, except for relatives who are allowed to live in outbuildings on the compound grounds in return for taking care of the premises. There is a separate character to the nonresident's village house that is reminiscent more of the residence patterns of the urban area than of the town. The house is walled in, like the compound model, but often its gates are large, constructed of metal, and remain locked against the "brothers" who make their day-to-day existence in the village. The owners of such villas rarely spend extended periods in residence, and they never involve themselves in cultivation, once a major forum for demonstrating masculine (and feminine) virtues.[28] Village residents see the material signs of their nonresidential relatives' wealth, but they do not see the less tangible signs of their commonality.

The key point here is not that the nonresidents have demonstrated themselves to be worthy of residents' respect because of their wealth (which seems to be partially Agu's position), but that they have not demonstrated this worth in village terms. A sorcerer can become wealthy by "stealing blood" and serving it to his *ikenga*,[29] an object that is the very embodiment of personal and even selfish accumulation and achievement for Igbo-speaking people. The unregulated accumulation of wealth is the type of urban practice that village elders most fear, because it suborns both their authority and the unity of the group itself. Overaccumulation and ill-gotten wealth can bring disrepute, or worse, on its recipients. The selfishness of accumulation is permanently attached to the wealth itself: it does not circulate; it is anticommunal. Therefore, resident villagers often look askance at unwarranted displays of useless wealth: wealth that is patently not being circulated, that accumulates to no understood purpose, like the uninhabited village houses of Nigeria's urban elite. The rural houses of Nigeria's wealthy serve as a temptation to many as well as markers of potential danger to village elders. The houses, sitting in their very solitary splendor, attract both thieves and envious thoughts. Wealth in motion—redistributed wealth—does not bring such *ihe njo* (ugly or wicked things) into a town.

An interesting twist in this complex set of witchcraft suspicions may emerge from the resident indigenes' fear of urban witchcraft and urban witches. An informant told Sylvia Leith-Ross in 1937 that a person whose household is being troubled by witchcraft may go to a diviner/healer and be made into a witch "'so that she may protect her children'" (Leith-Ross 1943:74). Agu is not suggesting that there are altruistic witches in his editorial; this makes no sense from the perspective of an accuser. It is possible, though, that some resident indigenes turn to a notion of witch-craft, or to its practice, through a desire to "protect their children" and their village from the effects of improper, urban accumulation. In some Igbo cosmological theorizing, there is a danger of infection to the land itself from the evil and unchecked actions of its inhabitants. The potential for "good" witchcraft to protect the land as well as its inhabitants is of particular interest if we recall the kinship foundation of most Igbo villages and towns.

In these lineage or clan-based villages, the group itself could be thought to be endangered by the emergence of group members who are not fully rooted in the group, who can claim full membership at their individual will, and who can appear on and disappear from the village scene arbitrarily. Igbo patrilineal society, by and large, maintains itself through a pattern of male stasis and female flow. That is to say, men remain in or around their patrilineal homeland, attending to the shrines of the patriline and working and living in a very direct connection to its ancestral forces. Conversely, women move across the landscape through marriage and trade, keeping pathways open and cementing intervillage alliances. Women's openness and their ability to be mobile both places them in a special relationship to purification and its rituals (particularly on a grand scale) and offers them more of an opportunity to come into contact with the dangerous wild forces that roam the spaces between patrilineage enclaves.

The movement of men into the urban areas, except perhaps for those Igbo groups who historically have sustained male migration because of trade or ritual duties, has helped to upset this ideology of male and female behavior.[30] Male movement out from the patrilineal lands has resulted in great pressure on the lineage model of authority and control, both in terms of gender and of seniority. For example, men who are too mobile come into contact with dangerous forces. Since men are characteristically less permeable to wild spiritual forces than women, these forces, once invoked, pose an intense danger for the men and their lineages. Women's evil actions are transitory in most Igbo lineages, because women are always moving, or being moved, out. Men who are tainted may stain the lineage forever, since there is a complete conflation of lineage men and lineage land.[31] For the majority of Igbo women, locale is necessarily fluid, a thing of the moment—or, perhaps, their locale is situated in a more generalized conception of space. For Igbo-speaking men like Agu, identity and locale are merged inescapably.

Classic anthropological literature on lineage in Africa (Radcliffe-Brown and Forde 1950; Fortes 1953; Turner 1957) suggests that local lineages have supported a mobile membership since the 1930s when migrant labor policies were well established in many areas of colonial Africa. The difference between what is being described here and those earlier analyses is that local Igbo lineages are now being called upon to support a mobile membership without some sort of a continuous tie to its home base, notably without maintaining ties through the presence of resident wives and children.[32] In the present case, certain models seem to help resident indigenes, who sustain older patterns of residence and relations, to understand and combat the trend toward isolationism emanating (as they see it) from those lineage members living elsewhere permanently. We might, as anthropologists, expect some of these intralineage tensions to manifest themselves in fission. As I have shown above, however, this does not seem to be true. Igbo kinsmen do not intend to go away permanently or to found their own villages elsewhere. Instead, they try to return, temporarily or sequentially, *n'obi,* to the heart or center of the lineage and expect to flourish and to acquire part of the good and the wealth found there. The keepers of the lineage and its resources, however, may feel it incumbent on them to barricade their towns against this alien, but still somehow familiar incursion.

What Agu sees as active mischief seems to be more in the line of admitting an ethical defeat: which is to say that rural townspeople have decided to take the last defense against witch-like behavior, itself always witchcraft. I am calling this an ethical defeat because it seems to implicitly recognize the power of selfishness and extreme exploitation and to capitulate to that power while capitalizing on it. The village witches/elders lose a valuable resource—their own lineage mates—in this tangle of defense and defensiveness. "Eating" the wealth of their alienated "brothers" offers no chance for the continuation, or what could be called the reproduction, of that wealth or of those persons. It only recognizes a temporal present for the nonresident kin, just as animals are only seen as existing in the present for human consumption. In a system where locality is what counts, and where locality can become a limited *commodity*—a thing that alienates people from each other rather than binding them together—when they no longer share a territorial space, kin can be transformed into strangers. Strangers do not share in the *mma* of a lineage nor in that lineage's infinite progression through time. Space is effectively privileged, divided from and given power over time.

Agu and his audience recognize the fact that their individual ancestral potential is in jeopardy; so must the resident indigenes recognize the fact that lineage spiritual potential stands at risk in this new permutation of the system. Witchcraft, and all the ways of thinking and being that it represents, finally emerges as a weapon of ultimate destruction—unless the witches can be brought to confess and to stop the cycle of intimate but alienating violence. As I have tried to show elsewhere (Bastian 1985), abomination, once allowed to take hold, has a tendency toward moving out from the center to the outside world. *Nso* (abomination) is only local in the sense that the earth itself is local. To conclude this essay, would like to return to a more direct consideration of Agu's editorial and demonstrate how confession and accusation is seen as playing a major role in defusing the destructive cycle of witchcraft—for Nigeria as a whole as well as for Igbo-speaking peoples themselves.

The Poison Ordeal: Editorial as Accusation
Confession or Accusation?

There are two common ways for an Igbo witch to be discovered. The first is for the witch to accuse herself. The second is for her victims to become suspicious, to consult a diviner on the matter, then to accuse her publicly. Both are dramatic moments of revelation which elicit retribution on the part of the community, but the difference between them lies in the identity of the accuser. The question of locale or space, which concerned us throughout the previous section, is also important for accusation and confession. Self-accusation, or confession, generally takes place in the most open of all Igbo spaces, the marketplace, if the witch is female—and in the most private of Igbo spaces, a man's deathbed, inside his house, if the man is a sorcerer or a witch.

The female witch will reveal herself physically by beginning to strip in the midst of the busy marketplace.[33] The sign of bodily nakedness almost always precedes actual, public confession. I would argue that a confessing witch's nakedness is a statement about wickedness (*njo*) and Igbo-speaking people's conceptions of a moral order. By discarding her garments, the witch promises to open herself to public scrutiny and to "come clean," in the parlance of American gangster movies. This act also demonstrates an awareness of her alienation from humanity, of her difference. The only other people who strip or appear naked in the marketplace are mad people. In Onitsha, at any rate, the insane are looked upon as less than human, almost animals, and lose their names and identities upon discarding their clothes.[34] The witch abnegates her separate identity with her clothes. This is significant since identity was the thing she cherished to extremes (in Agu's words, her "selfishness") and which first motivated her witchly transformation.

The verbal confession takes the form of an anguished recitation of the names of victims and why they were killed. There seems to be a sense here that the witch's heart is full—that she simply cannot accumulate any more life force from her victims, or stand any more of her own evil. As she confesses, her wrongful accumulation is spilled out through words (just as spiritual wealth is redistributed by elders through proverbs). Naming names is a significant action: a dead person's name is not called lightly, especially by the person who took his or her life. There is some sense that the dead respond to their names.[35] Naming the names of the dead in the marketplace, a locale where spirits are said to mingle freely with living human beings, may serve as a potent evocation to the prematurely lost members of the community as well as to those still living. The self-accusatory performance is thus a powerful one, and it attracts a large audience because of that power. Passers-by stop to hear (and to see) the infamy uncovered and to comment on those people whose deaths are being shown to be unnatural. The onlookers stay for the entire performance, not least of all because they will take part in its ending. When the witch is exhausted, all her crimes confessed, and power dissipated, the witnesses stone her.[36] The eradication of a witch requires communal participation. It would appear that Agu understands this principle and is attempting to muster broad-based support for his own proposal of eradication.

Matters stand differently for the typical male sorcerer who admits his guilt.[37] Again this appears to be correlated with locale. The self-accused sorcerer is usually dying before he makes a confession. He may even be boasting of his conquests rather than trying to expiate his guilt. He also may be trying to implicate his heirs in his activities, passing on to them the powerful medicines he has accumulated over time (with the exception of his *ikenga*, a very personal object) and exhorting them to continue in his successful path. This speaks directly to the problem of male evil addressed briefly above. The self-confessed witch openly exposes her guilt, taking as her forum the most public space in Igbo metaphysical topography. This is very much in keeping with Igbo-speakers' notions of female gender responsibilities and affinities. Male sorcerers or witches are more likely to confess to their kin group only—the people with most reason to keep the knowledge of guilt a secret. Witchcraft substance passed from one out-marrying daughter to another does not seem to generate the same sense of danger and concern that the idea of inherited medicines does. Male medicines do not circulate but remain rooted inside the lineage, for good or evil, like other types of male property. Evil medicine can taint the whole lineage, just as good medicines can enhance lineage credit in the public eye.

Male sorcery is also often connected to local politics, the area where men (especially middle-aged men) carry out their public responsibilities in an atmosphere of intense competition. I emphasize the age of Igbo "politicians" because middle age appears to be construed as the most dangerous time in the life cycle of all human beings. By middle age, men are expected to be well on the road to an accumulation of property and goods. Such an accumulation leads to an opacity, as opposed to a transparency, of the accumulator. When Igbo-speaking men enter into politics, they become "hot" and should begin to redistribute their wealth to "cool" themselves. This is an exchange for, or a transformation of, material wealth into spiritual wealth. There is always a danger, however, that political competition will engender a desire for further and unnecessary accumulation. It is this sort of accumulation that can lead to sorcery (the use of "medicines") or, in a very extreme form, witchcraft (becoming, in a sense, a "medicine" through the ingestion of eriri).[38]

The fear of overweening, prideful accumulation is part of the motivation for witchcraft suspicion and accusation. Agu fears that the village elders have decided to hoard the spiritual good (the true mma) of the land, ruining his future ancestral potential along with his present political hopes. Members of rural communities fear that present, material good is being siphoned away from them by the very people, their nonresident kin, who were initially sent out to capture that good and make village life more equitable to the life enjoyed elsewhere. Because the nonresident and resident villagers have begun to see each other as "other," separated somehow by choice rather than by circumstances, neither group expects to work out the witch problem through the medium of confession. Accusation, and a rooting out of the evil from the land must be the answer. In the next section, we will consider the Igbo idea of accusation and why such an accusation would find a place in the Sunday edition of a local newspaper.

Accusation, the "Stinging Sting"

In the Onitsha Igbo model of accusation, a victim will feel that he or she is being attacked (or his or her relatives will so decide after debilitation or death) and will consult a diviner to seek out the source of the attack.[39] Once a single source, or a group of potential sources, has been located through the spiritual mediumship of the healer, the relatives of the afflicted person will take his or her case to the elders of the town. This type of accusation would be made in the court of the Onitsha king, who was known as the Obi.[40] Accusation was generally enough to set the wheels of justice in motion, if the accusation was made by known and responsible people.

The Obi would decree that the accused must take the sasswood poison ordeal. The accused had to drink a cup of sasswood mixture at the break of day, just as a nocturnal witch's power was ebbing away, and survive for twenty-eight days (four "small" market weeks, or two "great" ones) after the draught. If the accused person survived, she would be allowed to dance in the marketplace, wearing white chalk and all her finery, telling her story of false accusation to everyone she encountered. Traders would be obligated to sympathize and to give her small gifts, just as they would give a bride or a woman who had just taken a title. Those who accused her would have to pay heavy fines to the Obi and would be publicly ridiculed. Most accused witches, one suspects, never made it to the marketplace as free women. The sasswood poison took rapid effect, causing respiratory failure.

Accusation was thus a fairly efficient means of eradicating witches— or, at least, of eradicating those so accused. The important point to take from all this was that an impersonal agent (the sasswood poison) was used to determine whether an accused individual was indeed a witch, and that the means of determination was also the means of carrying out judgment. Those who survived the sasswood trial were feted and given great freedom in the town, but those who did not were acknowledged (but unconfessed) witches whose bodies would not be given proper burial. We will next examine more closely the modern witchcraft accusation that inspired this chapter and try to see how it is similar or dissimilar to the model of accusation and judgment above.

Agu's editorial is a contemporary form of witchcraft accusation.[41] It also may be meant to serve as something of a poison ordeal as well, although the "poison oracle" in this case is made of words rather than of sasswood. The structure of the column so closely parallels a common Igbo oratorial style (one, for instance, used for public accusation) that it cannot have been accidentally chosen for the piece. In this style of oration, the speaker will begin by telling his or her audience what they already know: that, "from our fathers," we have heard such-and-such a thing (implying that, therefore, we know it to be true). Second, he or she will comment on some current situation—one not obviously connected to the piece of ancestral knowledge just expounded upon. Finally, the speaker will make the connection between the first two points explicit, ending with proverbial speech, which shows the depth of the speaker's maturity and spiritual wealth. The use of proverbial speech encapsulates, for those sufficiently experienced to understand the allusions, the main didactic points to be considered and hopefully sways the audience to the speaker's opinion. Agu clearly follows this pattern in the construction of his essay, although he takes some liberties with it that are particularly telling.

First, Agu tells us what is "known" about witches: their predatory nature, their selfishness, their affinity for darkness, their slipperiness in the face of accusation. It is interesting, however, to note that he does not begin his account with a reminder that "everyone knows" this, or that "our fathers told us" about this. This seems to be a deliberate omission because what is "known" is not presented as the old form of witchcraft, exactly, but as a more modern permutation. Here we begin to see how the medium is being used to bring a different message for a different audience. The newspaper is meant to tell what is "new," and Agu thinks that he has discovered a new form of witchcraft in the world. Such a discovery, especially since the witchcraft is directed against that audience, is fit for the pages of a newspaper published in English, for people who speak and read English on a daily basis.

Agu may or may not be taking account of the fact that it is this use of another language that was one of the things that initially set the nonresident villagers apart from their resident kin and that continues to serve as something of a barrier between them. A common, bitter complaint I heard from rural people was that their urban kin would speak English even "at home" and were not teaching their children to speak "proper" Igbo. This is a serious issue, since almost every major town group in the Igbo-speaking Southeast has a separate, "deep" vocabulary that differentiates its language from that of its neighbors. The loss of linguistic continuity between the generations is directly linked to the loss of territorial continuity. Elders told me that Igbo proverbs "can't be learned from book." The words of a proverb only represent half of the equation. The other half comes through seeing proverbial sentiment in action, through participating in the events addressed by proverbs. Without shared life experience, the richness and beauty of speech cannot be transmitted on to the future.

People in both the rural and urban areas express a certain ambivalence about the widespread use of English among native speakers of Igbo. On one hand, it is something to be proud of, because it is a marker of connection to the non-Igbo, wealthy world. On the other hand, it alienates people from their own culture because of the foreign wealth and attractiveness of English. Part of that wealth is that English is the written language of choice throughout the region. Unlike in other areas of Nigeria where indigenous languages have long-established orthographies and infrastructural support, Igbo is neither widely written nor read.[42] English is thus the language of long-distance communication and the language of secretiveness. For rural people, literate in neither English nor Igbo, or only functionally literate in English, the written word becomes more significant for what it hides than for what it reveals.

Agu's editorial is an excellent example of this selective secretiveness. He is writing for an audience that is not only literate in English but which prides itself on understanding the international, nonterritorially based culture English represents. Because of his flexibility in moving between Igbo and English notions, Agu is able to formulate a description of "modern" witchcraft that takes into account his fears (and those of his putative audience) about the actions of his resident village kin as well as his understanding of local level politics. What gives the text its selective secrecy is the recourse to what can be said in English—turning to a larger, cosmopolitan frame of reference in order to speak only to those for whom that frame has meaning. In a sense, it is a new form of proverbial speech, where the life experiences of the urban dwelling villager gives meaning to a set of arcane allusions taken from "deep" but nonlocalized language.

For example, Agu's witches are "bloodhounds," not the customary owl or rat, and it appears to be significant that he has conserved the form of witchcraft (being able to transform oneself into the shape of an animal) while using an idea alien to the indigenous model. As far as I know, there is no indigenous term for "bloodhound," because there are no dogs bred specifically for this purpose. Agu's use of the English word here, however, suggests a synthesis of Igbo and English convention. Witches do seek out blood (their favorite food), and they do transform themselves into animals, but the image of an unearthly, blood-seeking dog comes more from A. Conan Doyle than from Achebe. It also has connotations from detective fiction, movies, and other objects of American (anglophone) popular culture, notably those of wrongful imprisonment and the need to escape from unsuitable punishment. There is also a sense of the difficulty inherent in escaping such a beast: the bloodhound is reputed to stay on the scent of its prey through all obstacles. By calling upon this multivocal image, speaking both to the Igbo (rural, rich in the knowledge of the patrilineage) side of his audience and to its anglophone (urban, "sophisticated," literate) side, Agu constructs a new proverbial form concerning witchcraft. He asks his audience to recall what they have learned, from both sets of influence, and to put that knowledge to the test in understanding what he will now reveal to them about their immediate environment.

The second paragraph of the editorial is very similar to the first in that Agu suggests a Western, psychologistic explanation for the predatory behavior of the "bloodhounds" described directly above. The witch, according to Agu, has an "uncanny obsession with self." This is the type of behavior seen in so-called traditional Igbo models of witchcraft but with an added-on English concept, "obsession," that speaks to Western ideas about a distinctly un-Igbo lack of self-awareness. Obsessions in native-speaker English, however, are rarely "uncanny." Westerners do not necessarily think that what they classify as obsessive behavior will lead to witchcraft—although they may see these obsessions as evil or frightening. Agu is saying that human obsessive behavior can create a nonhuman person or community of persons, a witch or cabal of witches.

Agu, moving between English and Igbo, builds up a concept of witchcraft that incorporates his own experience as well as ideas from both languages and cultures. In doing so, he speaks directly to an audience who is involved in making the same sort of connections in their everyday lives.[43] He distances himself from two other audiences at the same time: those who are perceived as living exclusively and locally inside Igbo culture and language, his resident kin, and those who live exclusively and internationally inside anglophone culture, without any understanding of Nigerian norms and values. From the initial paragraphs, then, Agu accuses a group of people who are unable (because they lack his life experience and culturally transformative skills) to field a rebuttal. The same thing was generally true of women brought before the Obi's court to suffer the sasswood ordeal in Onitsha. The moral high ground for Igbo speakers is usually occupied by those with the knowledge to appropriately exploit the system—as in the case of elders whose claim to superior wisdom lies in their reputations and their specialized forms of knowledge, such as the proper use of proverbial speech. Agu's sophisticated use of English language (and metaphor) in the cause of accusation, especially since the accusation comes in a newspaper, gives his accusation authority in Igbo terms. This demonstrated ease of language enables him to make statements about the contemporary scene that bear weight for his readers.

The next part of Agu's oration/editorial is thus a recounting, from his own perspective, of the problems of political action in contemporary Nigeria. These problems are multifarious but seen as being inherently related. He speaks to issues like corruption and to a distaste in the country for "fair competition." He also questions whether the "New Breed" of Nigerian politicians will be able to think for themselves. Finally, he bemoans the fact that successful men like those in his putative audience have to lead double residential and, by inference, social lives in the urban-based commercial but rurally based social systems of the country.

From these general comments, he goes on to mention his specific problem: that nonresidents are not being allowed access to the platforms for political activity that their indigenous villages or towns offer them. Old-fashioned, town-based politicians, he has hinted earlier, have much in common with witches. The elders do not favor the "lucky" or the successful, unless they have had a hand in that luck or success. At this point we are meant to notice that village elders have much in common with old-style politicians. The rural elders to not intend to let their fledgling (read "eaglet") nonresident kin move from the nest, much less take on the adult responsibilities of leadership. The old-style politicians refuse to loosen their hold on the political future of the Nigerian state, however much they have harmed its past. Younger people, people with new and different experiences, are being shut out of all positions of trust, although their productivity is exploited on every side. In essence, politicians and elders have secured their turf (often through this exploitation) and do not intend to surrender it. If, as in the case of the banned politicians, that turf does them no good, then no one else will be given an opportunity to make good either. This form of witchcraft thus goes beyond the idea of a zero-sum game. Agu suggests that abomination, which benefits no one, may be the end result of such political selfishness.

Elders, old-style politicians, and witches are all represented here as full of malice. In Igbo it might be said that they have a sting in their hearts. This need to separate themselves from their companions, because of their own pain at being shut out from the new games of political and social power in Nigeria, has transformed them from resources for the community into forces for that community's potential destruction. What they cannot grasp themselves, because they do not have the education, or the government permission, or the ability to attain through hard work, they seek to deny to others. "Down here," notes Agu in disgust, "we have learnt nothing and forgotten nothing." The witch-like beings mull over their past glories (or victims), while ignoring the moral lessons that they might have learned in the process. What ought to be finished is contained in memory, at the center of life, and allowed to "spoil"[44] the chances of "our best." From this stasis of moral economy comes an abomination that threatens to destroy more than Agu's political future.

Agu and his fellows remember another time when witch-like activity threatened to wreck what must have seemed like the whole world—the Biafran civil war. He deliberately evokes the specter of the war, reminding his audience of who was in charge during that troubled period, and he juxtaposes that event with the problems of maintaining two residences. "Mischief makers" try to keep "brothers" apart in the present circumstance—consuming their productive lives by that action—just as they did during Biafra. Neither the rural nor the urban Igbo population has forgotten the horrors attendant upon Biafra's death throes. The selfishness of the alienated (and alienating) person is shown by Agu to be connected to the person who would be a traitor and, ultimately a witch. That type of nonhuman person seeks his own gain by making human life meaningless through an unceasing exploitation, even to death and beyond.

During the Biafran war, many of those Igbo-speaking politicians who are banned from participating directly in Nigerian politics today were active in the establishment of the rebellious enclave. These old politicians are thought to continue to manipulate local politics, pushing their own programs through the control they exercise over young relatives or other, junior persons. The overheated, uncontrolled atmosphere inside Biafra during the war—and the deaths due to bureaucratic ineptitude or outright corruption as well as from military action—is often, in private conversation, attributed to these would-be political actors. People connected to the government in Biafra often suffered the least, as is well known. Ojukwu[45] himself drives the Onitsha-Enugu expressway today in a Mercedes, ignoring the pathetic display of wheelchaired, veteran beggars who sit alongside the road. Much of the selfishness displayed during the war escaped punishment.

After reestablishing the memory of Biafra and its internal fragmentation in the minds of his readers and connecting it firmly to contemporary situations, Agu returns to Igbo rhetorical form and gives them an English proverb to think about: "A word is enough for the wise." In Igbo oration, it is common to use proverbs to sum up the speaker's position, and to show his rootedness in the community of the elders ("the wise," as we might say in English). Collective wisdom is public wisdom; the accomplished Igbo speaker wishes to be seen as vocalizing accepted truths. Agu uses the language of the urban area, the powerful and public written English, to reach his chosen audience. However, he uses the form accepted in the rural area, the proverb and Igbo rhetorical styles, to shape his words.

This notion of form is important because it is one of the primary categories of Igbo creativity. For example, Igbo ideas about conception make the creation of form the special province of the earth goddess, Ala/Ani. Along with Chukwu, the "great spirit," Ani is one of the most important of Igbo spiritual forces, and she is definitely the one most concerned with human actions. The word for "tradition" in Igbo is *omenala,* or *omenani.*[46] The "flesh" (i.e., the words) of Igbo speech is subordinated to its form, just as human beings must give respect to the earth responsible for the creation of their form. I would suggest that Agu is drawing attention to the special character and problems of his urbanized Igbo readership by his use of English for very Igbo purposes.

Using the languages of both the urban and the rural Igbo-speaking areas, the witches/bloodhounds have been named and accused; also, they have been effectively muzzled by Agu's demonstration of moral/linguistic superiority. Open, public recognition of witchcraft is the final and best sanction against the weapon that witchcraft, and all of its ills, represents, because the witch can only operate in secret, in the dark. Bringing the witch's acts into the light of day, as it were, allows for counteraction. The newspaper and Nigerian English are thus offered as new poison ordeals. Editorial accusation brings the supposed witchcraft into "public" discourse while, at the same time, it effectively limits the public and veils the discourse. To survive the ordeal's strictures, those accused must demonstrate equal adeptness and persuasive power while under its influence. They must be able to consume the poison (which is to say, to operate under its rules) and live to dance in the marketplace. The trick of this new ordeal is that many of the supposed witches do not know they have been accused, or even that the poison of words has been administered.

Agu's editorial is a call for community action and responsibility, but he has strictly defined the community he desires to reach by his use of language. It is the Western-educated, internationally aware Igbo community that must weed out the witch-like beings who have disguised themselves as powerful, successful humans. And it is the same community that must reestablish a sense of solidarity within itself, returning the benefits of community *n'obi* (to the center, or the heart).

The editorial represents a certain consciousness of evil and the need to alleviate that evil. It also demonstrates an awareness that people in the contemporary Nigerian situation have moved away from some sensed Igbo "norm" of decent behavior (*omenani*, the respect of the earth). What Agu does not allow for, however, is that there might be a different opinion as to whether what he is doing is *mma* (good, beautiful). He does not acknowledge the selective secrecy of his own use of a written text and an "Igboized" English. From the point of view of the rural elders he accuses, and for whom he offers no possibility of rebuttal, he looks very much like a witch himself. The editorial thus serves best as an example, not of doing the "right thing" but of how difficult it is to determine what the right thing may be in such a fragmented community.

Conclusions

Agu's editorial offers us an insight into how Igbo people consolidate their everyday life experiences and make sense of a world that contains both witchcraft and international capitalism. Contrary to earlier speculations about African witchcraft and the urban situation, ideas about witchcraft have not withered away under the cash economies of the continent's cities.[47] If anything, discussions of witchcraft flourish in popular media and provide new material for descriptions of the experience of deprivation and evil in the urban world. Igbo-speaking people in the southeastern part of Nigeria who have never been to Lagos or other points west, for example, now routinely talk about "*maggum*" charms—a type of magical preparation that seems to have come from Yoruba-speaking groups.[48] Tabloids out of Lagos feature this charm prominently in their reporting of scandal, and Yoruba-speaking people now live, for business purposes, in major eastern towns like Enugu. Through outmigration and literacy, formerly esoteric Yoruba knowledge is now common currency (literally, since *maggum* charms must be bought from Yoruba specialists) throughout the country.

Literacy, which some theorists have seen as offering a conclusive break between "magic" and "science" (Goody 1977), does not seem to work in quite the fashion advertised. Walter Ong's dictum that "[p]rint encourages a sense of closure, a sense that what is found in a text has been finalized" (Ong 1982:132), also seems to work less well in Nigerian and, I would argue, less well *more generally* in literary practice than Ong suggests. Although skepticism may indeed "accumulate" through reading about witchcraft, the idea of witchcraft (and, subsequently, the usefulness of the concept) does not seem to disappear under the weight of that skepticism. Goody's sense of "the awareness of alternatives" (1977:43) remains essentially correct: indigenous Nigerian people do become aware of alternative ways of understanding, and they do generalize from those alternatives. But the Western-centered argument breaks down when faced with the facts that not only Western ways of seeing and knowing will be disseminated through literacy—and that Western knowledge can be challenged and transformed to bring it more in line with the experience of non-Western peoples.

Wrapped in the newer power of English language literacy, the word does not lose its mystical efficacy for Igbo-speaking people. Indeed, efficacy may be seen to increase as urban-dwelling people who can read and write in English receive the best of the contemporary political and economic systems in Nigeria. Agu is a firm believer in the potency of words: he has staked a great deal on the idea that he can arouse those with similar experiences to his own by using the written, English word for Igbo ends. He also knows that one of the current, esoteric forms of knowledge in the country lies in the sophisticated use of English to accuse and exclude others who cannot write so persuasively in the same language.[49]

Witchcraft, when considered as a relatively empty category in the social lives of Igbo-speaking peoples, is broadly "about" selfishness, exclusiveness, and a pervasive evil. Rather than being antirational, or antiscientific, or antimodern, witchcraft continues to offer a possible description for actions that are morally wrong. With the proliferation of selfishness and exploitation under a still alien system of government and economics, Igbo explanations of evil remain important to Igbo-thinking—as well as Igbo-speaking—people. As Agu reminds us, "A word is enough to the wise." Our task, as non-Igbo readers of his editorial, is to consider which word and whose "wise," an ambiguity already present in the English proverb.

Notes

1. Thanks to all the participants in the African Studies Workshop, University of Chicago, for their comments and assistance on a primordial version of this essay. Professor George Bond and the other participants and audience of the panel on modern forms of African witchcraft at the ASA meetings, November 1989, were also more than helpful. Special thanks to Mark Auslander, Ralph Austen, Jean Comaroff, John Comaroff, Wendy Griswold, Randy Matory, and Ellen Schattschneider at the University of Chicago for their careful reading and comments on a

previous version. Luise White of the University of Minnesota and Lillian Trager of the University of Wisconsin at Parkside read the paper and gave me many insightful comments as well as raising critical issues with which I am still struggling. I am grateful for their lengthy, critical discussions of the material. More special thanks to Adam Ashforth for his very challenging comments on the current version of this essay.

2. This field work was undertaken with the support of a Fullbright Scholarship and could not have been successfully completed without the assistance of Professors Mark Anikpo and K. P. Moseley of the Department of Sociology, University of Port Harcourt, or the friendship and support of the Asika family of Onitsha, along with too many others to be named here.

3. I have seen no really good literacy statistics for Nigeria, but my own experience was that literacy (or semiliteracy) in English was fairly widespread in the urban areas of the Southeast. Literacy in Igbo seemed surprisingly low, although it is taught as a subject through secondary school. There also appears to be a paucity of material published in the country written in Igbo (unlike in the other major languages of Nigeria, Yoruba, and Hausa). I know of only two novels published in the language, for example.

4. In 1987 Nigeria's currency, the *naira*, was fluctuating in its value—and currently (1992) is in even worse shape. The *naira's* mean value continued around four *naira* to one dollar. (In 1992, the *naira's* exchange in relation to the dollar may even be as high as thirty to one.) There are 100 *kobo* in one *naira*. Newspapers in 1987 thus cost between ten and twelve cents.

5. I learned this from experience. Trying to find an old copy of *Lagos Weekend* to clip articles was a delicate task, requiring tact and a detective's sensibility. I once traced my paper halfway across Onitsha before giving up on its eventual return. Previously read newspapers passed from friend to friend, or relative to relative. In effect, their movement mapped out networks of consanguinity or affinity as well as of literacy.

6. It is not clear whether Bendel State lives up to its reputation as the prime source for Nigerian supernatural events, or whether the tabloid writers were playing to the established prejudices of their (largely) Southern audience. I heard the same sorts of stories about the powers of "Bendelite" witches and sorcerers throughout the Southeast and the Southwest. In one bizarre sports article I read while in the field, a Yoruba-speaking (but English-writing) reporter noted that he was surprised at the amount of "superstition" he found while following one of Nigeria's football teams to South America. Upon seeing broken pots smeared with the blood and feathers of a cock, he said he "felt like [he] was in Bendel State." Bendel State indigenes were not themselves averse to claiming that their area produced superior medicines and powerful supernatural actors. One educated "Bendelite" I knew proudly boasted to me that no Igbo diviner could "medicate" a building like a diviner from Bendel State.

7. This is certainly a possibility. Akin Omoyajowo, a Yoruba Christian, pub-

lished a pamphlet called *Witches?* that seeks to demonstrate his superior (read, Western) understanding of the psychological and sociological rationale for witchcraft in Nigeria. This pamphlet has been in print continuously since 1965 and was pressed upon me by a Nigerian friend who thought I spent entirely too much of my research time listening to "superstitious nonsense."

8. By "evil" in this case I mean a general sense of wrong or wickedness. Particular witches are seen as being particularly malicious and personally evil, but Agu seems to be talking about a larger malaise. Parkin (1985b:2) suggests that anthropologists have often resorted to witchcraft studies because of the very specificity of the evil action in so-called nonliterate societies. In a literate discourse, like Agu's above, witchcraft can also come to represent a more complex set of suppositions about the nature of evil throughout the society.

9. A good example of this is the *ogbaanje* mentioned above. Another example are those people marked out to become diviners, or spiritual mediators, through possession or simply because they are in communication with the world of spiritual forces in a way that living human beings are not supposed to be. Because of this closeness, these people are somehow more than human but less than true spiritual force.

10. I use the joint pronoun advisedly, because the Igbo language does not differentiate between the genders in the same way English does. *O* stands for a person of either gender. In this paper I may refer to a witch as "she," because witches are generally thought to be female. Agu, however, seems to disregard such a distinction in this column.

11. One of the greatest insults to an Igbo person is to call him/her an animal, an *anu*. The word also means meat, so the insult has even greater force. To call a person an animal is to imply that he/she has no consciousness, is meat on foot.

12. Igbo-speaking peoples recognize two forms of murder, "female" and "male." "Female" murder takes place when the murderer acts under extreme duress or when the crime is inadvertent. The usual punishment, prior to the introduction of the British judicial system, seems to have been banishment for a period of time. "Male" murder is premeditated and directed toward a specific victim or victims. Punishment for this crime could be death for the murderer and loss of lineage property and rights. See Meek 1937. Part of the plot of Achebe's novel *Things Fall Apart* (1959) hinges upon this distinction in Igbo moral thought.

13. For good examples of this, see Meek (1937:79–84) or Metuh (1981:100–102). This is one of the most common patterns in ethnographic descriptions of African witchcraft as a whole. See Marwick's essay "Witchcraft as a Social Strain-Gauge" (1970c:280) for a short discussion of the comparative material.

14. The powerful head of OMATA, the Onitsha Markets Amalgamated Traders Association, himself a non-Onitsha trader, tried to run for the chairmanship of Onitsha Local Government in December 1987. Although he maintained the support of his organization for the bid, and although nonindigenes are said to outnum-

ber indigenes three to one, he was not elected. The question of who was elected was never properly settled because of massive vote tampering and election-day violence.

15. See, e.g., Smock (1971).

16. Most villages in the Igbo area are based in lineage organization, either at the maximal lineage or clan level.

17. James Ferguson, in two unpublished presentations of his research in the Copperbelt (Ferguson 1987, 1988), makes a very similar point. The separate circumstances of migrant mine labor in Zambia and Nigerian migrant participation in trade, however, raise some interesting contrasts in the experience of the problem he calls "locality."

18. Note that the article comes from the *Sunday Statesman*, a longer version of the Imo State daily that contains an extended features section, including a two-page editorial section. This length implies an increased leisure time, with more time to read the newspaper, probably because of Sunday's status in the workweek as a permanent holiday. It was certainly my experience in Nigeria that Sundays were utilized for ceremonial occasions that required all-day attendance, ceremonies that would have disrupted people's weekly business schedules.

19. The *ozo* title-taking society, throughout the Igbo-speaking region, seems historically to have been a male hunters' and warriors' association. Today the *ozo* title often symbolizes male business and, more generally, life success. It is very expensive to obtain, since the initiand must pay a number of extraordinary fees and fines before he can even be considered for membership. The ceremonies surrounding initiation can cost much more than the annual income for most Igbo men. For a detailed analysis of Onitsha *ozo* title taking, see Henderson (1972:245–64).

20. One of his daughters was studying sociology at a local university in 1987. For a class project, she did a short study of *ozo* title taking in Atani. The two weeks she spent in the town during this undertaking constituted one of the longest stays she had ever made there. She even found it difficult to understand the "deep" Atani Igbo her informants spoke and had to ask her father to act as translator from time to time. She was praised for her interest in the Atani "traditions," but her interest was of a fairly limited variety, lasting until her paper was graded and the course passed. It is some measure of the villagers' desperation to recapture the interest of these nonresident young people that this young woman would even be told anything about *ozo* title taking, much less be praised for her enquiry. The *ozo* title is exclusively the province of men; women generally are discouraged from prying into its rituals or into the activities of the *ozo* society's members.

21. As I have only recently learned, the doctor was not being entirely frank with me. Another major Onitsha attraction during 1987 was his youthful mistress, whom he subsequently married (sometime early in 1989). The doctor's senior wife has left him to set up her own household, and he seems even more an Onitsha fixture than ever.

22. It is important to note here the Igbo belief in limited reincarnation. If a person is to incarnate in the future, to return to the world of living human beings, he or she must be an ancestor. Being denied ancestorhood is the same as being denied return access to the world and to life during the future. Since reincarnation is one of the hallmarks of successful humanity, this loss of ancestral potential equates to a real, felt loss of humanity.

23. "Enjoying" is a common Nigerian English term that can contain a wealth of satirical commentary. Its use generally implies that the "enjoyment" is at the expense of others.

24. Victor Turner's work about initiation naturally comes to mind, especially in *The Forest of Symbols* (1967) and *The Drums of Affliction* (1968).

25. Luise White, in recent work on prostitution in Nairobi (1990), shows how this improper (in village terms) accumulation of wealth often goes hand in hand with an equally improper sexuality. This is true of Onitsha as well. One of the major complaints of resident elders about their nonresident "brothers" is that the nonresidents think they can "just marry anyone they please" and that "loose women" live in the urban areas, looking to entrap innocent young men into marriage or worse.

26. There is an interesting Nigerian anglophone novel (by a Yoruba novelist) that speaks to just this sort of "unknown" activity: *Hero's Welcome* (1986) by Laide Anigbedu. In this story, a young man murders a number of his village rivals, runs away from home to escape punishment, then embarks on a life of crime and business in the commercial cities of the North. He becomes a wealthy man and decides to come home, take titles, and become respectable once more. The village elders cynically agree to take him back into the community after a judicious bribe, but he is killed before he can be reintegrated. The "hero's" death might be ascribed to poetic justice, but it might also be because of some mystical protection of the village's honor.

27. Lillian Trager, in a personal communication, pointed out to me that less wealthy nonresidents in the Yoruba areas also build houses in their home villages. This is also the case for the Igbo. Such houses do not exhibit the material luxury described above but may contain tokens of their owners' urban experience that seem as alien and alienating as any satellite dish to his or her rural "brother." One older man I visited in rural Imo State took great pride in seating me on his single, remaining plastic-covered chair. This chair has once been part of a "set," including a sofa and two matching chairs, which he purchased while working in the urban area. Although the rest of the "set" has been dismantled over the years, this chair was kept as a reminder of relative urban success.

28. Nonresidents sometimes become involved in agribusiness schemes or build "factories" in their natal towns. One such common business is the mill, whose products are more likely to be transported to and consumed in the urban areas than to materially benefit its rural base. In 1987, there was an urban-based busi-

ness fad for rural fisheries. These fisheries were specifically targeted at providing a luxury food for the urban middle and elite classes. Few rural Igbo people can afford to eat fish on any regular basis, unless they are able to catch them.

29. The *ikenga* is an object of great symbolic value to Igbo-speaking men and to some Igbo-speaking women. The scope of this paper does not allow me to discuss it at any length here, but it is mentioned in Meek (1937:39, 173), Cole (1982:xv; with citations of further discussions in the art historical literature), and Henderson (1972:120–21, 346–47).

30. Notably the Aro long-distance traders from the Southern Igbo areas, Awka blacksmiths, and Nri ritual specialists from the North.

31. When a man commits a self-conscious ("male") crime like murder, his compound is razed and all his belongings scattered. The lineage literally tries to erase him and his deeds from the ground so that man and those actions will not find expression again.

32. Luise White points out that the refusal or inability to maintain families in natal towns led directly to a loss in land rights for Kenyan urban dwellers (personal communication). See also Ferguson (1988) for an analysis of similar difficulties felt by Zambian urban dwellers. The importance of maintaining a "village wife" is not lost on Igbo-speaking men, some of whom make an effort to support families in both locations. The difficulties of this strategy, however, are graphically illustrated in Elechi Amadi's recent novel *Estrangement* (1988).

33. In the Nigerian English words of one of my informants, "to naked herself." It is interesting to recall that seventeenth-century English Quakers talked about "going naked as a sign." They stripped and went forth in public, according to Bauman, as a "public performance of shocking, dramatic [action], intend[ing] to convey, by nonverbal means, an expression of moral reproof and/or prophesy" (1983:84).

34. The identities of particular *ndi ala* (mad people) were never under discussion. My sense of the matter was that people simply did not want to acknowledge that the "madman" they saw everyday at the market might "be someone," i.e., that the insane were named or had families still living. Mad people, and, by extension, witches ready for confession, are like walking dead. They have bodies, but there is no life force inside them.

35. For instance, it may be some time after death before a well-known person's name or nickname will be given to someone else. My own Igbo name, Nkakagulanwaanyi, was the nickname of a famous Onitsha woman trader. She was killed, so I was told, during the fighting in Biafra. Twenty years had passed since her death when I received the name. The name was then considered "safe" for use. It seems that the dead, particularly the uniquely named dead, may be drawn to their namesakes.

36. I did not witness such a stoning in the marketplace myself. However, I did read and hear of several incidents during my stay in the country, and stoning as

punishment in the marketplace was hardly unknown for crimes like stealing. None of my friends or informants admitted to ever participating in this activity, but a number claimed to have heard at least one witchcraft confession.

37. Men are supposed to tend toward sorcery rather than witchcraft. That is, their powers involve skilled manipulation of sorcerous technologies, like the *ikenga* and other "medicines." It is, however, untrue to say that only men are sorcerers or only women are witches. I heard several cases in 1987 where Onitsha women were accused of using "medicines" and where men were thought to exhibit witch-like properties. The engendered dichotomy of witchcraft and sorcery has been much discussed in the literature, beginning with Evans-Pritchard (1976). See Austen (Chap. 4 this vol.) for a brief discussion of the European literature on gender and witchcraft.

38. Witches transform themselves using the dreaded *eriri* power, which they imbibe with the witchcraft "medicine" made from the genitalia of the civet. See Meek (1937:81) and Metuh (1981:101) for more on *eriri* and *ogwu edi*.

39. Williamson glosses the word *ebubu* as accusation. This is extremely interesting for the present case, because it is obviously related (tonally as well as in the reiteration of the sound) to the word *ebu* (sting), familiar to us from Metuh's description of the witch, above. Repeating sounds or phrases are a common feature of the Igbo language; they usually represent an emphasis or an enlargement of the core word. Thus, we might think of *ebubu* as meaning "the stinging sting" or the "big sting" or the "sting that stings." In terms of the current discussion, the significance of stinging accusations for stinging hearts seems quite poetic and speaks to an internal linguistic and cultural logic that cannot often be so easily traced.

40. See Richard Henderson (1972) and Meek (1937) for more detailed descriptions of the sasswood poison ordeal and the careful form of accusation that led up to it. Neither discusses why it should be the Obi who has authority over the poison. It may be that the Obi, who has been described as a "divine king," is himself a very potent witch. Note the sense given Leith-Ross, above, that it may take a witch to counteract a witch. Certainly the currnet Obi exhibits many witch-like qualities, including a propensity for extreme acquisitiveness.

41. Mark Auslander suggested this point to me upon first reading Agu's editorial.

42. There are many historical reasons for this, not the least of which is the very separateness of Igbo dialects mentioned earlier. People were loath to agree to learn so-called Standard Igbo, a pseudolanguage that stripped all local richness from the tongue. Even with the work of eminent Igbo linguists like Emenanjo, there is no universally acknowledged standardization of Igbo orthography, as can be seen from my own usages and from quotations in this essay. Those who do write in Igbo do not use tone markings, and I have heard long arguments about the meaning of a particular sentence of written Igbo, based upon whether one tone or another was meant.

43. Jean and John Comaroff have referred to this type of linguistic and social synthesis as "experimental practice." See their Introduction (this vol.).

44. More ordinary Nigerian English usage: it is common to hear that one's outfit has been "spoiled" by the rain or, more darkly, that "people" are seeking to "spoil the land" by their wrongful actions.

45. Lt.-Col. Emeka Ojukwu, the military and political leader of the Biafrans, at the time of the "Majors' Coup" in 1965 was stationed in the North and did not participate actively in the overthrow of the First Nigerian Republic. Later he was stationed in the Southeast and became the principal exponent of Igbo succession.

46. From the tone of *ome* in *omenala/omenani,* it would seem that the word might be glossed as "respect to Ala/Ani." Tradition is thus the giving of respect to the earth and her rules.

47. Richards's essay in Marwick's edited collection *Witchcraft and Sorcery* (1970*a*) is a particularly good example, because she is sure that the urban Bemba are losing their "wearisome taboos" in light of the "safety bought on a hard cash basis" (Richards 1970:176).

48. This charm is a favorite of the tabloid arm of the Nigerian press because of its sexual nature. A person will purchase a *maggum* charm if he or she suspects his or her spouse of infidelity. Once administered, the erring spouse will stick to his or her adulterous partner while having sex and will be unable to separate at the act's end. Public humiliation and even death is said to result from this unnatural coupling.

49. Note Bauman's ideas about the creation of communities united by "means of speech" (1983:5–6). What he does not emphasize, and what I think is just as important, is how such communities create otherness and exclusivity at the same time.

References

Achebe, Chinua. 1959. *Things Fall Apart.* London: Heinemann.

Achebe, Chinwe. 1986. *The World of Ogbanje.* Enugu: Fourth Dimension.

Amadi, Elechi. 1982. *Ethics in Nigerian Culture.* Ibadan: Heinemann.

———. 1986. *Estrangement.* London: Heinemann.

Anigbedu, Laide. 1986. *Hero's Welcome.* Lagos: Writers' Fraternity.

Barber, Paul. 1989. *Vampires, Burial and Death: Folklore and Reality.* New Haven: Yale University Press.

Basden, George T. 1921. *Among the Ibos of Nigeria.* London: Seeley, Service & Co.

———. 1966. *Niger Ibos: A Description of the Primitive Life, Customs and Animistic Beliefs of the Ibo People of Nigeria.* London: Cass.

Bastian, Misty L. 1985. Useful Women and the Good of the Land: The Women's War of 1929. Master's thesis, University of Chicago.

Bauman, Richard. 1983. *Let Your Words Be Few: Symbolism of Speaking and*

Silence among Seventeenth-Century Quakers. Cambridge: Cambridge University Press.

Cole, Herbert M. 1982. *Mbari: Art and Life among the Owerri Igbo.* Bloomington: Indiana University Press.

Evans-Pritchard, E. E. 1970. Sorcery and Native Opinion. In *Witchcraft and Sorcery: Selected Readings,* ed. Max Marwick. Middlesex: Penguin Books.

———. 1976. *Witchcraft, Oracles and Magic among the Azande.* Oxford: Clarendon Press. Abridged ed.

Ferguson, James. 1987. Economic Crisis and the Cultural Balance of Power: The Micro-Political Economy of Cultural Style on the Zambian Copperbelt. Paper presented at the American Anthropological Association annual meeting, November.

———. 1988. The Country and the City on the Copperbelt. Paper presented at the American Anthropological Association annual meeting, November.

Forde, Cyril D. 1950. *The Ibo and Ibibio-Speaking Peoples of South-Eastern Nigeria.* New York: Oxford University Press.

Fortes, Meyer. 1953. The Structure of Unilineal Descent Groups. *American Anthropologist* 55:17–41.

Gluckman, Max. 1970. The Logic of African Science and Witchcraft. In *Witchcraft and Sorcery: Selected Readings,* ed. Max Marwick. Middlesex: Penguin Books.

Goody, Jack. 1977. *The Domestication of the Savage Mind.* Cambridge: Cambridge University Press.

Green, M. M. 1964 [1947]. *Ibo Village Affairs.* New York: Praeger.

Henderson, Helen Kreider. 1969. Ritual Roles of Women in Onitsha Ibo Society. Ph.D. diss., University of California, Berkeley.

Henderson, Richard N. 1972. *The King in Everyman: Evolutionary Trends in Onitsha Ibo Society and Culture.* New Haven: Yale University Press.

Horton, Robin. 1967. African Traditional Thought and Western Science. *Africa* 37:50–71, 155–87.

Krige, J. D. 1970. The Social Function of Witchcraft. In *Witchcraft and Sorcery: Selected Readings,* ed. by Max Marwick. Middlesex: Penguin Books.

Leith-Ross, Sylvia. 1936. *African Women: A Study of the Ibo of Nigeria.* London: Faber and Faber.

———. 1943. *African Conversation Piece.* London: Hutchinson.

Macfarlane, Alan. 1985. The Root of All Evil. In *The Anthropology of Evil,* ed. David Parkin. Oxford: Basil Blackwell.

Marwick, Max, ed. 1970a. *Witchcraft and Sorcery: Selected Readings.* Middlesex: Penguin Books.

———. 1970b. Introduction. In Marwick (1970a).

———. 1970c. Witchcraft as a Social Strain-Gauge. In Marwick (1970a).

Meek, C. K. 1937. *Law and Authority in a Nigerian Tribe: A Study in Indirect Rule.* Oxford: Oxford University Press.

Metuh, Emefie Ikenga. 1981. *God and Man in African Religion: A Case Study of the Igbo of Nigeria*. London: Chapman.

———. 1985. *African Religions in Western Conceptual Schemes: The Problem of Interpretation (Studies in Igbo Religion)*. Ibadan: Pastoral Institute.

Nadel, S. F. 1970. Witchcraft in Four African Societies. In *Witchcraft and Sorcery: Selected Readings,* ed. Max Marwick. Middlesex: Penguin Books.

Njaka, Mazi Elechukwu N. 1974. *Igbo Political Culture*. Evanston: Northwestern University Press.

Nwala, T. Uzodinma. 1985. *Igbo Philosophy*. Ikeja: Litermed Publications.

Ogbalu, F. C. 1965. *Ilu Igbo: The Book of Igbo Proverbs*. Onitsha: University Publishing Co.

Omoyajowo, Akin. 1971. *Witches?: A Study of the Belief in Witchcraft and of Its Future in Modern African Society*. Ibàdàn: Daystar Press.

Ong, Walter J. 1982. *Orality and Literacy: the Technologizing of the Word*. London: Routledge.

Ottenberg, Simon and Phoebe. 1962. Afikpo Markets: 1900–1960. In *Markets in Africa*, ed. Paul Bohannon and George Dalton. Evanston: Northwestern University Press.

Parkin, David, ed. 1985a. *The Anthropology of Evil*. Oxford: Basil Blackwell.

———. 1985b. Introduction. In *The Anthropology of Evil*, ed. Parkin. Oxford: Basil Blackwell.

———. 1985c. Entitling Evil: Muslims and Non-Muslims in Coastal Kenya. In *The Anthropology of Evil*, ed. Parkin. Oxford: Basil Blackwell.

Radcliffe-Brown, A. R., and Daryll Forde, eds. 1950. *African Systems of Kinship and Marriage*. Oxford: Oxford University Press.

Richards, Audrey. 1970. A Modern Movement of Witch-Finders. In *Witchcraft and Sorcery: Selected Readings*, ed. Max Marwick. Middlesex: Penguin Books.

Schapera, Isaac. 1970. Sorcery and Witchcraft in Bechuanaland. In *Witchcraft and Sorcery: Selected Readings*, ed. Max Marwick. Middlesex: Penguin Books.

Shelton, Austin J. 1968. Causality in African Thought: Igbo and Other. *Practical Anthropology* 15:157–69.

Smock, Audrey C. 1971. *Ibo Politics: The Role of Ethnic Unions in Eastern Nigeria*. Cambridge, Mass.: Harvard University Press.

Turner, Victor. 1957. *Schism and Continuity in an African Society: A Study of Ndembu Village Life*. Manchester: Rhodes-Livingston Institute.

———. 1967. *The Forest of Symbols: Aspects of Ndembu Ritual*. Ithaca, N.Y.: Cornell University Press.

———. 1968. *The Drums of Affliction: A Study of Religious Processes among the Ndembu of Zambia*. Oxford: Clarendon Press and the International African Institute.

Uchendu, Victor C. 1965. *The Igbo of Southeast Nigeria*. New York: Holt, Rinehart & Winston.

White, Luise. 1990. "Bodily Fluids and Usufruct: Controlling Property in Nairobi, 1917–1939." *Canadian Journal of African Studies* 24:418–38.

Williamson, Kay, ed. 1972. *Igbo-English Dictionary: Based on the Onitsha Dialect*. Benin City: Ethiope Publishing Corp.

Willis, Roy. 1985. Do the Fipa Have a Word for It? In *The Anthropology of Evil*, ed. David Parkin. Oxford: Basil Blackwell.

Wilson, Monica Hunter. 1970. Witch-Beliefs and Social Structure. In *Witchcraft and Sorcery: Selected Readings*, ed. Max Marwick. Middlesex: Penguin Books.

7

"Open the Wombs!":
The Symbolic Politics of Modern
Ngoni Witchfinding

Mark Auslander

THE TITLE OF THIS ESSAY—"Open the Wombs!"—is drawn from a day-long witchfinding ritual I attended, in May 1988, in a rural Ngoni community in Eastern Zambia.[1] In front of hundreds of onlookers, a usually respected Ngoni matriarch found herself confronted by a young male witchfinder who accused her of rendering barren the village's young women. Ignoring her denials, the spirit-possessed diviner advanced toward the old woman, asking "Is it good that your friends should not bear children?" He demanded, "Open the wombs! Go bring the charm"—and then publicly struck her with his powerful flywhisk, ordering that her hut be searched by his assistants. As the day proceeded, many other senior village women (and a much smaller group of senior men) were publicly denounced as witches, their huts violently searched and incriminating witchcraft horns "discovered" in their roofs and under their beds. They were subjected to intense public humiliation and severe beatings, their skins incised with numerous cuts into which powerful antiwitchcraft medicines were impressed. The witchfinder and his young male supporters proclaimed that by means of this elaborate rite—and similar rites in neighboring villages—witchcraft would once and for all be eliminated from Ngoni society. Only then would villagers be capable of "making money" safely and successfully.

I take this cry, "Open the wombs" (*kuvula mamimba* in ChiChewa), as an evocative point of departure for understanding the extraordinary witchfinding rituals of 1988, rituals that swept unexpectedly through the Mpezeni Ngoni chiefdoms of southern Chipata District and petered out just as unexpectedly in January 1989. For during these complex ceremonies, numerous Ngoni elders stood accused of "closing wombs"—not only in the literal sense of promoting biological infertility but, more generally, of destroying socioeconomic processes of reproduction. Allegedly, they had subverted proper relationships within and among the household, the village, the nation-state, and the regional economy. These "jealous" old people, it was repeatedly asserted, were responsible for many evils: among them, frequent miscarriages, sickness, and death; the growing AIDS pandemic; and the failure by young Ngoni men to prosper either as short-term labor migrants or to take successful advantage of state-sponsored maize-for-cash schemes.

At the same time, the shouted command, "Open the wombs," exemplifies for me my enduring difficulties in coming to terms with these memorable events—at analytic, moral, and political levels. During my second year of fieldwork in Chipata District, as I first heard distant rumors of resurgent witchfinding and then directly witnessed village cleansing rites, I became increasingly obsessed with the conundrums they presented: Why were elderly Ngoni women, ordinarily treated with such great respect in village communities, the principal targets of verbal and physical violence in public witchfinding? Why were these women, generally honored as the "mothers" and "grandmothers" of the community, episodically attacked for subverting the very processes of biological and social reproduction to which they had devoted their lifetimes? Why did so many rural Ngoni, at other times capable of articulating cogent political economic explanations for the manifold ills of rural Zambia in the late 1980s, come to insist so adamantly that the local community's salvation lay in ritually reworking the ostensibly perverted bodies of their senior kith and kin? Subsequent political developments in Zambia have only sharpened these seeming paradoxes: How can it be that the same communities that two years later enthusiastically supported the Movement for Multiparty Democracy in its successful challenge to Zambian President Kenneth Kaunda and the UNIP party-state could have devoted so much of their energies during 1988 to a tortuous and divisive hut-by-hut search for presumed witches?

I do not pretend that the following analysis of the events of 1988 fully answers, or even fully addresses, these difficult questions. Nonetheless, through unpacking the witchfinder's striking admonition to "open the wombs," I believe we may begin to bridge the apparent radical disjuncture between modern Ngoni witchfinding practices and regional politico-economic processes. As the essays in this volume seek to demonstrate, ideologies of ritual agency, witchcraft, spirit mediumship, and divination in contemporary Africa are not archaic or exotic phenomenon, somehow isolated or disjointed for historical processes of global political and economic transformation. Rather, these are moral discourses alive to the basic coordinates of experience, highly sensitive to contradictions in economy and society.

This is not to argue that we can or should propose seamless unified analyses of events such as mass witchfinding, reducing such processes to folk versions of Western social scientific analyses. The search for witches should not be rendered simply as an illusory quest for "objective" economic forces, framed in an indigenous "idiom." To be sure, for all their extraordinary features (arguably no less puzzling and disturbing to many rural Ngoni than to Western-trained ethnographers), the witchfinding processes discussed below can and should be carefully located in long-term local struggles to understand and control specifiable social and economic dislocations generated by the global economy. Yet witchfinding must equally be located in a complex local ideological and symbolic field, which has arisen out of long-term historical articulations between African and European systems of knowledge and practice. In the ideological field of modern rural Chipata District, the presence and power of "selfish witches" is virtually as universal a premise as the ultimate omnipotence of the Christian deity, the profound authority of the Old and New Testaments, or the assumed proclivity of selfish state officials in Lusaka to steal money and goods from the poor people of Zambia.

The challenge in interpreting Ngoni witchfinding is thus to render explicit its intimate engagement with the regional political economy and with the local politics of class, gender, and generation—without rendering witchfinding excessively "transparent," as explicable solely within a universaling rationalist or economistic framework. We must, in effect, lose sight neither of witchfinding's partial intelligibility nor of its partial opaqueness to both local and external observers.

Witchcraft and "Moral Geographies"

To meet this interpretive challenge, I find it helpful to deploy the heuristic device of a "symbolic topography" or "moral geography." For nearly a century, rural Ngoni communities have been enmeshed in the migratory political economy of Southern Africa. By the late 1980s they had developed complex inchoate maps, "moral geographies," of recruitment networks, informal migration routes, and shifting patterns of urban-rural employment—a world of mines, prisons, pass laws, and passports: of national highways and RENAMO guerillas; of cinemas and beer halls; and "at home," of cash cropping, and chemical fertilizer. Yet in comparison to printed two-dimensional cartographic texts (with which most Ngoni are at least passingly familiar), these symbolic topographies are highly fluid and contestable, suffused with apprehended dangerous flows of persons and substances. As the 1980s proceeded, rumors proliferated in Ngoni villages and townships that corrupt politicians had diverted fertilizer and food staples initially destined for Eastern Zambia to neighboring Malawi, in illicit "truck convoys." Itinerant preachers and witchfinders warned darkly that the "bus" of prosperity was passing villagers by, as witches (mainly female) stole their neighbors' hybrid maize and flew off to the Copperbelt on nocturnal celestial highways. Senior men claimed that economically independent market women were bringing AIDS into the village, from "roads" originating in South African gold mines and rural slums. Women, in turn—in ritual songs and oratory—decried men who traveled "aimlessly" on the region's roadways. Female-dominated *vivanda* cults of affliction sought to restore biological and agricultural fertility by fabricating complex spirit provinces in which all traces of motor vehicles and roadways were excluded. Taken together, these imaginatively conceived flows of commodities and persons constituted contesting moral geographies—symbolic "maps" of the unequal relations between and within peripheral rural communities, the Zambian industrial core, and the wider Southern African political economy.

Modern witchfinding movements are, among other things, ritual attempts to work upon these inchoate, partially apprehended "maps," to distill and transform structural relations between the local and the global, between rural households and metropolitan sites of production and state power. Among contemporary Ngoni they seek not only to scapegoat "enemies within" but also to appropriate powers of production and reproduction not generally available in rural Zambia. Thus, as we shall see, these highly synthetic ritual processes creatively incorporate and symbolically play upon not only indigenous symbolic repertoires of affliction and healing but also upon the technologies and routines of bureaucracy, schools and missions, clinical medicine, and state surveillance including highways and roadblocks.

As we would expect, these processes feed into local schisms, struggles, and power relations: witchfinding tangibly attempts to produce a particular kind of moral "map," arguing for the empowerment of young men at the expense of women and older members of the community, most especially elderly women. Indeed, central to my discussion will be an attempt to explain why the battle to "make wealth" through witchcleansing is so often waged upon the mature female body. At the same time, I seek to demonstrate that since witchcraft discourses are profoundly implicated in local and regional contradictions and conflicts, they are not homogeneous even within one particular community. As we shall see, the particular moral geography that the witchfinders sought to inscribe on physical bodies and on the body politic was neither final nor fully efficacious but was itself open to query and contestation.

Meeting Doctor Moses: The Approaching Storm

My interpretive model of witchfinding as a novel symbolic topography partly arises out of the circumstances of my initial encounters with public witchcleansing. Following my return to the field in October 1988 (after a period of convalescence in North America) I found southwestern Chipata District abuzz with accounts of a new witchfinder, "Doctor Moses" (often simply called "the Doctor" or "Moses"), who was slowly making his way through the villages of the area. As perceived from my fieldsite in one of the leading villages of a Southern Ngoni chiefdom, Moses' reported progress rather had the quality of an approaching thunderstorm and at times resembled persistent popular narratives about *RENAMO*-inflicted atrocities in adjacent war-torn Mozambique. "Moses" was spoken of as an unstoppable force making its way across the landscape, bringing a temporary reign of terror and social disruption until moving on to another village, all the time drawing ever nearer.[2] Young male friends and informants assured me that a cleansed village "looked different" after a witchfinding and that they could more easily traverse its environs now that its huts, fields, and pathways were free of noxious witchcraft substances. A once-familiar landscape, it appeared, was being subtly altered.

These accounts at first appeared impossible to confirm directly, as I was widely assured that no white person would be permitted access to the secret rites. But in late January 1988, my friend the village schoolteacher insisted that he and I attend Doctor Moses' rite at a village three kilometers distant. We crossed the rain-swollen Msipazi river, precariously lugging my video camera over low-hanging branches and scrambling up the muddy riverbank to a large village I had often passed through before. Indeed, the social topography of the community appeared entirely transformed: its 450 inhabitants were all gathered in two lines in the open village center, facing a swaying red-capped figure speaking in a high reedy voice, surrounded by a large noisy crowd from adjacent communities. After a few minutes, the red-capped figure sent word that I was to video the proceedings, following him and his entourage as they rushed to a hut on the village outskirts, from whose grass roof he uncovered an incriminating witchcraft horn. Thus began my year-long encounter with Doctor Moses and modern witchfinding, as I followed him and his disciples across the landscape of southwestern Chipata District, chronicling and videoing the acrimonious debates proceeding his arrival, the public cleansing rites themselves, and the ambiguous aftereffects of his visits.[3]

Moses' Witchfinding Ritual

Although the eleven witchfinding rituals I attended all followed the same basic structure, each had its own peculiar mixture of tragedy and hilarity, excitement and boredom, violence and poignancy. I wish to stress that these practices were considered extraordinary and fascinating by all Ngoni—in large measure because of the unpredictable physical violence directed against older people. Violence in Ngoni everyday experience is generally confined to domestic disputes or contexts in which alcohol is consumed, especially roadside beer gardens. Within the village itself, public aggression against elders is virtually unheard of.

To illustrate the complicated gender and generational politics of such events, I present a scene from one that took place in a village near the Great East Road that connects Lusaka to the eastern Province and Malawi. The village is renowned for its especially independent women, who frequently travel as entrepreneurs and smugglers along the national highways. This scene is noteworthy, among other reasons, for being one of the few cases in which Ngoni women (or indeed, any person) publicly challenged the authority of the witchfinder.

From mid-morning, the "Doctor" and his "disciples" had been searching the assembly, which had been divided into two long lines at the center of the village. The day had begun with songs by the witchfinders and speeches from the village leaders. In one line stood the males, with small boys in front then older boys, young men and finally the *madoda*, male elders. The parallel line for women— considerably longer—began with girls, followed by younger and middle-aged women, many carrying babies, and ended with the oldest women. Young men, recruited for the day from the village, wielded long sticks to keep the line silent and to hold back the large crowd of excited onlookers from surrounding villages, "Noise! Noise!" the young guards would cry out from time to time, waving their sticks at talkative onlookers and occasionally hitting them. Nothing, however, could dim the festive, carnivalesque atmosphere of the occasion.

As they approached the head of the line, the villagers had their feet washed with a foamy medicine, which was believed to protect them against bad substances deposited on paths by witches. Then they were called, one at a time, to stand quietly in a circle drawn in the sandy ground, legs straddling a nail driven into the ground at its center. There they were examined by the "Doctor," wearing a white, red and blue uniform, upon which was embroidered "Doctor Moses the Senior." The Doctor, who that morning had been possessed by the biblical spirit of "John,"[4] held out a small hand mirror called *"temperature"* (the English word was used) as each person entered the circle. In a high reedy voice, he then called out a number or series of numbers: most children and youths received a low digit, from one to ten, signifying their relative goodness and purity of heart. The disciples then took the young person off to the side and tattooed that number of marks onto his or her upper chest with a razor. Black antiwitchcraft medicine was then smeared into these cuts and pressed in with a large tool shaped like a rubber stamp.

As the day continued, the interrogations became more prolonged. Elders, especially older women, were repeatedly asked by the Doctor, "What do you have in your house?" "Where are your medicines?" Head down, each woman and man responded in a barely audible whisper: "There is nothing," or "only medicines for coughing," and so forth. Invariably dissatisfied with their answers, the Doctor sent them off with some of his disciples to their huts to bring back all their medicines. In some cases, Moses had gone off with his assistants to search the suspect's house; thatched roofs and mattresses had been torn apart, hut floors dug up. In all cases, the Doctor found damning evidence: a *nyanga*, a small witchcraft horn believed to be used to afflict and murder people. The exposed suspects were then forced to perform a dance said to be done by witches at graveyards, while holding aloft the incriminating horn. After another examination with the Doctor's magic mirror, they were assigned a long numerical string in English—for example, *"Fifteen point seventeen sta-roke* [stroke] *twenty-seven."* This number of tattoos were then razored onto various parts of their skin, and the black medicine stamped into the cuts. This medicine, it was explained, would "cure" the miscreant of future witchy activity; if not, any subsequent use of evil substances would cause his or her death.

In a few dramatic cases, Moses called out *"Zimya Lait-i!"* (Extinguish the light/fire!) at elderly suspects. Upon hearing this, his disciples surrounded the elder; old men were forced to lower their trousers, old women had been forced to untuck their wrap skirts. As the crowd roared with laughter, the Doctor made a special medicinal incision just below the base of the spine and pressed in a special powder with the stamp-like tool. This medicine, reserved for especially dangerous witches, was held to block up the powerful flames which emerge from the anuses of witches, propelling them through the night sky as they travel about on their malicious errands.

Suddenly, the Doctor blew his police whistle at an elderly woman standing before him in the circle, "Eleven sta-roke nine," he shouted. As the disciples began to razor the cuts onto her legs, a middle-aged woman behind her, named Sarah, objected aloud to this treatment. The only person to voice any protest that day, she muttered: *"Angatenda chitende tende"* (They are just cutting anyhow/ without purpose).

Great commotion ensued. As the disgusted Sarah attempted to walk away, the disciples trundled her back to the village center, where she was publicly interrogated by the Doctor: "What are you saying? Why didn't you do this work? [i.e., if you are such an expert, why didn't you conduct a witchfinding]? What medicines do you have?"

The usually feisty Sarah immediately lowered her head and spoke in the whispered voice adopted by villagers when dealing with senior men or State officials. *"Paliye chanu ziwa* [I don't know anything]," she murmured repeatedly. "I only have medicine for 'pressure' [high blood pressure]."

Her husband was called forward and interrogated: had he heard what his wife had done? "What wrong," asked the Doctor sharply, "have we done to be so insulted by a woman?" Although Moses continued his examination, many onlookers became convinced that the insulted diviner was now refusing to catch the evildoers passing before him; "known" elderly witches were being assigned absurdly low numbers. The male elders—who had thus far kept themselves to the background—began to intercede with the Doctor, pleading that the old woman's foolishness should not condemn the village to death. They promised they would write a letter to the chief, detailling Sarah's monstrous conduct. Sarah was brought forth to plead forgiveness: "I am saying continue with God's work. It is me who is wrong. You won't hear me talk," she promised.

After about forty-five minutes of negotiation, the Doctor relented. To the apparent relief of nearly everyone, he turned his attention to one of the village's oldest widows, a widely suspected witch. Her house was searched, and a horn and (ostensibly human) bones were uncovered. Shoved by the disciples and whipped with the Doctor's magic cow tail, she was forced to dance the witch's dance in the village center and received over fifty razored incisions. Her name was written down in the witchfinders' notebook, as Moses turned to the next suspect standing in the magic circle.

Doctor Moses

As I attended witchfindings like the above and interviewed participants and spectators over the course of 1988, Doctor Moses' background began to emerge. A man of Ngoni and Luvale parentage in his early thirties, he had practiced healing and witchfinding throughout rural and urban Zambia and Zimbabwe since the late 1970s. In mid-1987, he announced that he would begin to operate in the southern Ngoni chiefdoms of Chipata District, where he had hitherto been relatively unknown.[5] For the next eighteen months, his operations were generally confined to southwestern

Chipata District, where he "cleansed" about twenty-five villages. When not detecting witches he was usually to be found at or near the principal roadside motels and bars of the area, supervising his small motor transport business or checking on his commercial maize farm in a Northern Ngoni chiefdom.

The arrival and activities of Doctor Moses thoroughly captured the local imagination. Bitter and prolonged controversy always preceded his arrival at any village. By and large, headmen and the *madoda* (elder male councillors) opposed his visits, while the *anyamata* (young men aged roughly eighteen to thirty-five) lobbied intensively for the witchcleansing to be carried out. In some cases, the latter overrode the resistance of the headmen by appealing directly to the local chief, who would ultimately sanction the rite.[6] In addition to generational differences, such disputes came to be implicated in a wide range of other local political processes, such as struggles over land use and succession to office.

As in parts of Zimbabwe, contemporary Eastern Zambian witchfinders tend to be loosely associated with the so-called Zionist independent churches of Southern and Central Africa. Most Ngoni dismiss Zionism as a small, bizarre, and troublesome (if not downright dangerous) sect. As "people of the Spirits" (*Mzimu*), Zionists are widely suspected by established Christian Zambian ministers of being satanic, doctrinally unsound, and ignorant of biblical interpretation. As Jean Comaroff observes of South African Tshidi Zionists, "their primary mnemonic is lodged not in Scripture but in the physical body and its immediate spatiotemporal location" (1985:200).

Paradoxically, it appears to be precisely the uncanny proclivity of the Zionists for ritually working upon the body, and space and time that renders them so highly appropriate for combating the scourge of witchcraft—which, as we shall see, is experienced as a fundamental perversion in space, time, and bodily integrity. Furthermore, Zionist prophets, healers, and preachers travel extensively along the highways and railroads of Central and Southern Africa. As both "men of the spirits" and highly mobile "men of the road," they are seen as capable of crossing over geographical and spiritual borders—borders closed to ordinary Zambians. The witchfinding rites have thus emerged as a key site of political struggle between the diviners (and their allies) and the lay and ecclesiastical hierarchies of the mainstream churches, in particular the Reformed Church of Zambia, which follows its parent Dutch Reformed Church in condemning such rites as "satanic."[7]

Defying the opposition of the established churches' clergy and lay leadership, the young males who campaigned for a cleansing devoted themselves assiduously to the task of collecting "donations" from each household for the witchfinder's fee, about 600 *kwacha* per village. This amount was substantial: approximately the sum a village man might save by working three months of short-term urban employment as a security guard or bricklayer in Chipata Township, enough to purchase sufficient hybrid maize seeds and chemical fertilizer to cultivate one hectare.

The collection of money was often a drawn-out, acrimonious affair. The young men kept careful records of which households had made the required donation.[8] Christian villagers who refused to pay—or who implied they might not attend the ceremony—risked accusations of being witches themselves and sometimes became the targets of physical violence.

Since the money from the compulsory donations was usually insufficient to meet the witchfinder's fee, the young men generally engaged in agricultural piecework to make up the difference. These work sessions were characterized by the high degree of enthusiasm, joviality, and male camaraderie that ordinarily was reserved only for "traditional" hunting. As they walked together to and from the field, the youths would boisterously sing the popular songs of the witchfinder and speak of themselves as an *"impi"* (regiment) and *"Freedom Fighters wachingoni"* (Ngoni Freedom Fighters), heroically making sacrifices for the good of the whole community. Even after most of the money had been collected, the hired witchfinder might repeatedly delay his coming because of other commitments or because, it would be widely rumored, he feared witchly conspiracies to assassinate him in that particular village. The young local organizers thus would often pay repeated visits to his home, pleading with him to come hurriedly.

Witchfinding in Ngoniland: Historical Background

As nearly all adult Ngoni noted, Moses was only the most recent of a long line of witchfinders to have operated in Ngoni and neighboring communities. Mass witchcleansing has had an erratic history in Chipata District (known as Fort Jameson District, 1900–64). In the years following the British South Africa Company's violent occupation of Ngoniland in 1898, Dutch Reformed missionaries and colonial officers suppressed the poison ordeal and other witchfinding rituals. Nonetheless, archival records and oral histories indicate that from the early 1920s witchfinders have periodically been brought in (usually from Malawi or Mozambique) by the Ngoni royal establishment to cleanse villages. Most widely remembered are the *Bamucapi* healers of the 1930s, who originated in Nyasaland and who operated over much of rural and peri-urban Northern Rhodesia. Over the past seventy years, antiwitchcraft movements and itinerant prophetic figures have surfaced intermittently in rural Eastern Zambia, few lasting over a year.

Their activities seem to be part of a general class of witchcraft eradication rites that have emerged throughout much of Sub-Saharan Africa over the past century or so.[9] By and large, the development of these rituals appears to have accompanied the incorporation of rural African communities into colonial capitalist labor markets. As Mary Douglas (1963) and others (e.g., Van Binsbergen 1981; Willis 1970) have noted, such colonial and postcolonial movements tend to differ dramatically from precolonial processes of divination and treatment. In contrast to late precolonial poison ordeals, the object of the modern ceremonies is usually not to kill witches but to cure them by confiscating their magical paraphernalia, and by medicinally rendering them incapable of doing evil. As this suggests, these ceremonies promise the wholesale eradication of witchcraft while making it possible to reincorporate the accused back into the community.

Many Ngoni villages have gone for ten to thirty years without being "cleansed" by mass divination. For most of the time, witchcraft is an "open secret" (see Munn 1986) in Chipata District: privately acknowledged by virtually all people, it varies from being a trivial annoyance to causing absolute terror. Yet it is rarely the subject of public discussion, being generally confined to conversations on paths, in fields, or in huts. An afflicted person who suspects witchcraft will usually be quietly counseled to go to a local healer for protective medication.[10] If references are made to mystical evil in public oratory, they tend to be heard at funerals or in disputes; and even in these contexts they are handled with subtle ambiguity by experienced speakers.

Ngoni Witchcraft Inferences: Fragmentations of Space, Time, and the Body

Why, from time to time, do young Ngoni men angrily reject the more cautious treatment of witchcraft by their elders and call for public, violent cleansings like the one described above? To understand the appeal of these rites, it is necessary (i) to look to the underlying symbolism of Ngoni witchcraft inferences, and (ii) to locate the eradication movements in the political and economic context of rural Eastern Zambia in the late 1980s.

Although the contemporary ideological field in rural Eastern Zambia is the site of numerous overt and covert disputes, certain premises appear to be nearly universally shared. As noted above, these include a belief in the omnipotence of the Christian deity, the profound importance and authority of the Old and New Testaments, the existence of *mizimu* (often glossed as "spirits"), and the ubiquitous presence of *bafwiti*, malicious persons prone to cause affliction and death through the operation of witchcraft (*ufwiti*). It should be noted, however, that these various premises do not all carry precisely the same discursive weight: most of my Ngoni friends and informants will willingly discuss at length biblical narratives or Christian church practice, but tend toward silence in issues of witchcraft or "evil spirits." The following brief account of Ngoni witchcraft inferences is thus highly abstracted, drawn from many conversations and observations in rural Ngoniland.

Among rural Ngoni, "witch beliefs"—to invoke Monical Wilson's oft-quoted dictum—can be fairly characterized as "the standardized nightmares of a group" (1951:313). As in many African contexts, the witch is imagined to be profoundly amoral, a person consumed with greed who excessively accumulates without redistributing to kin or clients; in so doing, he or she subverts the norms of reciprocity and circulation.

For many earlier social anthropologists, the relevant "group" in Wilson's dictum was the ethnically homogeneous "tribe." Witchcraft beliefs, it was held, varied from ethnic group to ethnic group as a function of contrasts in social organization. But this approach did not take account of differences within African communities, nor of the arguments over witchcraft sparked by their growing internal contradictions. As we now know, witchcraft discourses may divide a "tribe" along internal lines of social cleavage, lines that change as history unfolds. We shall see below, for example, that virtually all rural Ngoni in the late 1980s shared basic sensibilities about the omnipresence of witchcraft; but that young and old men had quite different ideas as to who the real witches are.

Let us begin with the shared assumptions. Ngoni frequently stress that any act of giving or sharing may potentially trigger later dangerous acts of witchcraft or poisoning by those left out. Reciprocity builds up social relationships and ultimately enables social reproduction, as in bridewealth transactions. By contrast, the witch—as the "excluded other" (Munn 1990:3)—who has been denied gifts, commodities, or assistance—is held to reciprocate subversively, by endangering the community. As this suggests, he or she may be represented as a marginal being excluded from redistributive networks or as an avaricious, secretly wealthy hoarder.[11]

The perversion of exchange and production by witchcraft is embodied in the terrifying image of the semianimate witchcraft horn (*nyanga*), a kind of antiproduction and antiexchange object. An extension of the witch's selfhood, it is believed to fly through the night sky from the hut of its owner to the body of the intended victim, causing illness, misfortune, or death. Significantly, many Ngoni assert that a horn is bought for one cow, nowadays the standard opening bridewealth or legalization payment, which guarantees that the children of a union will belong to the line of the cattle-giving family. Whereas marriage beasts ideally "open the wombs" of women, the witchcraft horn in effect "closes" them, rupturing biological and social reproduction.

Thus exchange and production—which constitute the lived-in Ngoni world of the daytime—imply a parallel world, largely operating at night. This is a terrifying world of inverted production and reproduction. Excluded by their nefarious avarice from regular diurnal transactions, witches enter the night to promote sterility, miscarriage, and infanticide. Too lazy to work, witches profit from the blood of others; they disinter corpses and use their genitals to capture more victims for their monstrous appetites.

Why, then, are elders—and especially elderly women—the usual targets of witchcraft accusations and of cleansings? The answer, I suggest, lies partly in Ngoni cultural preoccupations with negative production; in particular, with the gendered and generational bases of social exclusion.

Let us first consider the generational bases of witchcraft. For youths, elders may be said to constitute a class of "excluded others," prone to subverting the positive potential of the young. As "less beautiful," less able to procreate, and closer to death, old people are held to be deeply jealous of the good looks, procreative abilities, vitality and energy of the next generation.[12] Children speak of the severe challenge of living up to their responsibilities to provide for less energetic and less productive members of the community; "We can never give them everything they expect," is a frequent complaint. As omnipresent "excluded others," it is assumed that elders direct witchcraft at young adults, or at young adults' children. For the aged are thought to have secret powers of their own, associated with the knowledge they have gained over their long lives—in the village, on the mines, and in far-away towns.

As with generation, so with gender; women, too, may be said to constitute a class of "excluded others," being debarred from most public activities, be they bridewealth negotiations, credit extension schemes or village politics. Men who do not share resources to their womenfolk risk the negative reciprocity of witchcraft—as do those who routinely expropriate cash earned by their wives, or who physically abuse them. In polygamous households a woman may well remain silent if her husband favors a co-wife or a co-wife's children with extra money, clothing, or food. But, many Ngoni men told me, the excluded one will almost surely be driven by her anger to retaliate against her husband or those he holds dear.

According to Ngoni men (and to a lesser extent, Ngoni women as well), females are more prone than males to remember wrongs and to pursue vengeance without hesitation. Men are held, as a rule, to act upon the world more deliberately, and only after consultation with others. Indeed, their deliberateness is understood as a function of their authority; "Men's work," as older males present it, is to manage jural and economic relations. They are thus supposed to behave "calmly" and "slowly," since their actions have repercussions for the community as a whole.

Women's work by contrast is implicated in a different kind of temporality. Much of female labor is of the here and now and must be done quickly and immediately. Delays would lead to all sorts of bad consequences: children would not be born; water would not be fetched; fields would not be planted, weeded, or harvested; maize would not be pounded; beer would not be brewed or food cooked; and people would not be fed. In most everyday contexts women's capacity to act directly and quickly is a positive quality. In the alternate world of witchcraft, however, this same capacity—or, rather, the tendency to react without careful deliberation—has dangerous implications. Ngoni of both genders agree that females are the most vicious and dangerous witches, since they attack without hesitation or remorse. As two oft-quoted proverbs express it, *"Mfiti yacikazi sibwelela"* (The woman witch never turns back), and *"Mfiti yacikazi ilibe chifundu"* (A woman witch is without mercy). Ngoni often explain this principle by citing the hunting practices of lions. The male, it is stressed, is hesitant, indecisive, and may even decide not to attack its prey. In contrast, the lioness, the primary huntress of the pride, it said never to hesitate but always to attack swiftly and decisively. The analogy is highly evocative: witches are sometimes spoken of as *banyama,* people who nocturnally turn themselves into lions.

This association of lions and women is also partly rooted in the status of Ngoni as comparative "strangers" to Eastern Zambia. The mobile Mpezeni Ngoni polity only settled in what is now Eastern Zambia in the 1870s. In the process, they conquered and incorporated numerous local Chewa and Nsenga communities and married their women. In principle, these women—along with many men from conquered central African communities—were rapidly incorporated into the royal-centered Ngoni fictive agnatic sociopolitical structure. Yet the nagging sense still remains in much male Ngoni discourse that women and their descendants have especially intimate relations with the powers of the local landscape—especially with its terrestrial lion spirits and aquatic python spirits—and can regulate agrarian and biological fertility. This privileged knowledge includes female initiation, midwifery, contraceptive and abortificant techniques, and control over male sexuality; an extensive range of *materia medica,* known primarily to females, may arouse men or render them impotent.

Ngoni men in general—and younger men in particular—express ambivalence over women's privileged control over matters of sexuality and reproduction; they constantly assert that women are liable to abuse these powers, undercutting male authority and subverting the reproduction of households. For example, a man who is often out of the village as a labor migrant may attribute his wife's miscarriage to a conspiracy between her and her older female relatives to cover up her adultery during his absence. Alternately, as in the opening scene, a "jealous" elder woman may be accused of "closing" her womb without her consent, through nocturnal witchcraft.[13]

While the gender and generational bases of witchcraft have endured for a long time, the particular forms taken by Ngoni beliefs and practice have been affected by historical processes of the short run. First and foremost, they have been conditioned by the general collapse of the copper-oriented Zambian urban economy, which has precipitated an ever-deepening national crisis from the early 1970s onward. The period saw increasing rates of population return to rural Eastern Zambian communities, where village dwellers engaged in cash cropping on a small scale, balanced with some gardening and local-strain maize cultivation for domestic consumption. From the late 1970s onward, the state has pressured smallholders to grow hybrid maize using chemical fertilizer and to sell their produce to the government-run marketing board. By the late 1980s, however, Ngoni farmers were bitterly exasperated with the chronically mismanaged and corrupt state agrarian system, which seemed to fail them in every possible way. Each year, they were promised quick cash wealth, but each year the majority have found themselves without sufficient seed or fertilizer for the coming season. Hunger and debt became endemic threats.

Nonetheless, each year at least a few families in every community managed the maize-for-cash system fairly well, in large measure because of close kinship-based connections to the party-state patronage system, access to motorized transport, and so forth. Their healthy crops were an infuriating mystery to less successful villagers, who found themselves devoting more and more of their labor time each season to piecework for their more prosperous neighbors.

These inequalities have been translated largely into the terms of generation and gender, at least by younger men. Older people, especially former migrant males, struggle to maintain multigenerational households intact under their control, hoping to achieve prosperity while avoiding fragmentation. By paying bridewealth on behalf of their adult sons, fathers seek to retain their loyalty and to ensure that they contribute to the political and economic activities of the domestic group. In song and speech older men express fear that their children—caught up in the rage for chemical fertilizer and other commodities—will bewitch or poison them and sell their cattle for cash, undermining the proper order of social hierarchy, exchange, and reproduction.

For their part, young Ngoni men tend to desire autonomy. Most invest their money and labor in cash cropping exclusively; some speak of eventually acquiring a "transport business"—which would allow them to move back and forth between rural and urban contexts as "big men." For them, the barrier to their economic betterment is not the Zambian State or the International Monetary Fund but the elders of the community, and the moral, political, and economic obligations on which they insist. Old people, say the youths, resent their potential to succeed in a highly monetized economy: old men, they say, refuse to sell off cattle for much-needed cash. Women, in particular, are accused of hoarding the income they earn from marketing and brewing ventures. Inasmuch as they retain unto themselves goods and powers, allegedly impeding life-giving reciprocity and circulation, the elders are portrayed in the classic image of the witch.

Modern Ngoni discourses about witchcraft, witchfinding, age, and gender are also bound up in another central feature of modern Zambian culture and political economy—the world of the paved road or "tarmac." The romance of the national highways—celebrated in conversation, oral narratives, and song—offers symbolic commentary on the complex urban-rural networks that emerged in postcolonial Central Africa. Village-based Ngoni men and women of all ages express endless fascination with the road: with its informal economy of large and small-scale transport operators, its smugglers and black marketeers, prostitutes and con artists, she-been queens and beer gardens. As the virtually bankrupt state ceases to be the supreme source of wealth and power, popular mythology has increasingly come to portray the tarmac and the world through which it courses as a nearly magical pathway to wealth.

As elsewhere in Africa, however, the road is also seen as profoundly dangerous, as the horrific site of bloody road accidents, massacres by RENAMO guerillas, sabotage by South African spies, and other less visible disasters. At least among males, there is a distinctly *gendered* tone to much of this imagery, which plays upon the cosmological dangers of unregulated and extraordinary mobility. According to national politicians, it is female black marketeers—illicitly traversing the country's roads—who are the source of hyperinflation and chronic shortages of essential commodities. Significantly, this anxiety is projected onto the physical condition of women. Zambian men increasingly blame the AIDS epidemic on the uncontrolled passage of female entrepreneurs up and down the highways. These "free" women, whose movement and sexuality escape male authority and encompassment, are said to become pregnant and self-abort continually, thus altering their "wombs" in such a manner as to infect with AIDS those who cohabit with them.

These national male discourses have fed the disquiet of Ngoni men over the cosmological and economic autonomy of their womenfolk. In mid-1988, men's speeches at the public conclusion of female initiation rituals began to admonish the wives and daughters of the village to stay away from the "road," as it was from there that women were purportedly "bringing AIDS" into Ngoni households. This injunction was a practical impossibility; among other things, most households depended on the marketing and smuggling ventures of women along the highways to earn enough for hybrid seeds and chemical fertilizer. Not surprisingly, witchcraft accusations often were leveled by men against older females who subsidized profitable maize cultivation through their entrepreneurial activities; many young males, comparing their failed crops to the abundant yields of these women, asked rhetorically how "just a woman" could attain such wealth if not by mystical means.

Witchfinding Revisited

Let us return, then, to the symbolism of witchcleansing, to Doctor Moses' effort to redress disruptions caused by mystical evil. Note, first, that for the purposes of the ritual people are arranged spatially according to the two principal axes of social organization salient to witchcraft—gender and age. The Doctor creates, in effect, a moral "map" of the village, clearly exposing to public gaze just where the malefactors are primarily located: at the rear of the two lines, where the village elders stand, and especially at the rear of the left line, the line of women. The symbolic deployment of space also points toward the crucial organizing principle of the rite. Modern Ngoni witchfinding is profoundly different from precolonial Ngoni divination processes, in which the diviner functioned as an extension of the monarch and served the interests of the royal clan. Today, the power to transform the world and generate wealth does not reside within the remnants of the local kingdom, but is instead associated with distant sites: with institutions and practices of the nation-state, with Christian churches, with highways, with South Africa and the great universe beyond.

Thus, in seeking to remedy the twin evils of physical and economic affliction, modern Central African witchfinders rely on valued *foreign* substances, those associated with higher-level political and economic process. These are pressed upon or into the bodies of the afflicted The *Bamucapi* movement of the 1930s—the principal model for contemporary Ngoni witchfinding—used preparations popularly believed to have been purchased from whites in neighboring Nyasaland (Richards 1935). Like their modern counterparts, these witchcleansers inserted the "European" medicines into African bodies in the interest of restoring vitality and wealth to the local community.

Appropriately, these foreign substances are embodied through practices associated with European-style secular and mission rituals: for example, the straight lines of the *Bamucapi* cleansing appear to have emulated colonial census-taking and taxation-assessing techniques, as did the diviners' proclivity for writing down the names of the accused. Modern cleansings also recall mass inoculation and vaccination campaigns, cattle dippings, mission baptismal rites, and similar routines. In Moses' redemptive ceremony, the lined-up villagers initially had their feet washed in a liquid preparation, believed to protect them from noxious witchcraft lines drawn in paths, and then received medicated incisions to render them incapable of receiving or practicing witchcraft.

Similarly, Moses' magic mirror, called (in English) "Temperature," recalls the mercury thermometers of government clinics and hospitals.[14] As at clinics, villagers wait for hours in straight lines before being "examined" and "treated" by the witchfinder, who assigns a precise numerical value to the "health" (i.e., the moral state) of each individual. At clinics, a high temperature, read off as two digits followed by a decimal point and another digit, indicates illness and the need for active therapy; preferably hypodermic injections, that most Zambians hold to be more efficacious than oral medication. Similarly, Moses insists that a high number—such as "thirty-seven point fifteen"—read in his magic mirror, proves that the examinee is in a perilous moral state and requires treatment. His ritual technique, in short, synthesizes classic Southern and Central African medicinal incisions with Western clinical practice.

Witchfinding and Roadblocks

The primary symbolic model for Moses, however, was the roadblock or security checkpoint, a ubiquitous feature of postcolonial Zambian highways since the Zimbabwean independence struggle. Through his mystical activity, the world of the city, the state, and the "tarmac"—normally remote from village life—was brought into the heart of the community. Its center was reorganized into a kind of obstructed highway; two straight, parallel lines moved slowly forward, were searched as they passed through the ritual barrier, and were then either detained or allowed to move on. At government roadblocks and customs checkpoints, officials seek to regulate the movement of persons and objects, in the interest of state military and economic "security." In a similar way, the goal of Moses' cleansings is to locate and confiscate "horns," the witchly familiars through which witches threatened the collective well-being.

Doctor Moses evoked the experience of the roadblock in other ways as well. In the course of the cleansing, he gave each person a magical version of the government-issued National Registration Card, which all Zambian citizens must present at security checkpoints. Just as the state photographs, interrogates, and classifies all Zambians for their cards, the diviner used his hand mirror (itself the size of an I.D.) to capture the image of each individual. Having "photographed" everyone, the diviner—like his official counterparts—then certified in writing whether they were "good" or "evil." Long numerical strings assigned to accused witches were also reminiscent of the long National Registration numbers assigned to each citizen. These were then inscribed in razored lines on the accused's skin, which itself became a kind of bureaucratic document upon which moral evaluations were imprinted.

Furthermore, the potent antiwitchcraft medicines were impressed into these incisions with a large object modeled on the ubiquitous rubber stamp, which closes all transactions at state offices, banks, hospitals, clinics, and border crossings. All of these usually entail interminable waits in line before one finally stands before the stamp-wielding official—where, recall villagers, matters are suddenly conducted with bewildering speed. Likewise, Moses' clients stand queued up, often for hours, before they are swiftly dealt with by being assigned a number and "stamped." Like a visa stamped in a passport officially verifies and authorizes passage from one country to another, this act of medicinal stamping authorizes and enables passage from one moral state to another.

But the stamp evoked more than geographical and moral transitions. For Ngoni males its most important association was with the passes and pass books that regulated the movement of migrant labor throughout Southern Africa. Older men, recalling the mysterious and degrading rituals of apartheid, emphasized the arbitrary power of the stamp, when wielded by white policemen or mine officials: one stamp might suddenly separate friends or relatives, determining whether a man would be allowed to work or would be sent to an impoverished rural area.

The witchfinders played upon precisely these seemingly arbitrary features of rubber-stamping and bureaucratic rituals. Among Ngoni, witches—especially female ones—were particularly feared for their unpredictability and ferocious anger. As in many Southern and Central African healing processes, the diviners thus sought in effect to counteract the violence of the witch through their own symbolically elaborated violence, which was presented as the just anger of the morally self-righteous. Using the most potent signs of state power, they emulated soldiers and state officials, who are free to chastise, threaten, and even beat old people at roadblocks and in other situations.

In this sense, witchfinding may be understood as an attempt by young males to preempt the mystical power of their elders and the structures of gerontocratic authority, by constituting a kind of masculine "imagined community." Just as the police and army control movement along national highways in search of South African "spies," "subversives," and women "black marketeers," so the diviners, playing upon images of state military prowess, sought to regulate movement within a novel ritual space in order to search out the "real" internal enemies. In so doing, these young men confronted their elders; in particular, they probed women's bodies and living spaces, hoping to "open their wombs" and gain access to the fabulous wealth associated with the "tarmac" and the wide world beyond.

The Efficacy of the Ritual

Yet, how effective were the young men in seizing control of the capacities of their elders? In the short term, the youths were enormously pleased with the ceremony. Most reported that they no longer dreamed of witch-sent fires coming into their huts, and no longer suffered from impotence, fatigue, and other illness. Instead, they dreamed of beautiful maidens and of cattle, and felt healthier, more energetic, and more confident about the future. For older men, on the other hand, the consequences of the witch-finding were decidedly mixed. For a few, the physical and psychic scars of public humiliation never went away. But for the class of elders as a whole, and for many of the village leaders in particular, the witchfinding seemed to have no long-term impact—either on their status or on their power. Here, as elsewhere, the youths found, to their dismay, that experienced and charismatic elders soon regained control over village public affairs. Recall the crisis after Sarah's protest: within minutes, the village headman and his principal aides had effectively reasserted their authority, interceding on behalf of the entire community for the diviner to continue with his work. Indeed, some prominent men seem even to have turned their "uncovering" to their advantage. The confirmation that they owned potent "medicines" made them even more feared than before—especially when sentiment began to spread through the area that Moses was not so thorough (or honest) a witchcleanser after all.

Similarly, while a number of older women were deeply traumatized by the violent ceremonies, most appeared to recuperate with time. Female church organizations, at first devastated by the accusations against their senior members, regrouped and once again became the backbone of local efforts to build schools, hold revival meetings, and so forth. Girls' initiation continued under the supervision of older women—sometimes the very women who had been publicly beaten and humiliated a few months earlier. In short, the control over sexuality and reproduction, like the capacity to "open wombs," remained ultimately in female hands.

Finally, women played a major part in discrediting Moses, causing his eventual departure from southwestern Chipata District. Sarah's public attack on his legitimacy might have been extraordinary. But many others campaigned quietly to keep him and his ilk out of neighboring communities. At grinding mills, at small markets, and along the Great East Road, women told each other about Moses' abuses of old people. This intelligence, which also made its way through women's church networks in the area, gradually produced a widespread sensibility that the Doctor was an ungodly, selfish scoundrel; all the more so after he was caught having sex with "another man's wife" at his favorite roadside motel. By early 1989, even the young male supporters of Moses had to acknowledge that somehow a consensus against him had filtered throughout the district.

Witchfinding and "The Informal Sector"

As the case of Doctor Moses illustrates, the complex dynamics of power and resistance in modern Africa thoroughly defy such classic analytic dichotomies as state and peasant, core and periphery, the global and the local. Consider, for example, the ambiguous ramifications of state power in Moses' ritual. On the one hand, the state, especially in its military and "Party youth" incarnations, presents a powerful paradigm of young male empowerment for those youths otherwise disillusioned with the promises of independent nationhood. Yet although Moses and his ilk adapt and redeploy important signifying practices associated with the state, they are scarcely signs of the state; in many respects the witchfinders are more closely related to certain interstitial figures—the notoriously corrupt "big men"—who ambiguously mediate socioeconomic relations between smallholder communities, the Party-State patronage structure, and the global political economy.

Moses, after all, brings no long-term routines of bureaucratic discipline; his disruptive therapy lasts only a day or two before he departs (rather to the relief of all concerned) taking the confiscated horns and his unsavory persona away with him. His visits have a certain carnivalesque quality, full of broad, even scatological, humor, as well as unexpected displays of petulance, anger, and violence by the witchfinder and his disciples. During a cleansing, conventional structures of generational authority are largely suspended, as youths chastise their elders with insults, even at times with physical blows. And as noted above, elder male political control of the community is usually reestablished within days.

These short-term, rather anarchic features of the witchfinder's *bricolage* are themselves highly significant. For Moses' enthusiastic young male followers were not oriented toward entering the dominant Party-State patronage structure with which they were profoundly disillusioned. They do not aspire simply to be good smallholder hybrid maize producers within the confines of the state-regulated market and cooperative union system. Rather, their imaginations are most often fired by tales of striking it rich in the informal sector—in black marketing, smuggling, and transport ventures—combined with lucrative commercial farming projects. They speak of wanting to be independent economic actors, encumbered neither by gerontocratic authority nor by the extensive redistributive obligations of rural kinship networks. The stories and fantasies of economic success they most often tell among themselves are of sudden get-rich schemes, of dramatic cons, scams, and scores by South Asian merchants or Zambian "big men."

I suggest that the precipitancy and jerky unpredictability of the witch-cleansing rites presents in microcosm the imagined precipitancy and excitement of the transnational African informal economy, which is encompassed neither by international boundaries nor by formal governmental structures. Indeed, like fabled transport magnates and smugglers, many modern African witchfinders over the course of their careers move from country to country, just as they move in and out of governmental favor. Consider the case of Chikanga, the famous witchfinder described by Redmayne (1970) in the earlier 1960s. Exiled from newly independent Malawi, he spent much of the ensuing three decades in Southern Rhodesia and South Africa, before returning at the end of the 1980s to a flourishing practice in northern Malawi—this time under the apparent aegis of the Malawi Congress party. Like Moses, Chikanga is also reported to use a rubber stamp in his therapeutic practice.[15] Like Moses, Chikanga thus may make use of the signifying practices and administrative organs of the state from time to time, without any long-term adherence to either a particular regime or to the nationalist program in general.

Indeed, it could be cogently argued that Moses and his fellow witch-finders are more closely attuned to the major trends of late twentieth-century African history—that is, to periodic popular withdrawals from the state, to the proliferation of complex informal economic networks, and to the emergence of global popular cultures—than are the One-Party State regimes that alternately attempt to suppress or co-opt these charismatic healers.[16]

Conclusion

As we have seen, even these popular interstitial figures—who seem to embody and exemplify so much of the modern African experience—may themselves be subject to censure, subversion, and resistance from unexpected, ostensibly disenfranchised, quarters. For what is perhaps most striking about the case of Doctor Moses—and perhaps all symbolic processes of this kind in the subordinated communities of the Third World—is its strange mix of overdetermined and indeterminate features. Local struggles, both ritual and secular, waged to regain control over a world run amuck, tend to play ambiguously into local conditions and cleavages, local patterns of domination and difference. In the Ngoni witchcleansing of the late 1980s, old tensions of generation came to the fore in a manner that has been well documented in other African colonial and postcolonial contexts, expressing themselves in physical, symbolically charged violence against "enemies within." This symbolic violence—like all signifying practices—drew at once from distant and proximate elements: the culture of precolonial kingship, the ideology of the modern Zambian nation-state, Christian mission values, the folklore of the motorway, and even the draconian procedures of the South African superstate. In constructing their "bodily politics," the witchfinders played mimetically upon these sources; in particular, they seized upon appropriately potent corporeal and disciplinary routines to empower their new moral order and to make tangible their novel social geography.

Yet, in the long term, such local efforts to regain control over the world are often thwarted in serendipitous and indeterminate ways, by the very subjects on whom they seek to act. The human body, after all, is never simply the silent, passive recipient of meanings others try to inscribe upon it. Even at the most local, "subordinate" levels of the world system, zones of comparative cultural autonomy may emerge, simultaneously reclaiming and reworking the corporeal body and the body politic. And so states and witchfinders alike may find themselves subtly subverted as they strive to remake people in their own image. As the struggle over witchcraft and witchcleansing among the Ngoni so poignantly suggests, people do not easily surrender control over the material and symbolic production and reproduction of their lives.

Notes

1. Previous versions of this paper were presented at the 1989 African Studies Association meetings, the Conference on Ritual, Power and History (Committee on African and African American Studies, University of Chicago, February 1990), and the Yale Anthropology Department Seminar, January 1991. Field and archival research in Zambia was conducted from January 1987–April 1989 and was supported by grants from the National Science Foundation, the Wenner-Gren Foundation, and I. I. E. Fulbright. Writing support was provided by the Charlotte W. Newcombe Foundation and the Harry F. Guggenheim Foundation.

Many people have commented on previous drafts of this paper. I especially acknowledge the generous editorial assistance of John Comaroff as well as careful readings from Adam Ashforth, the anonymous external reviewer for the University of Chicago Press, George Bond, Jean Comaroff, Gillian Feely-Harnik, Ellen Schattschneider, and members of my dissertation writing group—Misty Bastian, Adeline Masquelier, Debra Spitulnik, and Brad Weiss.

2. Indeed, a number of elderly informants described the tumultuous preparations for Moses' visits as "like a RENAMO raid."

3. I believe that my extensive videoing and still photography of the witchfindings may have, ironically, furthered my access to these rituals, which were in prin-

ciple illegal under Zambian law and are grounds for excommunication or severe discipline in many established Zambian churches. Doctor Moses and his followers appeared to value greatly the photos I gave them. On several occasions the Doctor indicated his hope to use these materials in a television series, which he hoped to broadcast eventually on Zambian or Zimbabwean television. As noted below, the symbolism of optics, photography, and telecommunications is of critical significance in these rites: my presence videoing and photographing the proceedings unquestionably played into these symbolic dynamics.

I continue to ponder the ethnical dimensions of my decision to video the witch-findings, given the extreme sensitivities involved. Permission to video was always obtained from chiefs and village authorities, but I recognize that in a Ngoni village this procedure does not guarantee individual consent on the part of all members of the community. At times I was so disturbed by the verbal and physical abuse of suspected malefactors that I turned off the video camera and walked away. In a few cases I believe the presence of the camera prevented verbal abuse from escalating into physical violence. In the vast majority of cases, the witchfinding process appeared so deeply absorbing to participants that my presence and that of the video camera may not have mattered much either way. Yet, on some occasions I unquestionably increased the anguish of participants: in one case, a woman whose husband's house had just been searched, cried out at me, "Why are you photographing me now, when I am old and ugly?" I immediately turned off the camera for the duration of the rite.

I have, of course, refrained from showing photographs or videos of witchfinding to anyone who might have direct knowledge of the participants, such as government officials or church ministers. I remain uncertain, however, as to the propriety of showing these video materials in the classroom, in seminars, or in professional meetings. I plan to address these issues in a forthcoming paper.

4. The medium later stated that this spirit was both John the Baptist and John the Apostle.

5. As it later emerged, he had been forced to suspend witchfinding in the Northern Ngoni chiefdoms, largely because of shifting popular opinion.

6. Karen Fields (1985) discusses comparable alliances in the 1930s between *Barnucapi* witchcleansers and "traditional authorities" throughout Northern Rhodesia. As in colonial times, witchfinding is technically illegal in Zambia; however, nearly all rural Ngoni believed that Doctor Moses was fully sanctioned by the District Executive Secretary in Chipata and by the Zambian One-Party State.

7. It was widely known throughout the region that Zionist witchfinders tended most often to accuse lay elders of Established Church congregations and imply that church ministers were themselves covert practitioners of witchcraft.

8. This practice of collecting compulsory "donations," and keeping written records was fairly standard; all villagers contributed several *kwacha* to the annual *Ne'wala* First Fruits ceremony and would occasionally be expected to give to spe-

cific causes, such as to pay for deputation of elders to visit an ill chief's wife in a Lusaka hospital.

9. Well-known examples of such large-scale cleansing movements include the *Bamcapi* of Central Africa in the 1930s (Richards 1935), the Bwanali-Mpulumutsi in Northern Rhodesia (Marwick 1950) in the late 1940s, the Kamcape of Southern Tanzania in the 1950s (Willis 1961), and witchfinding among the Mijekenda of Coastal Kenya in the 1980s (Ciakawy 1989).

10. In many cases, people may even leave the village out of fear of neighboring witches, taking up residence in urban or peri-urban locations, in the hope of escaping such malicious sorcerers.

11. These images are by no means mutually exclusive; I recorded numerous cases of elderly widows living in poor huts at a village edge, who were nonetheless rumored to have amassed secret hordes of money and maize through nocturnal mystical activity.

12. When I asked younger informants if the political power and authority enjoyed by elders in any sense compensated for their lack of physical beauty or vitality, and hence defused the temptation to turn to supernatural means, I was often treated to a bemused smile and asked in return, "How do you think old people become powerful?" One of my closest informants flatly asserted that all chiefs made use of witchcraft substances and sighed, "All powerful people are terrible people."

13. These dynamics are not simply a case of "men" against "women." Young married women often share young men's apprehension over older women's control of reproductive processes. A newly married woman experiencing illness, difficulty in conceiving, or a troubled pregnancy quite often will suspect one of her husband's father's wives (usually not the biological mother of her husband). Witchfinders thus promise young women security within her husband's community, generally an onerous place for the early years of a Ngoni woman's married life.

14. Many other Central African witchfinders—like healers and diviners elsewhere in the colonial and postcolonial world—have used hand mirrors. Such practices appear to synthesize indigenous notions of water reflections and divination, with European forms of power, knowledge, and selfhood (see the discussion in Comaroff and Comaroff [1991] on the use of hand mirrors in early missionization in South Africa).

15. Chikanga is said to stamp the letters his various clients bring with them from their local chief or headman, thus certifying that the accused person has been fully cleansed of the capacity to practice witchcraft (A. Wendroff, personal communication).

16. The events described in this paper preceded the emergence of the popular Movement for Multiparty Democracy in Zambia, which in October 1991 defeated President Kenneth Kaunda and ended one-party rule in the nation.

References

Comaroff, Jean. 1985. *Body of Power, Spirit of Resistance: The Culture and History of a South African People*. Chicago: University of Chicago Press.

Comaroff, Jean and John. 1991. *Of Revelation and Revolution*. Vol. 1. Chicago: University of Chicago Press.

Douglas, Mary. 1963. Techniques of Sorcery Control in Central Africa. In *Witchcraft and Sorcery in East Africa*, ed. John Middleton and E. H. Winter. London: Routledge & Kegan Paul.

Fields, Karen F. 1985. *Revival and Rebellion in Colonial Central Africa*. Princeton: Princeton University Press.

Marwick, M. G. 1950. Another Modern Anti-Witchcraft Movement in East-Central Africa. *Africa* 20, no. 1:100–112.

Munn, Nancy. 1986. *The Fame of Gawa: A Symbolic Study of Value Transformation in a Massim (PNG) Society*. Cambridge University Press.

———. 1990. Constructing Regional Worlds in Experience: Kula Exchange, Witchcraft and Gawan Local Events. Man, n.s. 25, no. 1 (March):1–17.

Redmayne, Alison. 1970. Chicanga: An African Diviner with an International Reputation. In *Witchcraft Confessions and Accusations*, ed. Mary Douglas. ASA Monographs no. 9, London: Tavistock Publications: 103–28.

Richards, Audrey. 1935. A Modern Movement of Witch-Finders. *Africa* 8, no. 4:448–61.

van Binsbergen, Wim. 1981. *Religious Change in Zambia: Exploratory Studies*. London and Boston: Kegan Paul International.

Willis, R. G. 1968. Kamcape: An Anti-Sorcery Movement in S.W. Tanzania. *Africa* 38, no. 1:1–15.

———. 1970. Instant Millenium: The Sociology of African Witch-Cleansing Cults. In *Witchcraft Confessions and Accusations*, ed. Mary Douglas. ASA Monograph no. 9. London: Tavistock Publications.

Wilson, Monica Hunter. 1951. Witch-Beliefs and Social Structure. *American Journal of Sociology* 56:307–13.

8

Black Stomachs, Beautiful Stones: Soul-Eating among Hausa in Niger

Pamela G. Schmoll

AS LUCK WOULD HAVE IT, I slept through my first encounter with a soul-eater. The head of our household was away. His young wife, Zeinabou, their three-year-old daughter, and newborn son were asleep in their *banco* hut. Another boarder (a primary school teacher) and myself also had huts in the compound, but neither of us was awakened by the incident. I did not hear the "dog" enter our compound, nor hear its eerie human-like howl. Only the next morning was I told how it had prowled the compound, trying to enter first the door, then the window of Zeinabou's hut. It had stalked restlessly from the door to the window, sniffing and scratching, terrifying the woman inside who had immediately suspected this was no ordinary dog.

The animal had gone past the cooking area, leaving untouched pots of food from the previous evening's meal. This, and its insistence on trying to enter the hut, seemed proof to all who heard the tale that the "dog" had really been a soul-eater or *maye*.[1]

Such attacks can occur at random, but it is also possible that the jealousy or nastiness (*bak'in ciki*)[2] of a neighbor or acquaintance was behind the incident. Zeinabou had had no open conflicts with anyone. Still, like most villagers, she was well aware of the dangers posed by the jealousies of others and recognized that one never knows what is truly in the hearts even of one's friends.

In fact, there was much that others could envy about Zeinabou. Young, very beautiful, and popular she was known for her kindness and generosity. She had two lovely, healthy children and a handsome, kind husband who, as a civil servant, had the luxury of a regular income. Thanks to his income, Zeinabou was free of some of the arduous chores that dominate the lives of most village women. She could afford to buy water and wood and hire someone to pound her millet. She and her husband had a garden in the summer, but they were not dependent on farming for their survival and so were not subjected to its physical and psychological stresses.

This is not to say they had an easy life. The crushing need for money in this Hausa society brings its own brand of anguish, and any salaried person is faced with never-ending demands from family and friends. Nonetheless, for many she was in an enviable position.

There was also her friendship with me—the "rich" American—and the access this permitted to what most imagined to be unlimited resources. That she did not visibly profit excessively from our relationship seemed irrelevant; rumors were always circulating as to the special Zeinabou exerted over me. That such ability is perhaps more coveted than actual material gain is evidenced by the popularity of medicines designed to procure this kind of influence. Commonly peddled as *mahibba* (lit.: "love, popularity, being of respect-inspiring or redoubtable mien"; Abraham 1978:681–82), such medicines (*magani*) are reputed to make one not only liked and respected but almost irresistible, the implication being that one will be so loved that others will be loyal, kind, and generous to him.

Fortunately in this instance the attempt on the life of Zeinabou and her children was unsuccessful, but the family remained in danger. There was no way to know the identity or the motives of the attacker. Even if we had, little could have been done except avoidance of that individual. The only reasonable resource was simply to purchase amulets and medicines (incense and a powder to be mixed with gruel and drunk) from local healers that would protect the family from future attacks.

Soon Zeinabou's brush with the soul-eater was, if not forgotten, at least no longer discussed. But the incident continued to intrigue me. Soul-eating was clearly felt as a real and constant threat. The plethora of anti–soul-eater medicines (*maganin maye*) available, sold by virtually every type of healer, was additional testimony to that. Furthermore, it seemed to be a problem of universal concern, cutting across both economic and social boundaries.

Its obvious importance to individuals in this community raised a broader question: How in the face of significant economic and social change, when many "traditions" and beliefs appear to be dying, do the images, symbols, beliefs, and practices surrounding soul-eating continue to be meaningful? And how is it they provide a viable discourse not only for ascribing meaning to crisis but for contemplating the human condition, social relationships, and the place of a specific kind of evil in that social universe.

Although many works have mentioned soul-eating in passing (Nicolas 1975; Faulkingham 1975; Tremearne 1968; Darrah 1980), to my knowledge none has chosen it as a primary focus of study. Yet, such analysis promises insight not only into Hausa culture but into (i) the broader questions of how "traditional" institutions mold and are molded by historical experience, and (ii) the role of these institutions in helping local populations make sense of and cope with changing social and economic conditions.

This chapter is an attempt to begin such analysis by looking at soul-eating as a culturally constituted, more-or-less coherent network of images, symbols, beliefs, practices, and values that not only provide people a conceptual framework for thinking about and making sense of certain kinds of experience but also establishes practical guidelines for action. Using ethnographic data gathered over a three-year period of research in the Gulbi Valley (Republic of Niger), I seek to show, in specific ethnographic terms, the nature of that framework. I emphasize soul-eating as a symbolic and semantic space in which particular hardships and struggles of contemporary life are brought together and made sense of using symbols and images that resonate throughout the broader society. I suggest that soul-eating has remained meaningful in this area of Hausaland because the kinds of destructive forces it has long addressed have, in the eyes of those with whom I worked, been exacerbated by colonialism and the far-reaching changes that have come in its wake.

Rooted in the past, these symbols provide a sense of familiarity, and thus continuity, to experience. At the same time, their malleability makes possible the incorporation of new socioeconomic and political realities. While "traditional" concepts have helped shape subjective experience of history past and present, soul-eating itself has been transformed as its categories and beliefs have been expanded and modified to accommodate changes in the material and social world.

An examination of soul-eating thus raises the complex question of cultural dynamism. How are societies able to move through time in such a way that core cultural beliefs and practices change enough to remain relevant and meaningful, yet continue to help individuals find a sense of identity and stability. Why are some signs and practices able to survive and transform themselves this way while others are not? What drives this dynamism? Is it simply a reaction to external events; or is there a more subtle, intricate, and less predictable interraction between the various dimensions of human experience that must be accounted for? Finally, as a phenomena that is not accepted as "reality" by most Westerners, soul-eating also challenges us to consider once again the familiar question of the nature of reality itself—in particular, the manner of its cultural construction.

Implicit here, too, are questions of responsibility for and influence in shaping and giving meaning to one's own history. In this instance, it is tempting to see this group of Hausa as simply victims of colonialism and its aftermath—all the more so since, historically, the population's reaction to domination has been one of outward submission and withdrawal. Yet, despite apparent feelings of powerlessness and frustration, and recognition of the significant impact of colonialism and capitalism, most villagers do not seem to view the situation in such a clear-cut way. Indeed, a look into soul-eating forces us to consider the extent to which peoples help make their own history as well as write it. I would argue that soul-eating is not only a medium for defining and categorizing evil and its newly emerged dimensions but that it is also a means of redirecting the social gaze. Not only does it compel people to reevaluate where the world is going but, by establishing a moral code, it creates pressure for and against certain types of social action.

Any ethnographic discussion also faces the problem of how to account for a culture without, on the one hand, essentializing and dehistoricizing the people who possess it or, on the other hand, particularizing them to the point that commonalities evaporate. Students of the Hausa need to be especially careful in this regard since the extent to which the latter constitute an ethnic group, as opposed to merely a linguistic population, is in itself a subject of debate. Indeed, each village and region has its own particular history, and while there are certainly many shared features among them, there is also a wide range of differences in custom, belief, and even in language. The significance of these differences is a question that has received little attention in the literature. Although I am also unable to discuss it here, it compels me to address the issue of how to refer to the people with whom I worked. This analysis is based on fieldwork done with rural Hausa living on the eastern side of the Gulbi Valley south of the town of Maradi in South Central Niger. Though centered in Djirataoua, much of my work was done with residents of neighboring villages and the surrounding bush areas. As these people identify themselves as Hausa, this is the easiest way for me to refer to them; it is the term they themselves would choose if asked. Nonetheless, my account refers specifically and exclusively to the inhabitants of a limited geographical region during the period of November 1983 to August 1986. I acknowledge, too, that even the homogeneity of this population cannot really be taken for granted.

The Social Context of Soul-Eating

Though historically this area of Hausaland depended heavily on subsistence agriculture and exchange in kind, today a discussion of soul-eating inevitably raises the issue of money (*ku'di*). Soul-eating seems to have traditionally centered on desire for and jealousy over *arziki*.[3] Glossed as "prosperity" (*arziki*), a primary goal of most villagers in the area I studied includes all types of moral, physical, material, and spiritual wealth (e.g., children, money, land, success in one's job, abundance of friends, good harvests, etc.).

With increasing "monetarization" of local society, however, currency has become indispensable in procuring and sustaining these various forms of wealth. Categories of goods once distinct but worked together to paint a multifaceted portrait of the luck (*sa'a*) and "prosperity" of an individual and his family can increasingly be reduced to the common denominator of money.

For example, a man with money is likely to have more wives and children. He can afford the large sums of money that are a necessary part of marriage negotiations. More wives mean more children and more status. He can provide well for his dependents. He can assure them not only material comforts (good, adequate food, medicines, comfortable living arrangements, clothes and other material possessions, and a considerably lighter work load than the average villager) but also the status that comes simply by being a rich man's wife or child.

The ability to provide these things makes him very attractive as a spouse—an attribute that is, in and of itself, a dimension of "prosperity." Likewise, his ability to provide monetary favors, plus his general prestige in the community (stemming from his many possessions, wives, children, etc.), make him more desirable as a friend, thus further augmenting his social status and "prosperity."

A man cannot get or keep a wife without money. One cannot even court a woman without money, for in addition to material gifts (which require currency to buy) he is expected to give her small monetary gifts (*ku'din hira*) just for talking to him. When one considers that an unmarried man or a man who is unable to provide for his family is not considered a responsible adult in Hausa society, one begins to get a glimpse of the vital role money plays. In short, money has become not only a form of "prosperity"[4] but, indeed, a symbol of it.

Likewise, the complex system of gift exchange through which the intricate fabric of social relations is woven has undergone a similar transformation. From baptisms to marriages to Islamic holidays, currency is gradually replacing goods in kind (goods to which villagers had relatively equal access) as the standard and preferred gift. Even occasions of more informal gift giving such as visiting a sick friend or calling on a relative require money. And though men are responsible for the family's official monetary obligations such as taxes, the extensive "monetarization" of daily life means the pressure for money is as intense for women as it is for men. In other words, money is not a nicety used to procure luxury items; rather, it has become integral to physical and social survival.

Not surprisingly, then, the pursuit of money (*neman ku'di*) has become a major preoccupation of the Hausa villager. Although this penetration of money into virtually every aspect of Hausa life has its roots in the colonial period with the introduction of French currency, the institution of taxation, the importation of consumer goods, and the commercialization of agriculture (in order to get cash needed to pay taxes and buy consumer goods; Raynaut 1977), the need and scramble for money seems, in the minds of most villagers, to have accelerated in recent times. Raynaut claims that the limited amount of currency in circulation, together with an escalating gap between increasing monetary obligations and decreasing revenue from agricultural products, accounts for this situation (ibid).

The sale of agricultural products (in particular, millet, sorghum, peanuts, cotton, and vegetables) is the primary means of income for most villagers, although secondary occupations (such as pottery making, selling of cooked foods, calabash carving) and gifts are also sources of money. A few, such as civil servants, are salaried.[5]

However, the pressing need for money combined with unstable agricultural prices and periodic drought have rendered income from agriculture unreliable and have led to the splintering of the extended family, as this traditional economic unit is no longer able to meet the monetary demands of its members (ibid., 161). As a result, the economic, social, and to a large extent "religious" unit is being reduced to the nuclear family. Villagers increasingly are moving away from defining their well-being and "prosperity" as a function of their relationship with spirits (*bori*) linked to lineage and land and are adopting an attitude of "each man for himself," approaching life more and more as a game of chance (ibid., 161–62). Thus, for many, disregard for one's heritage (*gaado*), alienation from traditional values and morals, and the effects of money are interrelated—an interrelationship that, as I shall show, finds expression in soul-eating.

This intense need for money to meet subsistence and social needs seems to be experienced as an inability to hold onto money, almost as if currency had a momentum of its own. Money is transient; it disappears. This elusiveness is epitomized in a phenomenon referred to as "wind money" (*ku'din iska*). Such magical money, used in a purchase, later simply disappears from the coffer of the seller. Given the incredible demands on monetary resources, the average seller of goods, particularly agricultural goods, must indeed experience a similar sensation even if he has not been the recipient of "wind money."

It is interesting that "wind money" does not return to the person who passed the currency. Unlike the baptized money discussed by Michael Taussig (1977; 1980:126–32) that reaps the peasant profit by leading the contents of the seller's coffer back to the owner of the magical money, for the Hausa there is virtually no profit. This seems consistent with Raynaut's (1977:165) comments that the average Hausa villager does not experience money as profit generating; he deals in cash, not capital. The goal of "wind money" is to meet an exchange need, while for the South American peasant it is the profit-reaping capacity of currency that, although illegitimate (immoral), is nonetheless sought.

The problem, according to Raynaut (1977), stems from a situation in which a limited amount of currency must try to meet the needs of a highly "monetarized" society. As he portrays it, money comes into the local economy from the sale of agricultural goods, and it must circulate at an extraordinary rate of speed to meet the needs of individuals before being pulled back out of the rural economy through taxes and the purchase of consumer items. I suggest that the stress this situation produces on the local population is marked and finds expression in "health"-related contexts, most particularly in soul-eating. I suggest that the average villager is not in a position to see the more global factors responsible for this keen pressure and so experiences the threat and alienation in the much more personal and familiar idiom of soul-eating. Also, while money, materialism, and colonialism are clearly identified by villagers as key factors, popular belief places ultimate responsibility on human nature and the reaction of villagers to these influences rather than on the influences themselves.

Body and Soul

Human beings consist of a body (*jiki*) and a soul (*kurwa*). The soul seems to both have life (*rai*) and be life. It has life in that it can be captured and itself killed, that is, lose its life. It *is* life, however, in the sense that its existence and that of the body, though not totally synonymous, are linked. For example, when the soul has been captured, the body begins to deteriorate and to lose strength. The body cannot live once the soul has been destroyed;[6] yet the death of the body is not necessarily simultaneous with the death of the soul. For example, failure of the victim to respond to medicines indicates the soul has already been slaughtered and death of the body is imminent.

The soul is also associated, though again not synonymous with, the person's shadow (*inuwa*). A soul-eater can capture the soul by touching the victim's shadow. One sign that a person has been "caught" by a soul-eater is that he has no shadow. This close affiliation is also signaled by the fact that in cases of possession of an individual by the soul of a deceased person the attacking soul is referred to as a shadow.

Most villagers would not even speculate as to where the soul was located in the body. Since only soul-eaters can see into the body, to claim such knowledge would either raise suspicions that one was a soul-eater (or associated with them), or make one appear foolish.

Those who would admit such knowledge were healers (some of whom were themselves soul-eaters but of a type devoted to helping others). They said the soul is located in the interior of the head, between the mouth and the nose, between the breath and the saliva, thus close to the two essentials of life: breathing and eating. The soul does not roam around the body.

It appears to soul-eaters as an insect or, most commonly, as a chicken.[7] Raynaut (1977:162) has pointed out that the soul and strength are also associated with luck (*sa'a*) and wealth, the latter two being outward manifestations of the former two.

The Anatomy of Soul-Eating

Maita, also called *k'ank'ara maita*, or simply *k'ank'ara* (lit.: "hail"), is the source of the soul-eater's power. Described by those I talked to as "pebbles"[8] or "seeds" (*k'wayoyi*), it is portrayed as a living, reproducing substance having gender and a will of its own. The "stones" live deep in (and are confined to) the belly (*ciki*) of the soul-eater and enable him to see, capture, and eat the soul of living things.

There are two types of soul-eaters: "savior" soul-eaters (*mayu ceto*) and "ant" soul-eaters (*mayu tururuwa*).[9] The former are known to be soul-eaters. Being benevolent, they use their powers to identify malevolent soul-eaters and protect the population. They publicly display their stones on special occasions and never turn their abilities to evil purposes.

If the savior soul-eaters are public, however, the ant soul-eaters are private, secretive, and evil, and it is essentially to them one is referring when speaking of soul-eating. Their identity is unknown (except to a savior soul-eater who can recognize them instantly), and they use their powers only for antisocial purposes. Their lust and desire for souls is so great that if they cannot satiate themselves on human souls they will go into the bush at night to an anthill and eat the souls of the ants, hence the name "ant soul-eaters." These soul-eaters, while very dangerous, were not extremely numerous in the past (at least in villagers' reconstruction of the past) and were dominated by the savior soul-eaters who traditionally were able to seek them out and punish them for attacking villagers.[10] I was unable to get a clear explanation of the relationship between the two types of soul-eaters. My impression is that the difference is not a question of differing capacities for evil but rather of differing abilities (or willingness) to control it.

Soul-eaters are able to transform themselves into any kind of animal, even snakes. But despite a familiar shape, there is generally something strange about the animal—a horse without a tail, a dog with a human-sounding howl. Such a sight terrifies (*hirgita*) the victim and, according to some, can so startle the soul that it jumps out of the body. In that split second it can be snapped up by the soul-eater.

Although this is one way to trap a soul, it is not in fact the usual scenario. Most often the soul is captured by the soul-eater touching the person or his shadow. Still another, though less common, means is to stand to the east of the victim and to catch his soul in the wind.

Once taken, the soul is imprisoned, generally in a bottle or gourd, and hidden in the hollow of a tree or buried. When the soul-eater decides to kill the victim, the soul is retrieved, its throat is cut (the same way an animal is customarily slaughtered or sacrificed), and the meat is "roasted" and eaten by the soul-eater. I will return to the importance of this imagery later.

Though anyone is a potential target, soul-eaters are described as preferring infants. Not only is the meat of babies more tender, but their inability to speak insures that the identity of the soul-eater will be difficult if not impossible to discover. In addition, given the high infant mortality rate from other diseases, choosing a baby, especially one that is already ill, means added camouflage for the soul-eater. Likewise, hospital patients are more vulnerable since death from attack by a soul-eater can be masked by other illness. Given that the hospital is frequently the last resort for villagers, many patients are indeed already at death's door.

In describing someone whose soul has been taken, most emphasized the total collapse of the individual, noting that the neck and back are particularly affected. The body becomes "soft" and weak, suffering a (sometimes very sudden) loss of strength. "The body breaks down" ("Jiki na lalace"), it "becomes weak [*sanyi*; lit.: "cold"] as if it doesn't have any bones."

The victim may start to waste away, especially if the soul-eater is letting the soul linger imprisoned before slaughtering it. This, I was told, is the mark of a particularly vicious soul-eater (*bak'in maita*, "black" *maita*) because he wants the soul to suffer. Sometimes such a soul-eater will bury the captured soul near a cooking fire so that every time the fire is lit, the soul will suffer from the heat.

Some mentioned that the victim may start to babble or not be able to speak at all. The eyes frequently roll to the back of the head and the person barely breathes.

Most spoke of terrible headaches: "It's the head the soul-eater grabs and makes it hurt." "It's the head that is afflicted, it hurts as if it is being chewed." Although the victim may appear conscious, in fact he is not. If the soul is returned, the individual will not be aware that anything has happened. A few people noted that the victim may shake. All mentioned that the victim has no shadow.

Although the individuals I spoke with seemed quite confident that they could identify attack by a soul-eater, discussion of actual cases revealed that such diagnosis was generally difficult to make. Clearly the symptoms can be associated with other debilitating conditions. What *is* specific to attack by a soul-eater, however, is the symbolic message encoded in the corporal symptoms.

The affliction seems to speak of the total dehumanization of the individual as life is drained out of him. At one level he becomes deprived of those functions which help make him human: he cannot speak (or only babbles), he is unable to work (he has no strength, his back and neck are useless), he is deprived of reason and intelligence (consciousness; terrible headaches as if the soul-eater is chewing on his head).

As part of this process of dehumanization the victim is transformed from consumer to consumed—from eater of food to becoming food himself. The soul, changed by the soul-eater into a chicken, is killed, cooked, and eaten. Even the method used to elicit the name of the soul-eater from the victim (i.e., putting the cord from the neck of a black goat around the neck of the victim) evokes the image of a trapped animal ready for slaughter.

What is considered "food" in this case is not the victim's body (i.e., his flesh, meat) but his soul, that is, the very essence of his life, and according to Raynaut (1977:162) the very source of the individual's "prosperity." Once a soul is killed, I was told, it is as if the person never existed, for there is virtually nothing left of the individual either in this world or the next. This seems to imply that soul-eating is an ultimate act of dehumanization since it is not simple destruction or death; it is total annihilation of the person.

Identification of attack by a soul-eater does not rely on symptoms alone but requires placing them in a social context. Firm diagnosis of almost all diseases, but especially attack by a soul-eater, is generally done in retrospect since only the cure truly identifies the malady. Still, a sudden onset of violent debilitating illness with no apparent cause or after a particularly suspicious encounter with someone would point to soul-eating.[11]

Treatment is extremely difficult, since generally the soul-eater must be identified and made to release the soul. I was told that the victim is given medicines or, more commonly, as mentioned above, the cord from around the neck of a black goat is placed around his neck. When this is done the victim will begin to cry out the name of the attacker. This, however, depends on the person being well enough to speak. Even when the soul-eater does not kill the victim immediately, the attack can debilitate the individual to the point that he is unable to talk.

In many instances the soul-eater is named only long after the fact (and death of the victim). In the majority of cases recounted to me, the identity was discovered virtually by accident. The soul-eater, caught for some current offense, ultimately confessed to numerous past cases that had been unsolved.

But even when the soul-eater is identified, punishment and "cure" is a tricky business. Traditionally, once named, the soul-eater was sought out, stripped naked, and made to jump over the victim three times without touching him, thereby releasing the soul back into the person. The soul-eater would then perhaps be beaten and exiled from the village.

Today, however, matters are more complex. Soul-eating is not a legally recognized offense, and villagers explained that to accuse someone of being a soul-eater is to risk being summoned to court oneself.[12] Pursuit of soul-eaters can be dealt with through the traditional power structure, but in the area where I lived some of the most influential traditional leaders were not trusted. As a result, many were reluctant to turn to them for help. Furthermore, attack by a soul-eater is a crisis where time is of the essence. Going through the proper channels requires valuable time that the victim may not be able to spare. Then, too, this is a society where money and status speak, and the average peasant is reluctant to pit his meager resources against those of the soul-eater which might be considerable.

Preventive medicines are felt to be the best method of dealing with the threat posed by soul-eaters. According to several specialists with whom I consulted, a person who is satiated with medicines is safe from harm (provided the medicines are genuine, of course), for soul-eaters prey on those who do not resist, that is, those who do not use medicines.

Anti–soul-eater medicines work in several ways. Some make the soul in one way or another invisible to the soul-eater. For example, one puts tears in the eyes of the soul-eater so it cannot see the victim. Others make the soul distasteful by, for example, giving the soul of the person a terrible stench, thereby ensuring the soul-eater will not come near it. Still others make it impossible for the soul to remain trapped. Even if it is enclosed in a bottle and put in the hollow of a tree or buried, the soul will be able to escape.

Desire (*kwa'dayi*),[13] especially jealousy over the "prosperity" of others, was the motive for attack most frequently cited by villagers. Ironically, while the soul-eater uses his special "stones" to act on this jealousy, he is, at the same time, imprisoned by their power. Portrayed as having a force, a will of their own, the "stones" periodically rise up in what is likened to hunger and demand to be satisfied. A healer described the sensation this way: "The 'stones' rise up from the belly and go towards the throat, they cause piercing pain . . . they strangle [the throat]."

If the "stones'" needs are not met, they become frustrated almost to the point of killing the soul-eater. According to this same healer, "[Not receiving souls] this is what incites the 'stones' to daze the soul-eater . . . it's as if they are going to kill the soul-eater but don't." He added, "[When the 'stones' rise up] it is as if the soul-eater is in a trance . . . it's not that he is ill . . . he curls up and belches. They cause him piercing pain . . . [until] they become tired [or are fed] and calm down."

In such a state the soul-eater attacks indiscriminantly;[14] whatever comes his way—even his own flesh and blood—is fair game. As one individual commented, "Now [for example] a person has some chickens, if he wants to catch one aren't they all the same? . . . even if it's his [soul-eater's] son, his own flesh and blood, the soul-eater will attack him."

Although at one level these two causes of attack (i.e., malice and "hunger") seem to be considered unrelated, at another they are implicitly linked. "When it the 'stones' begin to move, desire is aroused. In fact, if they want him [the soul-eater] to eat someone, they begin to move by themselves." In other words, there seems to be a causal connection between the arousal of the "stones" and the awakening of feelings of desire in the soul-eater. On the other hand, desire and jealousy not only seem able to excite the "stones" but are the motivating forces behind individuals' seeking to become soul-eaters in the first place.

The Commoditization of Soul-Eating

The ability to eat souls is inherited bilaterally through the mother's milk or through the father's semen. Traditionally such abilities were only inherited. Recent times, however, have witnessed the commoditization of soul-eating, and now such powers can be purchased with money. I was assured by an elder in the savior soul-eater's clan that it was generally those who have become soul-eaters through purchase of "stones" and sometimes the ant soul-eaters who sell the "stones." The buyer acquires and swallows one male and one female "stone" from a soul-eater who has vomited them up from his/her own gut. Both a male and female "stone" are necessary since it is only once they have begun to reproduce that the person becomes a true soul-eater.

Once the "stones" have been activated, the status of this person is permanently transformed; not only will they forever be a soul-eater but so will all their descendants. Symbolically, this suggests that many feel that once desire is fully awakened, there is no going back. It takes on a life of its own, growing only bigger and stronger.

While the sellers of the "stones" are usually seeking money, the buyers are generally motivated by envy and greed (frequently over money). They see others with more wealth (monetary, material and nonmaterial) and want to destroy them. As one villager described the scenario:

If you don't have anything and you go to a relative's place or to someone's place that you are always with and you see he has more monetary wealth, or more kids, you become jealous of these things and you say to yourself, "o.k. if I don't have more than this person then he shouldn't have more than I do . . . I know what I'll do with him." So he goes and hangs around those who possess it [soul-eating "stones"].

The implication is that he will buy the "stones" and become a soul-eater in order to destroy the individual he envies.[15]

But in procuring the ability to eat souls the buyer is described as being himself enslaved and, in a moral sense, destroyed. I was told that some purchase the "stones" erroneously assuming that once their evil deed is accomplished, that will be the end of the affair. In fact, the "stones" ultimately take control. As one individual explained, "[Once the "stones" have matured] he [the person] can't control himself anymore, he can't calm himself . . . since he has already tasted [souls] he will continue to kill."

Whether inherited or purchased, the seeds must mature and reproduce before the individual can begin to consume souls. Hence children of soul-eaters, though congenitally soul-eaters, cannot exercise their powers until they are adults. The implicit connection between the maturation of the "stones" and what we might call the "loss of innocence" of the individual adds an interesting twist to the image of the soul-eater as himself the helpless victim of soul-eating. People used the expression "when he has reached the age of being cunning, clever, intelligent" (*sai ya yi wayo*) to describe the point at which the "stones" are activated. This belief typifies a view many Hausa in this area seem to hold that a child is not responsible for his actions insofar as he is too young to understand their implications. Parents, for example, are not particularly bothered by their children swearing or saying things that would be serious for an adult to say, because they are ignorant, innocent. Therefore, if at one level the soul-eater is cast as the victim of the "stones," at another he is still ultimately responsible, for the fact he is old enough to be aware of the consequences of his actions implies he should be able to control the desire. This view is further substantiated by the fact that even the "good" soul-eaters appear to have the same terrible urges but are somehow able to surmount them.

Soul-Eating and the Subjective Experience of Socioeconomic Change

Perhaps one of the reasons soul-eating is such a potent and pervasive set of images is that using the symbols *ciki* (lit.: "stomach, abdomen, pregnancy") and *ci* (lit.: "to eat"; fig.: "to kill," "to have sexual intercourse") it provides a framework for a sophisticated and nuanced commentary on the problem of uncontrolled desire for power and wealth and the use of immoral means to achieve them—precisely problems many Hausa claim have been exacerbated by the socioeconomic changes set in motion during the colonial period. Soul-eating draws images, symbols, and metaphors from the core human experiences of consumption, reproduction, and destruction (killing), and the cultural values that surround them. Thus soul-eating is not only grounded in the realities of human existence but it gives powerful expression to important contradictions and paradoxes particular to the experience of Hausa villagers in this region. By touching aspects of daily life that have been profoundly affected by colonialism and capitalism, soul-eating provides an appropriate and meaningful language for expressing, interpreting, and evaluating these historical influences.

The Symbolism of Ciki and Ci
Ciki

Ciki has several literal meanings: (1) inside, (2) the stomach/belly/abdomen, (3) pregnancy/womb. Figuratively, however, *ciki*, along with the heart (*zuciya*), is associated with both an individual's character and his temporary disposition. For example, *farin ciki* (lit.: "white stomach") is translated by Bargery (1957:306) as "happiness, pleasure, gratification." Bargery adds that in Katsina *farin ciki* is also used as *farar zuciya* (lit.: "white heart").

In contrast, *bak'in ciki* (lit.: "black stomach") means "sadness, sorrow, displeasure, being or feeling annoyed" (Bargery 1957:65). I found it interesting that two states or emotions—sadness/being upset and annoyance/nastiness—which, for us are distinctly different, should be linguistically paired. The explanation given by one individual was that a person who is unhappy is more likely to be nasty, so the two emotions actually go hand in hand. As concerns the soul-eater, the stomach is where the soul-eating "stones" as well as jealousies, greed, and desires reside.

In describing the human personality Hausa villagers implicitly refer to two components: desires and reason (*hankali*). Emotions and desires (both positive and negative) are centered in the heart and stomach (*ciki*), while reason is in the head (*kai*). It is clear that one of the most highly valued traits in a person is his self-control and discipline, in other words, the ability of his mind and reason to master or temper his passions and desires.

Living among the rural Hausa of this area, impresses one with the value placed on self-control and discipline. Displays of anger, sorrow, pain, even happiness are all highly controlled. Emphasis on self-mastery extends beyond emotions, however, to include basic human drives such as hunger. Darrah (1980) explains in great detail the importance placed on eating etiquette and the shame involved in showing one's hunger. As one friend explained to me, only children show they are hungry and rush to eat because they do not know any better; they are not yet old enough to know how to control themselves. For an adult to be too anxious to eat, however, shows lack of self-control and is, therefore, shameful.

Much of child rearing and socialization appears to center on developing the power of reason to temper desire. This is seen in part in the way adults talk about children. A child who shows maturity and self-control will be described as *"yana da kai"* (lit.: "He has a head"; fig.: "He is wise, intelligent, in control"). In contrast, a child who is wild, impolite, or improper will be described as *"ba shi da kai"* (lit.: "He has no head"; fig.: "He's senseless" (Abraham 1978:450).[16] To a significant degree, then, the ability to master one's emotions and desires (symbolically signified by the ability of the head to dominate the stomach and heart) appears crucial in defining the socially acceptable individual. This would appear to make self-control more than simply a value in Hausa society, but rather something of a linchpin—a foundation for the rest of the moral system.

Returning to the context of soul-eating, it appears, then, that the situation is one of Hausa morality being "stood on its head." The stomach, symbol of the individual's emotions and desires and the seat of soul-eating powers, has risen up and triumphed over the head (reason).[17] The soul-eater, incited by nastiness, desire, and jealousy, or simply controlled by the lust of the "stones" themselves, seems to be the quintessential anti-social individual since he is literally out of control. In representing the inversion of the normal moral and social order (or as Turner 1964:323) would argue the lack of any such structure), he also appears to represent the ultimate threat to society since uncontrolled desire is antithetical to and destructive of social order.

Ci

Also part of soul-eating imagery, and clearly intertwined with stomach imagery, is the symbolic element *ci*. This verb literally means "to eat," but it also has a number of figurative meanings which relate back to the image of consumption. For example, *ci* can mean to have intercourse. *"Ci uwaka!"* (lit.: "Eat your mother!"), a very serious insult, means "Have intercourse with your mother!" Here we see not only the idea of consumption, in this case it is consumption out of control. Perhaps one reason this is such a powerful insult is that it suggests submission of reason to passion. Since reason prohibits incest, an accusation of incest implies the person is out of control, a slave to desires (*ciki*).

Ci can also mean to master or control in a general sense. A student who has just done well on an English exam might be heard to say, "na ci Inglishi!" meaning that he mastered, literally, "ate up" the English exam. Another example of a related use of *ci* would be "ciwo yana cina" (lit.: "The pain is eating me up"; "The pain is overcoming me").

The Discourse of Soul-Eating

Stomach and eating imagery come together in a number of different ways in the context of soul-eating to evoke several themes prominent in Hausa society as a whole. However, even though these themes can be distinguished they are, at the same time, inextricably intertwined since each evokes the other by virtue of the symbolic multivocality of the terms *ciki* (stomach) and *ci* (to eat).

Food/Hunger/Consumption

As I have already mentioned, the inability to control literal and figurative hunger is scorned in this society. It seems to be considered a mark of antisociality because it shows lack of control over one's desires. Hunger, however, appears to imply other aspects of social deviance as well. Exclusion from the social fabric to the point one is hungry in a society where the extra person is always welcome to share the family meal marks the individual as a misfit, alienated from the family and the larger social community.

The symbols of hunger and food also involve a moral dimension. "Prosperity" is viewed as a state of physical, emotional, material, and spiritual grace, for there is the underlying notion among the Hausa that Allah rewards the pious and makes sinners suffer. An abundance or lack of food, therefore, has latent moral implications as well (Darrah 1980:3).

Hunger, in all its forms, is thus a threat both to the individual and to the society at large. Literal hunger (i.e., the need for food) renders the individual vulnerable physically and socially. To the extent that a person who suffers is more likely to become jealous and mean, hunger also potentially threatens society. Symbolically, it appears to signify strong desire and the challenge posed by controlling, or keeping in balance, that desire. It is, therefore, suggestive of the threat posed by a failure to keep desire in check.

The hunger metaphor is further reinforced and elaborated by the symbols of the tongue and licking. Darrah (1980:70) points out that the image in a range of afflictions referred to as "the mouth" is of the tongue licking at the "prosperity" of the person.[18] Likewise, a licking gesture is sometimes used to refer to a soul-eater. The image here is of the soul-eater licking the soul—the very source of the victim's "prosperity."

Consumption imagery also evokes the sociology of food. What constitutes proper food, and what an individual eats (or does not eat) is, in this society, an important and nuanced statement about who that person is, where they fit into the social order, and their abundance or lack of "prosperity." Ordinary villagers, for example, eat millet, functionaries eat rice,

Muslims do not eat pork, Christians do, and so on. Meat and to a certain extent rice and macaroni are considered luxury foods and a mark of prosperity. A diet of *tuwo and* gruel rather than just gruel, and being able to add milk to one's gruel, are all indicators that one is not suffering.[19] On the other hand, *tuwo* made from sorghum, in particular red sorghum, is something of a poor man's diet. Worse, still, is not being able to afford *tuwo* at all, but subsisting almost solely on gruel.[20]

The language of food is equally relevant in the context of soul-eating. The fact that the food is human renders it highly illicit and antisocial. That the soul is trapped and slaughtered in the same way an animal would be killed reiterates the cannibalistic image of human reduced to food source. The soul-eater's willingness to attack even his own children epitomizes this cannibalism. For if human flesh is taboo, children are doubly so. They are helpless and innocent and can have done nothing to offend anyone. In addition, they are seen to represent the future both of their family (lineage) and of society as a whole. The symbolic message seems to be that the inability of individuals to master desires, in particular greed and jealousy, ultimately destroys society since it leads man to prey upon and destroy his fellowman and himself (his lineage).

The antisocial character of the soul-eater is further suggested by the fact that the diet is solely meat. Meat is considered a luxury item, one that even royalty do not eat to the exclusion of other foods. In fact, due to the high amount of grease (fat) in meat, most people argue that too much meat will make a normal individual ill. That the soul-eater not only has such a diet but in fact thrives on what would sicken the average person again suggests a lust for the finer things in life, a "*gourmandise*" as well as social deviance.

Reproduction

The terms "eating" and "stomach" can also refer to intercourse and the womb, respectively. These usages provide the basis for a set of images surrounding reproduction—images that are ultimately intertwined with those of hunger and consumption.

To begin, I submit that the "food" of the soul-eater is not simply the life essence (soul) of individuals, but the "soul" of society—social reproduction. Eating is a metaphor for intercourse, and food (*tuwo*) a metaphor for children (Darrah 1980:38, 171, 184). This symbolic association reappears in the context of soul-eating but in inverted form since the child is transformed from *tuwo* (legitimate food) which is *created* through socially condoned "consumption" (of the mother) to meat (a luxury food and, therefore, more likely to weaken self-control) which is *destroyed* through illegitimate consumption. The emphasis on children as preferred targets suggests that many perceive the very core of Hausa society to be at risk, literally, in the destruction of its children, and figuratively, in the robbing of its collective "prosperity" (of which children appear to be both a concrete manifestation and a symbol).

This is expressed even more directly in the belief that if a soul-eater has intercourse (ci) with an ordinary woman, once he has ejaculated into her, all her subsequent children (even those fathered by other men who are not soul-eaters) will be soul-eaters. The woman herself, however, will not become a soul-eater. In other words, the soul-eater has permanently contaminated the woman's capacity to reproduce. Through intercourse (ci) he has taken control (ci) of her reproductive ability (a form of wealth) and in so doing has virtually destroyed (ci) it in terms of creating normal individuals.

The control or destruction of reproductive capacity is evidenced in another way as well. Sometimes a soul-eater will give or sell the "stones" (usually disguised as some sort of other medicine) to the children of someone he dislikes. Since all descendants of those children will be soul-eaters, the soul-eater has seriously damaged the reproductive wealth of that individual.

Killing/Cooking

Another theme prominent in soul-eating is that of killing, in particular killing by spilling blood and then roasting the victim. The symbol of fire is a complex one. On the one hand, it appears to represent life and strength. For example, Darrah (1980:220) reports that a newborn child (i.e., new life) is regarded as a metaphorical fire. The mother, considered "raw" from being opened during childbirth and thus weak and potentially near death, is given hot baths for forty days to "roast" her, close her up, and give her back strength (and by extension, life).

But if fire and heat are life-giving, in excess they are life-taking. This paradox is nicely portrayed in the image of the soul buried by the soul-eater near the hearth. The heat of the cooking fire tortures and weakens the soul below while preparing life-giving food for those in the household.

Fire (heat) seems to represent yet another contradiction, for it is both legitimate strength, and immodesty or strength out of control. It is both raw emotion and the maturity to control one's emotions. As Darrah states:

> Fire has multiple referents. Fire, or rather its thermal properties, symbolizes emotion. *Zafi*, the word for heat, means anger and discord. Immodesty and braggadocio are also associated with heat. On the positive side, generosity, courage, and maturity are functions of a person's heat. An individual's life is symbolized by a fire which must

be kept under control in order to avoid the consequences of excessive heat. The cooling effects of ritual and proscriptive modesty are the means by which this balance is achieved. (1980:211)

Perhaps this is precisely why the soul-eater is considered so dangerous, he lacks the cooling modesty (*kumya*) needed to temper the flame of desire. Indeed, this Hausa community seems to feel that balance and control are fundamental to the well-being of the individual and society. Any emotion—even love—is dangerous in excess.[21] Therefore, it may be that extremes are threatening because they not only indicate lack of individual self-discipline but because they threaten to disrupt the harmony (health, *lahiya*) of the broader social environment as well.

The Transformation of Soul-Eating and Its Implications

Although the attack of the soul-eater has always been feared and guarded against, the number of soul-eaters and the frequency of their attack are perceived by most villagers to have increased in recent times. The explanations given centered on three interrelated themes: the increasing nastiness of people, the commoditization of soul-eating, and the lack of respect for tradition and heritage.

Jealousy over the "prosperity" of others, in particular the inability to tolerate others having what one does not have, was commonly cited by villagers as the motivating force behind soul-eating and its spread. Jealousy, desire, and nastiness, though not new to man's nature, are felt by the local population to have become increasingly problematic. Most associate this dilemma with European colonialism and the material and social culture that accompanied it. They accuse the French of having whetted local appetites and desires with money and material goods. Many claim that as the search for money (*neman ku'di*) has intensified, traditions have been progressively scorned or disregarded, respect is gone, and no one has "shame" (*kumya*) anymore. One friend described it as follows:

It's you [the whites] who provoked this! It's because of you that all this has happened . . . [The problem] is that nowadays men and women, old and young, everyone wants to get rich . . . For example, young people, well before they are married, break away from their families in order to find their own fortunes . . . today the world has become a place where everyone is constantly coming and going. When I say that soul-eating has spread in the last forty years its because today there are few people who respect their heritage, their patrimony. Whenever one talks of the olden days, one is told that it's passé.

Another person explained it this way:

> In the past we didn't sell *maita* because people didn't have anything of their own [they didn't have lots of possessions]. But now, since the whites came, they make people work and they pay them. This is what opened up the black man's eyes to jealousy.

A third villager added,

> Before [the coming of the French], even when there weren't any cars here, you could send me to get something [in another village]. When I returned, even if you didn't give me anything, it would be o.k. by me. But nowadays, if you send me to get something there, if you don't give me enough money when I return, I will refuse the next time you ask me.

Yet another individual assessed the situation this way: "That's right! In today's world it is money alone that speaks. However little you work for someone, you expect him to give you money."

Arousal of this baser side of man is, as I have already mentioned, also held responsible for the selling of soul-eating capacities and thus doubly responsible for its proliferation. The sale of one's heritage—which normally is part of one's identity and cannot be the object of exchange—is, in and of itself, a dramatic statement. Suddenly a unique part of the person is transformed from a quality to a commodity. The results are far-reaching and potentially devastating. The stranger can now acquire powers to which he has no legitimate right.[22] The lineage is made vulnerable: family secrets are exposed, and access is created to one of the family's main sources of material and nonmaterial wealth (i.e., its heritage).[23]

However, danger is perceived to extend beyond the family and lineage. At a very concrete level such sale unleashes unknown soul-eaters into the community. At a symbolic level it suggests that many feel the very foundations of local custom have been shaken by selling something that should not be the object of any form of exchange at all. Equally as devastating is that a crucial vehicle for determining individual and group identity and for orchestrating social relationships is now unreliable. In short, you do not know who anyone is anymore. Even more important, you do not know who YOU are anymore.

The commoditization of soul-eating has frightening implications for the perpetuation of evil as well. Historically, the spread of soul-eating was limited to natural reproduction, since one had to be born with it. The damage of any one soul-eater was also contained in that Allah would only allow him to consume 999 human souls; if he consumed 1000 he would die. However, with the commercialization of soul-eating these limits have been removed.

The act of selling the power to consume souls, as well as the act of buying it, seems to represent for many Hausa a breakdown of tradition and the system of ethics it embodies, which in the past served to contain these destructive forces. Once again money is implicated in this disintegration. When asked if the soul-eaters who sell their powers have any qualms about spreading evil and endangering others this way, one individual replied:

> what do they care about something being good? . . . [to them] soul-eating is what's good, that is, affliction [is what's good] . . . if you can attack your own children, why not someone else's? . . . they do not care [that they are increasing the numbers of soul-eaters by selling their "stones"], there is nothing that bothers them.

In short, many people seem to feel that these soul-eaters and, by extension, an increasing number of villagers, have no sense of morality.

According to many villagers, the powers of soul-eaters were as potent precolonially, but soul-eaters were less numerous. They were also controllable, through the limits of biological reproduction and through the power of values and traditions to prohibit its sale and punish its use. Then, too, while the soul-eater's inability to master the drives of the "stones" were scorned and feared, they were nonetheless somewhat in the natural order of things. After all, they had not sought to be soul-eaters, they were born that way; it was, in a way, their fate. They represented a sort of natural evil that could, nonetheless, be socially controlled.

Colonialism helped to alter that by introducing a system that, in the eyes of villagers, has fueled the proliferation of soul-eating while seriously impoverishing social controls over it. Furthermore, it has challenged or made untenable many traditions. Without the ethical guidelines historically provided by such traditions, that enable one to know the value of things, individuals and society as a whole are threatened. This is exemplified in one man's description of the spread of soul-eating:

> Today, one thing that has caused the spread of soul-eating is that people travel all over and as soon as they see a beautiful young girl, they marry her without caring who she *is*.[24] So she has children and because she is a soul-eater, her children are also. They grow up, boys and girls, all very handsome children, so handsome that everyone in the village and beyond wants to marry them. Thus, *maita* is spread. You see through marriage is one way in which it is bought. One person can contaminate many people.

I suggest that this example can be understood as a metaphor for what a significant number of Hausa villagers of the Gulbi Valley (especially older people) perceive as the response of many villagers to the changes set in motion by colonialism. As the scramble for money has intensified, people (particularly the youth), out of necessity or choice, have abandoned many of the values and practices that have historically helped define morality in the Hausa universe. Like the young boy tempted by the beautiful woman, many are so entranced by money and the desirable things it can obtain, they give little thought to the implications or value of their goals. Dismissing tradition as backward and passé, they give full rein to their desires. They pursue their fortunes blinded by the glitter of "modernity" to the moral reality of what that "modernity" might mean. In such a context, it is not surprising that many feel their ability to reproduce, in the sense of reproducing the world of their values and priorities, is threatened if not already destroyed.

In short, all these factors—the commoditization of soul-eating, disregard for tradition, and the lack of control over man's dark side—speak to the broader dilemma of how one copes with contemporary crises when the underpinnings of one's moral system are being challenged. Many villagers emphasize man's vulnerability to desire and to the allure of attractive things when he has no traditions to guide and protect him. The discourse surrounding soul-eating suggests that numerous villagers, though forced by the exigencies of physical and social survival to participate in the money economy and capitalist culture, are nonetheless deeply troubled by its moral implications in this particular context.[25] The increasing appeal of Islam is perhaps, in part, born of this conflict.

Thus, in certain respects, soul-eating seems to have become a metaphor for "the search for money." Both take on an existence and power of their own, and can corrupt the individual to the point of destruction both of himself and those around him. One thinks one is in control, but in fact, it is easy to become victimized oneself. Gnawing like a hunger, both the soul-eating "stones" and the desire for money push people to abandon tradition (represented by the sale of one's heritage), to commit acts that are, in traditional terms at least, morally despicable, to prey on the wealth and well-being of others (represented by the soul-eater eating the soul of others), to abandon respect and self-control (epitomized by the soul-eater's willingness to eat his own children). They loosen the control of the head (reason) over the stomach (emotion), that is, they inflame desire and dampen reason. They speak of desires that continue to grow inside the individual, never truly satiated, only temporarily satisfied.

The power to consume souls can result in social alienation and ostracism. On the other hand, such power can also enable the individual to supersede the normal social order—thus being freed from many of the social constraints and regulations that bind the ordinary members of society. Money, too, is capable of altering one's social status. It has multiplied avenues to both wealth and power in a society where a small group of elite (*sarauta* or royalty) have traditionally dominated and in certain cases exploited the peasantry (*talakawa* or commoners). Western-induced economic and political opportunities have helped blur these boundaries, though one's roots are never completely forgotten.

Though the ability to eat souls is generally talked of as an evil force, in fact it can be harnessed for social good (as exemplified by the savior type of soul-eater). Similarly, while money is seen as the root of many contemporary problems, villagers readily admit that it is not categorically bad. It both liberates and enslaves, placates and creates insatiable desires, weaves social relations (marriages, friendships, patron/client relationships, etc.), and tears them apart.

The key for money, as for the soul-eating "stones," is control, balance. It is not money per se people have trouble with, but rather the way its universality and access to it have reconstituted social categories and reconfigured the social terrain, thereby lessening man's ability to control his own desires and wants as well as those of his fellow villagers. Money, symbol of the historical confluence of political and economic factors, has helped to radically alter the rules of the game, and in so doing has significantly affected the peasant's ability to maneuver within his social world. "Prosperity" dangled before the peasant by luck seems, like the wind, to evaporate in his hand.

That soul-eating continues to be meaningful even for individuals such as civil servants who have been educated in Western-type schools (both in Niger and abroad) and who have adopted many of the trappings of a Western lifestyle, is in many ways not surprising. Indeed, the social and financial pressures on them are in some ways perhaps greater than on any other segment of the population. As a group, they have the most consistent access to money, even though their salaries are quite low. However, the demands put on them for money—from family and peers—are generally beyond what their meager incomes can bear. This situation is further aggravated by the fact that civil servant positions are not numerous, and there is considerable stress and competition involved both in getting and in moving up in such jobs. In short, no one feels the paradoxes surrounding power and money as acutely as the civil servants.

Conclusion

Beliefs and values surrounding soul-eating provide poignant commentary about a changing world and changing social relationships—the transformation of the sociocultural system and its values as a whole. Traditionally a discourse about desires and wants—a metaphoric hunger, out of control—soul-eating continues to be not only a reality in this part of Hausaland, but a polyvalent and meaningful set of images that speaks to the jealousies, expectations, and frustrations that have come in the wake of capitalism, colonialism, and the disruption of the traditional balance of power and wealth. It gives voice to a "hunger" perceived to be so powerful and so uncontrollable that it can incite the selling of one's most prized form of wealth, one's heritage.

Using symbols that reverberate to the very core of human experience—consumption, reproduction, death—soul-eating can be viewed as addressing the threat posed by uncontrolled desire and jealousy in society. I suggest that it provides a complex language for expressing and understanding not only the nature of the beast but the paradoxes that surround it and the way it has been affected by changes in the social, economic, and material world of the Hausa. Embedded in this discourse is important exegesis concerning the complexities of a people's struggle in today's world, particularly as regards their very difficult and stressful economic position. Thus, although soul-eating speaks of an age-old kind of evil, this imagery continues to provide villagers with a viable framework in which to understand contemporary experience.

Notes

1. *Kaman maye* (lit.: "catch of the soul-eater") is generally translated as "witchcraft." However, as Turner (1964) and Macfarlane (1970), among others, have pointed out, cross-cultural differences in the perception and categorization of activities we gloss as "witchcraft" and "sorcery" make the development of a universal lexicon for discussion such phenomena challenging. Not only does ethnographic data fail to fit neatly into these categories, but we are faced with the dilemma that the English terms "witchcraft," "witch," and "sorcery" carry, at least for Western audiences, implicit cultural and historical baggage no matter how explicitly they are redefined.

In an effort to minimize this problem, I will use the terms "soul-eater" and "soul-eating" or "attack by a soul-eater" as glosses for the Hausa terms *maye* and *kaman maye*, respectively. Although men and women are, according to villagers, equally prevalent as soul-eaters, for convenience sake I will use masculine pronouns in general discussion to refer to the soul-eater and his victim.

There is not even a rough English equivalent for the substance that, traditionally inherited from either parent, enables an individual to capture and consume souls. Since the term used for them can be translated as hailstone, I will refer to them as "stones" with the understanding that they are not believed to be real stones but simply small round hard objects.

As concerns other Hausa terms, I have tried to use only the English gloss so as not to encumber the nonspecialist reader with too many terms. Where the gloss is only roughly approximate, however, I have, in its first occurrence, provided the Hausa word as well so as to make the analysis more meaningful to other students of Hausa culture.

2. This is translated literally as "black stomach." More will be said of this imagery later.

3. In order to minimize the confusion introduced by using too many indigenous terms, I will hereafter use the word prosperity for *arziki*. I will put it in quotations, however, to remind the reader that it is only a very rough gloss, and includes many aspects of spiritual and personal wealth we would not automatically think of as being included in the term "prosperity."

4. That this is the case is evidenced in Bargery's translation of "wealth" as *"azziki; dukiya; ku'di; samu; tajirci; wadata; zarafi; bogi"* (1957:1223). Of these synonyms, only *ku'di* (money) has such a specific meaning. All others refer to general wealth.

5. Raynaut (1977) argues that in terms of community wealth the money earned through secondary occupations, gifts, and services is more apparent than real. Agriculture is the only true source of income, since it is the only revenue brought in from outside the community. Money exchanged within the local society in the form of gifts and services is merely a rapid distribution and redistribution which enables individuals to discharge financial obligations before the money is siphoned out of the community again via taxes and purchase of consumer goods.

6. The converse, however, is not true. In normal death the soul continues to live after the death of the body.

7. The implication seems to be that the soul is to the soul-eater what chicken is to the ordinary Hausa, that is, food.

8. Although Bargery (1957:54) defines *k'ank'ara* as hail, when asked to translate the term my Francophone friends unanimously translated it as *cailloux* (stones, pebbles) and not *grele* or *grelon* which would be an exact translation of hail or hailstone. In any case, the point seems to be that *maita* are envisioned as round, hard, brilliant objects. Bargery (1957:554) defines *maita* as "glass beads produced from the mouth by a magician, supposed to be a form of solidified saliva." Some described them as bright and clear, others as being wonderful colors. There did not seem to be any connection in their minds, however, between the *maita* and saliva.

9. For more information on these types of soul-eaters see Nicolas 1975:330–32.

10. Of course, this raises the question of whether such perceptions indicate actual changes or a mystification of the past (i.e., "in the good old days" syndrome). While this is a legitimate point of debate, for the purposes of this chapter I am limiting myself to examination of villagers' construction (both conscious and implicit) of reality and leaving comparison of such perspective with other historical facts to another discussion.

11. For example, if someone who had worked all day in the hot fields came home and immediately took a cool bath without giving his body time to rest, and then fainted, soul-eating would not immediately be suspected since the individual clearly neglected to let his body rest before bathing. On the other hand, if that same person fell ill without any apparent reason, soul-eating might be suspected.

12. When I discovered that a woman I had worked with for several years had been exiled for being a soul-eater, I wanted to go see her. I was warned by friends, however, not to go for several reasons. Not only would I be endangering myself to possible attack, but if I mentioned anything about her being a soul-eater she would probably have me summoned to court.

13. This word is defined by Abraham and Bargery as "keen desire." It is interesting that it was frequently translated by French-speaking Hausa as *"gourmandise."* While the literal translation of *"gourmandise"* is "gluttony" or "love of good food," it is clearly used metaphorically here to describe a "hunger" for good things in general.

14. No medicine will calm the "stones" once they have been aroused, although one healer mentioned that putting powdered hot peppers in the mouth of the soul-eater may help calm the "desire."

15. Rivalry over inheritance was another reason cited by those I talked to for procuring *maita.* Sometimes women who do not want their children to have to share the father's estate with his children from other marriages will buy *maita* so as to eliminate the competition. Note that this is but another variation of the main theme that *maita* is sought as a response to jealousy over other's access to wealth, in particular, money.

16. Other similar expressions include *"mai farin kai"* (lit.: "the one with the white head"; fig.: "the well-educated one") and *"mai bak'in kai"* (lit.: "the one who has a black head"; fig.: "the uneducated one").

17. Although in the case of soul-eating the desires are negative ones, the lack of control is as much an issue as the negativity of the desires. That this is the case is suggested by the fact that "good" emotions (e.g., love) are equally dangerous when "out of control." Certain instances of attack by a soul and even attack by a spirit where a deceased person's soul or a spirit (*bori, aljanu*) afflict the person because they like them and want to be with them exemplify this. *Baki* (lit.: "the mouth," a range of afflictions caused by speaking, for good or ill, about someone) is another case in point. Compliments can be just as damaging as insults if proper precautions (i.e., controls) are not taken.

18. *Bak'i* (lit.: "the mouth") or *Bakin duniya* (lit.: "the mouth of the world") refers to a range of afflictions that occur when an individual imbued with certain innate, but not necessarily recognized, powers talks (for good or ill) about another person. As it was explained to me, most people's words are harmless (*zama k'asa*). But the words of some individuals are not benign (whether they be praise or curse). Rather they go to the person being talked about and stick (*lik'e*) to him, thus causing illness or misfortune.

19. *Tuwo* is a cooked paste made from millet or sorghum and occasionally wheat or rice. It is eaten with a tomato or herb-based sauce and is the basis of the local diet. *Fura (hura)* is a type of gruel made from cooked millet.

20. Unfortunately, there is not time here to do justice to the very complex role

of food in Hausa social relationships. These few simple examples merely illustrate that there is indeed a language of food.

21. For example, if a mother shows too much love to her children, this can arouse jealousies thereby provoking attack (by soul-eaters or other evil villagers) on herself or her family.

22. Here the theme of illegitimate consumption (in particular of life and of reproductive powers) reoccurs in the symbolism of the soul-eating "stones" which are swallowed (one male and one female) and which must *reproduce* in the *ciki* (stomach, abdomen, womb) for the powers to become manifest.

23. "A ruhe mini asiri!" ("please conceal my secrets") is a common supplication in asking for health from God and spirits (*bori*). This phrase signals the importance of safeguarding personal and family "secrets" in maintaining both health and the integrity of the self.

24. In this context he is referring particularly to a disregard for the girl's lineage.

25. I say this with due respect to the questions and criticisms raised by Parry and Bloch (1989). Clearly this ethnographic context can and should be more fully elaborated in light of their insights. Such an endeavor, however, is not possible here.

References

Abraham, Roy C. 1978 [1958]. *Dictionary of the Hausa Language.* London: Hodder and Stroughton.

Bargery, Rev. G. P. 1957 [1934]. *A Hausa-English Dictionary.* London: Oxford University Press.

Darrah, Allen C. 1980. A Hermaneutic Approach to Hausa Therapeutics: The Allegory of the Living Fire. Ph.D. diss., University of Michigan, Ann Arbor.

Faulkingham, Ralph. 1975. The Spirits and Their Cousins: Some Aspects of Belief, Ritual and Social Organization in a Rural Hausa Village in Niger. Research Report no. 15, University of Massachusetts, Department of Anthropology.

Macfarlane, A. D. J. 1970. Definitions of Witchcraft. In *Witchcraft and Sorcery,* ed. Max Marwick. Baltimore, Md.: Penguin Books.

Nicolas, Guy. 1975. *Dynamique sociale et apprehension du monde au sein d'une société Hausa.* Paris: Institut d'Ethnologie.

Parry, J., and M. Bloch. 1989. *Money and the Morality of Exchange.* Cambridge: Cambridge University Press.

Raynaut, Claude. 1977. Circulation monetaire et evolution des structures socio-economiques chez les Haoussas du Niger. *Africa* 47, no. 2:160–274.

Taussig, Michael. 1977. The Genesis of Capitalism amongst a South American Peasantry: Devil's Labor and the Baptism of Money. *Comparative Studies in Society and History* 19, no. 2:130–55.

————. 1980. *The Devil and Commodity Fetishism in South America*. Chapel Hill: University of North Carolina Press.

Tremearne, Major A. J. N. 1968 [1914]. *The Ban of the Bori*. London: Frank Cass & Co.

Turner, Victor. 1964. Witchcraft and Sorcery: Taxonomy vs. Dynamics. *Africa* 34, no. 4:314–25.

CONTRIBUTORS

Andrew Apter is assistant professor of anthropology at the University of Chicago. He has done extensive research in Nigeria, is author of *Black Critics and Kings: The Hermeneutics of Power in Yoruba Society,* and has published several papers on ritual and power. His current interests include popular culture, modernity and politics, the African diaspora, and religious discourse and practice.

Mark Auslander is completing his graduate studies in anthropology at the University of Chicago. He did his doctoral research in Zambia and is writing a dissertation on "State Cosmologies, Subversive States: Ritual, Power, and History in the Mpezeni Ngoni Polity." His current interests, in addition to ritual, power, and history, include the study of commodities and symbolic geography in Southern Africa.

Ralph A. Austen is professor of history at the University of Chicago. The author of numerous works on various aspects of African economic and social history, his most recent book is entitled *African Economic History.* He has done extensive research in Northwest Tanzania and coastal Cameroon. His current interests include the slave trade, and the heroic figure in African narrative.

Misty L. Bastian is a Fellow of the Academy Scholars Program at the Center for International Affairs, Harvard University. She recently completed a dissertation on Ibo market women in Nigeria entitled "The World as Marketplace: Historical, Cosmological, and Popular Constructions of the Onitsha Market System." Her research interests include gender, popular culture, religion, and cosmology.

Jean and John Comaroff are both professors of anthropology at the University of Chicago. Their most recent books are *Of Revelation and Revolution: Christianity, Colonialism, and Consciousness in South Africa,* vol. 1, and *Ethnography and the Historical Imagination.* They have done research in South Africa and Botswana and write on, among other things, African culture, society, and history.

Deborah Kaspin is assistant professor of anthropology at Yale University. She has worked among Chewa in Malawi and wrote her doctoral dissertation on "Elephants and Ancestors: The Legacy of Kingship in Rural Malawi." Her research interests include ritual, history, and the construction of nationalism and ethnicity.

Adeline Masquelier has recently completed her Ph.D. degree at the University of Chicago and is about to take up an assistant professorship in anthropology at Tulane University. She did her doctoral research in Niger on spirit possession, history, and the politics of healing in the Bori cult. Her research interests include gender, the body and personhood, and ritual processes in the postcolonial world.

J. Lorand Matory is assistant professor of anthropology and of Afro-American Studies at Harvard University. He has conducted fieldwork among the Yoruba of Nigeria and the Peoples Republic of Bénin as well as in the Candomblé of Brazil. His forthcoming book is entitled *Sex and the Empire That Is No More: Women's Religion and the Politics of Metaphor in an Oyo-Yoruba Town.* His current interests include ritual, gender, and politics in Africa and the African diaspora.

Pamela G. Schmoll recently completed her Ph.D. at the University of Chicago. She did research in Niger and wrote a dissertation on Searching for Health in a World of Dis-ease: Affliction Management among Rural Hausa of the Maradi Valley." Her current interests include comparative systems of healing, ritual, the body, witchcraft, and commodities in cultural perspective.

INDEX

Van Gennep, xxxiin.9

Vessels, 61. *See also* Calabashes; Pots

Violence, and ritual, 171–72, 173, 174, 176, 185, 187, 189

Wages, 103

War, 12, 31; as avenue to riches, 20; backbone of Mawri society, 9, 14; and fame, 10, 20; as holy, 11; pillage, 9; prisoners of, 28n.4; suppression of, 12; as unifying force, 11. *See also* Jihad; Peace

Wealth, 115, 117, 118, 122, 124. *See also* Money; Commodization

Weapons of the Weak (Scott), 94

Weber, Max, 101–2

Weiss, Brad L., xxxiin.12

West Africa, 89

West Central Africa, 92

White, Allon, xv

White, Luise, xxxiin.2, 157n.1, 160n.25, 161n.32

Whitting, C. E. J., 20, 33

Wikan, Unni, 75

Williams, Raymond, xxvi

Willis, Roy, 177, 191n.9

Wilson, Monica, xx, xxviii, 125n.5, 178

Wilson, Peter J., 3, 33

Winter, E., 125n.5

Witchcraft, xiv, xvii, 68, 79, 89–110, 114, 116, 129–30, 132–34, 136, 138–42, 144–56, 158nn.8 and 13, 162nn.37, 38, and 40, 163n.47; and cannibalism, 114, 115, 116, 118, 123; and capitalism, 89–106; classical Africanist accounts of, 125n.5; and colonialism, xxv, xxviii; comparative history of, 87–105; covens, 114, 118, 119, 123, 126n.9; and cowives, 116; as discourse on contradictions of modernity, xxv, xxvi,

xxviii, xxix; Eurocentric analyses of, xviii; European, xxvii, 97–103; and female form, xxvii, xxviii, 115; and female wealth, 177–78; impersonal vs. antipersonal, 91; logic of, 113, 120, 122; in North American popular film, xxviii; official, 91, 98; and political sabotage, 118, 119; rural vs. urban, 91–92, 97–103; and the state, 121–25, 126n.13; and trading capital, 120. *See also* Modernity; Practice; Ritual

Witchfinding, 114, 115, 167–92; Ngoni procedure described, 192–94

Wolf, Eric R., xxiv

Wombs, and ritual, 167, 170, 182, 186

Women, 58, 111, 117; and barrenness, 78, 80; as chiefs, 67, 79; and capitalist contradictions, xxvii, xxviii, xxxin.2; as daughters, 60, 61; and economic autonomy, 120; mistrust of, 61; as mothers, 64, 77; reflected in mirrors, 114; as traders, 79, 120, 121; and uterine fertility, 68; as widows, 60; as witches, 113, 114, 117, 123; as wives, 60, 64, 65, 72, 76, 80. *See also* Body symbolism; Bridewealth; Divorce; Marginalization; Witchcraft

Woodcuts, 101

Works, John A., 8, 20, 33

Worldly asceticism, 102

Writing, and ritual action, 173, 174, 184, 185, 191n.15

Yoruba, xxi, xxvii, 58–82, 94, 111–25

Zambia, xxiii, xxvii, xxxiin.13

Zero-sum economy, 92, 100, 102, 105n.6

Zionism, 175, 190